Adaptive Reuse in Architecture

A Typological Index

Liliane Wong

Birkhäuser

Table of Contents

Preface

An index is a list, typically in alphabetical order, of some specified datum. There are word indexes (also known as concordances) and subject indexes; in either form, they are devices for introducing order and organization to a particular object set and easing the tasks of search and location. An index reveals the structure of a work at multiple scales from alpha-numerical listings to the architecture of an intended framework. Subject indexes disclose particular positions and dispositions. An index is a guide for the different journeys of one's choosing.

Adaptive Reuse in Architecture: A Typological Index emerged from an investigation of two seemingly unrelated observations: the first use of the term "adaptive reuse" in 1973 and the exponential increase in notable projects of adaptive reuse in the 21st century. The chapter titles reflect this journey, which began by looking backward in time to the 1970s. The many discoveries made along the way evolved over time into a hypothesis that firmly connected the two observations as a phenomenon over a half century from 1973–2023. The different chapter subjects emerged from a pattern discerned in the notable projects of reuse since the end of the 20th century. It was not happenstance that they were the transformation of buildings used for very specific functions. The individual chapters, like subject indexes, offer journeys in time of the development of certain aspects of our social, cultural and geopolitical context. The graphs, selected projects, diagrams and charts are alternate paths to explore those ideas, separately or as a whole. As the term "adaptive reuse" was only first used in 1973, this work aspires to describe this particular phase of an otherwise ancient practice of reuse.

These ideas did not emerge from a void. My many Rhode Island School of Design (RISD) Interior Architecture students, graduate and undergraduate, were wonderful sounding boards for queries on the year 1973. The enthusiasm of the BFA class of 2020 served as encouragement to press on. Special thanks to Charlie Kramer and the Board of APTNE (Association for Preservation Technology North East) for inviting me to deliver the keynote at their February 28, 2020 Annual Meeting and Symposium on "2020 Vision: New Uses for Old Buildings." On the eve of the pandemic, the audience was wonderfully receptive to the graphs from "Immortality Comes of Age: Adaptive Reuse in the Millennium." These were the first iterations of the graphs that precede each chapter of this book. It is thanks to Kent Kleinman, former Provost of RISD and founder of an initiative to offer internships to graduate students unable to travel home in the pandemic, that I had the opportunity to work with two graduate students studying adaptive reuse at RISD's Department of Interior Architecture. Now alumnae of RISD's Master of Design (MDes) program in Adaptive Reuse, Kayci Gallagher and Yara Hadi were instrumental in the making of this book. Over many Friday Zoom meetings, we explored the idea of an adaptive reuse index together.

Our conversations are woven through this book. While the many words we exchanged are now invisible, their physical manifestation as the diagrams of each project are reminders of their participation in, and contribution to, this project. This book would not be what it is without the generosity of architectural firms, photographers, colleagues and friends whose images populate this volume. I am most grateful for the designs of Sebastian Schmitt and Bureau Est. Their graphic design concepts brought a new legibility to my words and ideas while their cover design connects to 1973 with a reference to the cover color of Daniel Bell's *The Coming of Post-Industrial Society*, a book that was invaluable to my research. Special thanks to my editor Michael Wachholz whose guidance was invaluable, as was the time he made for Zoom meetings conducted from Berlin at Eastern Standard Time. And to Andreas Müller, with gratitude for his guidance on the first book on adaptive reuse that was the genesis of this companion book and the music of the 70s that, I hope, can be heard within these pages.

I will always be grateful to have been one of the last cohorts of students taught by Professor Eduard F. Sekler at the Harvard Graduate School of Design. From his many history and theory classes I learned to see architecture through the lens of an expansive context. The journeys he offered in the lectures on those distant mornings at the Carpenter Center inspired the journeys explored in this book.

Providence, Rhode Island
August 2022

Looking Back

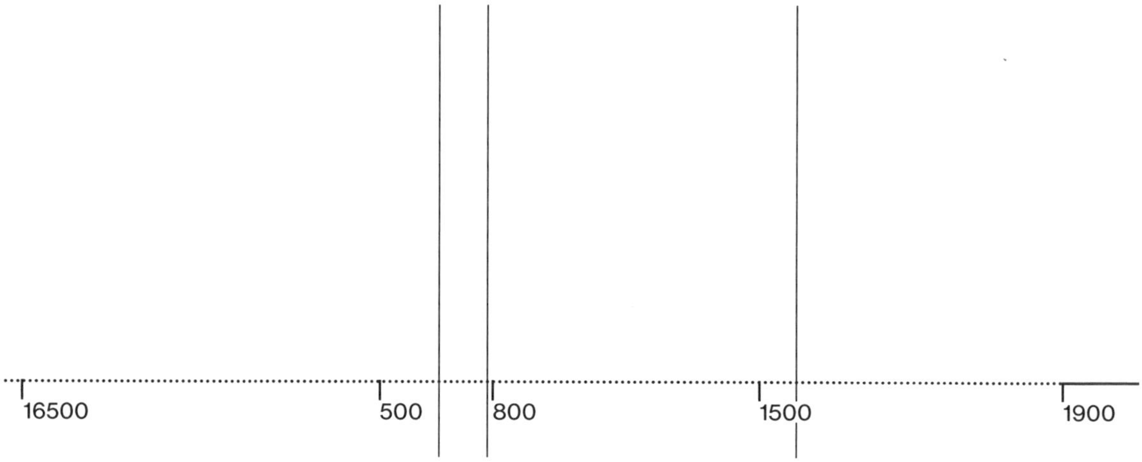

16500 Caves of Lascaux

+600 Reuse of Palace of Diocletian in Split

+700 Arles Amphitheater fortress

785 Mosque of Cordoba

1562 Santa Maria degli Angeli e degli Martiri

1947 Auschwitz-Birkenau Museum

1958 Olivetti Store

1959 Castelvecchio

1967 Hedmark Museum

1971 MoMA PS.1

1972 The Clocktower

1973 The Factory

1977 SESC Pompéia

1979 S.21 Tuol Sleng Genocide Museum

1985 Eremitani Civic Museum

1986 Musée d'Orsay; Tower of the Winds; Museum of Roman Art

1996 Hiroshima Peace Memorial

1997 Centrale Montemartini; Piazza Alicia; Le Fresnoy Art Center

1998 Comme des Garçons

1999 Mass MOCA; MKM Museum Küppersmühle; Yellow House

2000 British Museum; Tate Modern Museum; La Piscine

2001 Library of San Fernando; Bunny Lane; Vienna Gasometers

2003 Mill City Museum; Ferry Building Market; Yin Yu Tang House at the Peabody Essex Museum

2005 Frøsilo/Gemini Residence; Barcelona Supercomputing; Santa Catarina Market

2006 Manufaktura; Jaegersborg Water Tower; Pixel Hotel

2007 Zollverein Coal Washing Plant; Selexzy Dominicanen Bookstore; Kraanspoor; Park Ave Armory; Boros Bunker; Liberty Hotel; Klan KOSOVA TV Station; Torre de David

2008 CaixaForum Madrid; 1933 Old Millfun Shanghai; 185 Post Building; Moritzburg Museum; Pace Gallery – 789 Art Zone

2009 Neues Museum; Fortress of Fortezza; Andel's Hotel; RCA Sackler; Dovecote Studio; The High Line; The Why Factory; Residenzschloss

2010 Bunker 599; Art of Americas Wing; Waterhouse Hotel Shanghai; David Barton Gym; Im Viadukt Arches; Bastide Niel; La Fabrique

2011 Milstein Hall; Cineteca Matadero; Bois-Le-Prêtre; Dresden Military History Museum; Downton Abbey; Joanneum; San Telmo Museum

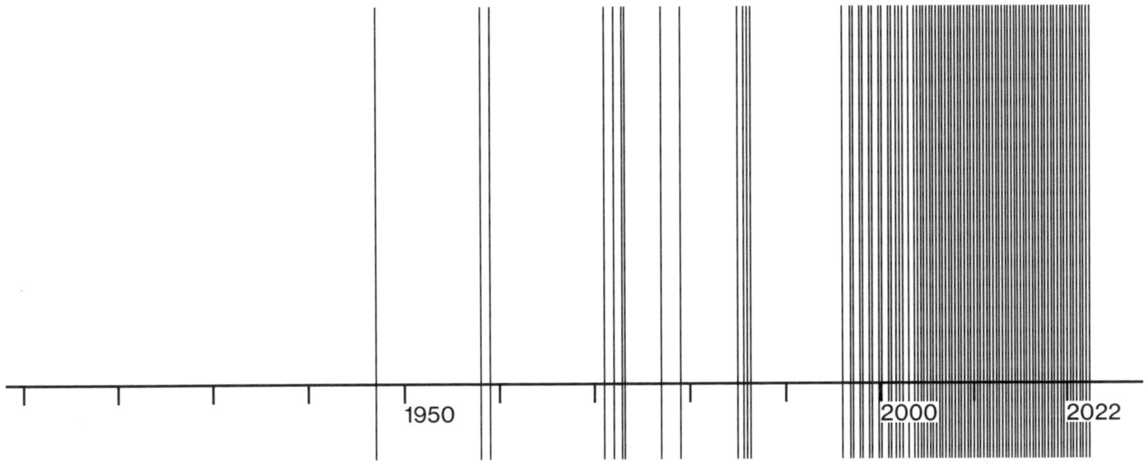

2012 Memorial to the Abolition of Slavery; Biblioteca Hertziana; Convento das Bernardas

2013 Castillo de la Luz; FRAC Grand Large; Danish Maritime Museum; Dharma Niaga; Kindl Centre for Contemporary Art Berlin

2014 Long Museum; Hotel Herman K; Royal Abbey of Fontevraud; Art Space, Seville; Pombal Castle Visitor Centre; Launch Labs; Stedelijk Museum Schiedam; Palais de Tokyo

2015 König Gallerie; Garage Museum; Gasholder Park; St. Ann's Warehouse; Kaos Temple; The Kommandant's House Learning Center; Monastery of San Juan; Rosa Parks House Project

2016 Crystal Houses Amsterdam; Elbphilharmonie; Fondaco dei Tedeschi Venice; Wencun Village Transformation; The Design Museum London; Woods Cathedral; Gucci Aeronautic HQ; Nyamata Genocide Memorial Centre; Port House; Katyn Museum; Transformation of 530 Dwellings; Tour & Taxi Development

2017 Zeitz MOCAA; The Silo; Tempelhof Refugee Center; Tsingpu Yangzhou Retreat; Seoullo 7017 Skygarden; Young City Gdansk; Medieval Mile Museum Kilkenny; Wuyuan Skywells Hotel

2018 Coal Drops Yard; Royal Museum Madrid; Wrightwood 659; Helsinki Bread Factory; Pier 70 San Francisco; Conversion of Olympic Tower Montreal; Jaffa Hotel; Tirana Pyramid conversion; The Plant; Streetmekka Viborg; Bicycle Parking Main Station Karlsruhe; Goldsmiths Centre for Contemporary Art; Google Spruce Goose Hangar; Fondation Galeries Lafayette; Fondazione Prada; Shipyard 1862; Neville Holt Opera; The Idea Exchange Old Post Office

2019 Loc-Hal Library; Apple Carnegie Library; The Detective Building Pittsburg; Prisengracht Hospital Co-Working; Egg Shed Heritage & Community Centre; TWA Hotel; WERK-12; Roskilde Festival Højskole; Magasin 13; The Malthouse Theater

2020 Resource Rows; Concordia Design; Dutch Pavilion World Expo; Tainan Spring; ETAM Paris; POST Houston; Baoshan Exhibition Centre; Phase Shifts Park; TaoCang Art Centre; Crye Precision Headquarters; KB Building Offices; Carnival Arts Centre; Youth Activity Center in Miyun District; Argo Factory Art Museum

2021 GES-2 Art Center; Village of Ruesta; Site Verrier de Meisenthal; Idea Factory; Ombu; MKM Museum Küppersmühle Extension; Kitakami Health and Childcare Support Center; NoMad London; Monastero Arx Vivendi Hotel; Hauser & Wirth Menorca; Chilean Headquarters for Culture, Arts & Heritage; Aaltosilo; Bodmin Jail Hotel; Bourse de Commerce – Pinault Collection; Urban Research Institute Company in Nantou; Glorya Kaufman Performing Arts Center

2022 One Green Mile; Bob Dylan Center; Camino School; Red House School; Wilmina; Wunderlocke Hotel; Lantern Art Factory; Visitor Center in Reus; Digital Factory of Luxottica; Kabelovna Studios; The Beams Cultural Center; Generator Building Bristol; Norwegian Press House; Glorya Kaufman Performing Arts Center

Adaptive reuse is a practice born of resourcefulness. Evidence of it can be found in various guises through the centuries from ancient times to present day. Materials scavenging mandated by scarcity, built legacies of conquerors knit into the structures of the vanquished, and architectural plunder reused in the far-off cities of the victors have their modern counterpart in systems facelifts for aging office complexes and conversions of old school buildings to apartment blocks. Unsung and without a name, architectural reuse was a branch of professional practice throughout the 20th century, providing an unremarkable but steady staple of refurbishment projects for architecture and design offices around the world. In the second decade of the 21st century, however, adaptive reuse practice exploded onto the forefront of the architectural profession, with award-winning projects of transformational reuse by sought-after architects. In 2008, an Internet search for the term "adaptive reuse" yielded few results.[1] In 2022, the same search produced 45,700,000 results in 0.60 seconds.[2] How did this development come about? And, why now? These two questions require us to go back in time, not just two decades but thousands of years, to understand the development of reuse as practices dictated by the demands of unique contexts. Operating without a formal name for millennia, the practice of reuse of existing structures and buildings was driven by the distinct preoccupations of different eras: economics, power transitions, conservation of heritage, war recovery. In order to understand the current phenomenon of adaptive reuse, a term first defined in 1973, it is essential to explore its different iterations through the centuries.

The Need for Resources

With the birth of societies, the need for economy dictated the reuse of materials and structures. In the built environment, this approach led to the salvaging of obsolete buildings for parts to reuse in new construction. This common practice was named *spolia* by the Romans. With Latin roots, it refers to "the reuse of building materials, especially in Christian Rome."[3] Examples such as the Arch of Constantine or St. Peter's Basilica in Rome, Italy, exemplify the extent of such reuse: of reliefs from earlier monuments in the former and columns of the arcade from Hadrian's Mausoleum in the latter.[4] Existing structures were also reused in their entirety and not simply in parts. The Mezquita of Córdoba in Spain is such an example. Upon the 7th-century Muslim conquest of the Iberian Peninsula, the Christian church was converted to a mosque, with subsequent additions in the following centuries, before it was reconverted in the 13th century. Similarly, the 8th-century Saracen invasions of Arles, France, inspired the reuse of the 90 CE Roman amphitheater as a fortress. Two hundred homes were created within its walls and watchtowers were added, three of which remain today. In the adaptation of an entire building for a new purpose, the existing structure is host to new programs of use.

Iconoclasm

Transformations such as those at the Mezquita of Córdoba allude to a reuse over and above the dictates of economy. Acts of iconoclasm reflecting centuries of religious power shifts speak to an intentional change of use. Notable intentional reuse was sporadic throughout the centuries with few remarkable examples. The Santa Maria degli Angeli e dei Martiri in 16th-century Rome, Michelangelo's 1563–1564 conversion of a Christian church from the frigidarium of the 3rd-century CE Baths of Diocletian, underscores the importance of architectural fit in intentional reuse. In this instance, the architecture of the monumental pagan bath was equally well suited to the architectural characteristics desired in a Christian basilica. The grandeur of three colossal cross-vaulted spaces in the shape of a Greek cross that served well as a civic place of Roman life and, later, as a Christian place of worship, demonstrates both the appropriateness and economy of spatial correspondence. The conversion of the Baths of Diocletian to the Santa Maria degli Angeli e dei Martiri is a perfect example of intentional adaptive reuse that was ahead of its time. A reuse project of this stature would not occur again for centuries. Nor would intentional adaptive reuse be definitively formalized for another 400 years.

Conservation of Heritage

In the Western world, a critical development on this long path came in the form of the French Revolution and the upheaval rent by the struggle for political and societal change. The damage inflicted on the structures of the monarchy and the church led to questions of how best to safeguard the country's built cultural heritage. In France, it resulted in government intervention and a first national inventory of damaged structures. This subsequently led to the creation of France's Commission des monuments historiques in 1837, to provide the protection and maintenance of built heritage.[5 6] Such action to protect national heritage structures would reverberate decades later with the First World War. In the wake of the damage inflicted on the structures of multiple countries in two world wars, it eventually expanded to an international discussion of heritage protection. The Athens Charter of 1931 was the product of a first international congress convened by architects and technicians of historic monuments after the First World War. Its recommendations for modern conservation included "the occupation of buildings, which ensures the continuity of their life, should be maintained but that they should be used for a purpose which respects their historic or artistic character."[7] This recommendation formally advocated for the reuse of heritage structures. It was a critical recognition of the importance of a host structure of historical significance and connected its longevity to reuse. The Second World War and the deadly weapons that wreaked a new level of devastation, not only on buildings but on whole cities, mandated international discussions of heritage. The Venice Charter of 1964 reexamined and enhanced the recommendations of the Athens Charter of 1931. Article 5 reiterates the recommendation of the Athens Charter for the occupation of the structure, stating that "the conservation of monuments is always facilitated by making use of them for some socially useful purpose."[8] Article 1, however, is groundbreaking in extending the definition of heritage with the recommendation that "the concept of a historic monument embraces not only the single architectural work but also the urban or rural setting in which is found the evidence of a particular civilization, a significant development or a historic event. This applies not only to great works of art but also to more modest works of the past which have acquired cultural significance

IMG 1 — The Arles amphitheater as a medieval housing community.
IMG 2 — The Arles amphitheater today as a tourist site.

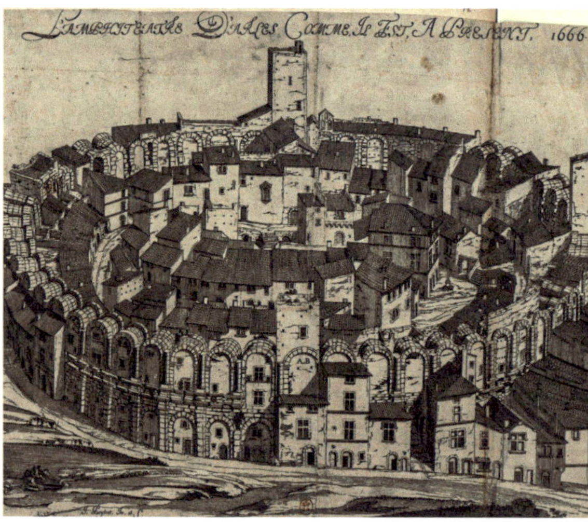

with the passing of time."[9] This recommendation broadened the scope of heritage structures to all works that have acquired cultural significance over time, from a classical temple to an entire city, a farm and a factory. Nine years later in 1973, the term "adaptive reuse" was officially defined in the American *Merriam-Webster Dictionary* as "the renovation and reuse of pre-existing structures ... for new purposes."[10] This definition included works of heritage but was in no way exclusive to them. It instead expanded the breadth of reuse projects and formalized work that had otherwise been unnamed.

Obsolescence

Adaptive reuse as the practice of reusing existing structures is premised on building obsolescence. The state of "no longer being useful" that triggers reuse arises from two different natural conditions. First, all structures require maintenance, the upkeep of the basic systems that support a building and its functions. Without proper and consistent maintenance, the building would eventually fail as a whole. Over time, even with regular maintenance, building structures and systems become antiquated and are no longer able to serve the needs and standards of a current society. This type of obsolescence is part of a natural cycle in the life of a building. Adaptive reuse in the form of upgrades and renovations can stay this obsolescence, albeit not indefinitely. Eventually, the building becomes underused or decommissioned and is possibly demolished due to an inevitable aging process. Alternatively, a structure becomes obsolete when it no longer serves its intended purpose to accommodate a specific function or functions. Such obsolescence results from evolving requirements of use and/or changes in the functioning of a particular program. An automobile factory from the early 20th century, designed for a human production line, is an example of this type of obsolescence in today's automated society. Different from age-related obsolescence, these changes result from the evolution of a society and the manner in which it operates. Conversely, such changes also spawned new functions. For example, the invention of the electric light is the origin of the structures related to "night-life."[11] These two conditions – the age of a building and the relevance of a building's use – trigger adaptive reuse. Aging structures require upgrades and irrelevant structures require a pertinent and meaningful purpose. These two types of triggers result in two distinct types of adaptive projects: refurbishment, which improves and upgrades an existing structure, and transformation, which intentionally changes an existing structure to give it a new purpose. In many ways, this differentiation of reuse project types sheds light on the recent focus on adaptive reuse as projects of transformation rather than centuries-old projects of upgrades.

The second trigger for adaptive reuse, the loss of relevance of a building's function, is not necessarily a singular event. When a group of buildings becomes obsolete all at once because they belong to a particular building use type, it speaks to dramatic changes in that type and perhaps in its relevance as a type in the functioning of that society. For example, the decommissioning of coal mines in Europe reflects a shift away from fossil fuels toward the production of renewable energy. When multiple groups of different building types fall out of use and/or are decommissioned over a defined period of time, there are complex forces at play. The search for an explanation requires an assessment of both the different building types as individual subjects and the time period itself. Such a phenomenon occurred in the second decade of the 21st century when whole groups of different building types/uses – from religious buildings to factories and power production plants – were adapted and intentionally transformed for a new use. Churches were converted into bookstores, hotels and galleries; factories into sports facilities; coal mines into cultural venues; train stations into museums, concert halls and libraries; sports stadiums into offices; and silos into residential buildings. These transformations allude to societal values, upended. A phenomenon of such vastness and variety does not occur in an instant. Instead, it is the culmination of events over time that together spurred an enormous surge in the architecture of reuse. With hindsight, this phenomenon is not unexpected. Rather, it is the result of a half-century of change reflected by the introduction of the term "adaptive reuse" in an American dictionary in 1973. Why was adaptive reuse formally defined at that particular time? What was particular to the 1970s that led to the defining of adaptive reuse in the United States, when the reuse of existing structures had existed for centuries? What role did this event play in the burgeoning of transformational reuse projects in the 21st century?

The 1970s

The defining of the term adaptive reuse took place following a decade characterized by counterculture. The latter half of the 1960s was marked by a demand for social change: the sexual revolution, the anti-war movement, the civil rights movement, feminism, the gay rights movement. While the idealism of these movements was overshadowed in the final years by war, riots, protests and assassinations, the pursuit of new social values continued, although amid a set of circumstances created by the geopolitics unfolding in the 1970s. Often overlooked in the aftermath of the turbulent and tumultuous 1960s, the 1970s were a time in which the ideals of the previous decade were tried and refined in the workings of a new global arena. Shaped by the context of a different generation, many ideas from that time led to societal shifts that irrevocably altered life in the half-century that followed. Specific and seemingly disparate events and ideas of the 1970s such as the first Earth Day celebration, the Yom Kippur War, the Munich Olympics and the advent of the Intel 4004 chip would lead to dramatic changes in six aspects of modern society. These areas related to energy production, manufacturing practices, agricultural practices, advancement in transportation, religious practices and new ways of memorializing. Dramatic changes within these six areas affected the structures related to each of those areas in turn. This book is an investigation of the particular events of that time period and how they led to significant implications for the built environment. The following six chapters examine the development of each of these areas as they evolved over a half-century, illustrated by distinctive reuse projects arising from those developments. The graphs depicting various trends over 50 years are an invitation to speculate on the unexpected relationship between global affairs and the built environment. Together, the six chapters offer a whole insight on adaptive reuse and its flowering in the 21st century.

Impactful change over time is not readily apparent except in hindsight. Changes in the built environment similarly occur slowly over time. Transitions from one way of operating to another span decades. An example of this relationship of change and time in the built environments can be seen in the impact of telecommunications on domestic spaces. Alexander Graham Bell's 1875 invention of the telephone established a direct connection between location and voice communication. Over the next century, telephone calls were place specific: home, office, telephone booth. In the 1970s, the character of a room within a house was influenced by its proximity to a telephone jack. Communal spaces such as living rooms and kitchens were spaces of more public conversations. Studies and bedrooms were retreats that permitted private and intimate discussions. The advent of cordless phones rendered these relationships moot. Today's phenomenon of speaking wirelessly has transformed the concept of place and conversation. The world is a room

IMG 3 — The assembly line at the Ford Motor Company, Detroit, Michigan, 1913.
IMG 4 — The Ruhr Museum, located in the converted coal washing plant of the former Zollverein Coal Mine in Essen, Germany, by OMA.

without walls from which all conversations take place. But today's ubiquitous use of the cell phone did not occur overnight. Invented by American engineer Martin Cooper in 1973, 98 years after Bell, the DynaTAC (Dynamic Adaptive Total Area Coverage) phone weighed 2.5 pounds (1.13 kg), was battery operated and permitted 35 minutes of use. Its commercial production by Motorola in 1983 required a decade and a unit price of $4,000 USD.[12] Flip phones were introduced in the mid-1990s and the industry-transforming iPhone in 2007, almost 35 years after the introduction of the DynaTAC. 1G cellular service was introduced in 1983, 2G in 1991, 4G in 2009 and 5G in

2019.[13] In 1993, there were 34 million mobile subscriptions worldwide, in 2021 that number had risen to 8.648 billion.[14] When the iPhone was introduced, approximately 75% of Americans owned a cell phone.[15] In 2021, 97% do. Begun in 1973, it required almost a half-century to become a societal norm. Societal transitions similar to "energy transitions are not sudden revolutionary advances that follow periods of prolonged stagnation, but rather continuously unfolding processes."[16]

The following chapters examine the transitions in energy production, manufacturing, agriculture, transportation, religion and heritage as they unfolded over a half-century, since the first noted use in 1973 of the term adaptive reuse in the *Merriam-Webster Dictionary*. Founded in 1831, the *Merriam-Webster Dictionary* traces its roots to *An American Dictionary of English Language*. This origin, which reflects the influence of the United States and the West in the 1960s and 1970s, takes forefront as a viewpoint of this investigation. It is an investigation to understand and to explain the phenomenon in the 21st century of a surge in specific groups of decommissioned buildings that were subsequently transformed into notable adaptive reuse projects. Why were there so many converted power plants, factories, silos, train stations, churches, military structures and sites of atrocities? Why those types and in such quantities within such a narrow time frame, after centuries of sporadic examples?

This work is a broad brush glance at the past to learn about circumstances that, over time, reveal a connected chain of seemingly unrelated incidents. With the purpose of probing these trends, the following investigation explores factors that ultimately contributed to the extinction of long-established ways of functioning and, in turn, the extinction of the buildings that accommodated those functions. Through six topics that experienced dramatic change as a result of events in the 1970s, a modern history of adaptive reuse appears. It is a story of society as it grappled with new and previously inconceivable ideas, and the slow process by which such ideas became the norm. This is the story of a half-century of change and its physical reflection in the built environment.

IMG 5 — Martin Cooper and the first hand-held mobile phone, 1973.

Notes and Sources

1 In the co-founding of the *Intar Journal of Interventions and Adaptive Reuse*, this was part of my research in 2008.

2 Google search of the term "adaptive reuse," accessed 17 January 2022.

3 https://www.oxfordreference.com/view/10.1093/oi/authority.20110803100524626, accessed 18 January 2022.

4 Ann Thomas Wilkins review of Lex Bosman, *The Power of Tradition: Spolia in the Architecture of St. Peter's in the Vatican.* https://www.oxfordreference.com/view/10.1093/oi/authority.20110803100524626, accessed 18 January 2022.

5 https://www.culture.gouv.fr/en/Thematiques/Monuments-Sites/Monuments-historiques-sites-patrimoniaux/Un-peu-d-histoire, accessed 20 January 2022.

6 In a report to the king, Ludovic Vitet, the first inspector general of historical monuments, summarized his responsibilities as: "To observe the existence and to describe all the buildings of the kingdom which, either by their date, by the character of their architecture, or by the events of which they were witnesses, deserve the attention of the archaeologist, the artist or the historian, this is the first aim of the functions entrusted to me; secondly, I must see to the conservation of these buildings, indicating to the government and to the local authorities the means either to prevent or to stop their degradation."

7 The Athens Charter of 1931, Section 1. Doctrines. General Principles. From the website of ICOMOS, International Council on Monuments and Sites. https://www.icomos.org/en/167-the-athens-charter-for-the-restoration-of-historic-monuments, accessed 20 January 2022.

8 The International Charter for the Conservation and Restoration of Monuments and Sites (The Venice Charter 1964).

9 Ibid.

10 https://www.merriam-webster.com/dictionary/adaptive%20reuse, accessed 17 January 2022.

11 Daniel Bell, "The Coming of Post-Industrial Society," *The Educational Forum*, May 1976, p. 575.

12 "Dynatac Cellular Telephone," The Smithsonian National Museum of American History. https://americanhistory.si.edu/collections/search/object/nmah_1191361, accessed 26 May 2022.

13 Richard Galazzo, "Timeline from 1G to 5G: A Brief History on Cell Phones," CENGN, 21 September 2020. https://www.cengn.ca/information-centre/innovation/timeline-from-1g-to-5g-a-brief-history-on-cell-phones/, accessed 26 May 2022.

14 "Number of Mobile (Cellular) Subscriptions Worldwide from 1993–2021," Statista, December 2021. https://www.statista.com/statistics/262950/global-mobile-subscriptions-since-1993/, accessed 26 May 2022.

15 "Mobile Fact Sheet," *Pew Research Center*, 7 April 2021. https://www.pewresearch.org/internet/fact-sheet/mobile/, accessed 26 May 2022.

16 Vaclav Smil, "Energy Transitions," *World Economic Forum* 2013, p. 10. https://vaclavsmil.com/wp-content/uploads/WEF_EN_IndustryVision-12.pdf, accessed 26 May 2022.

Energy

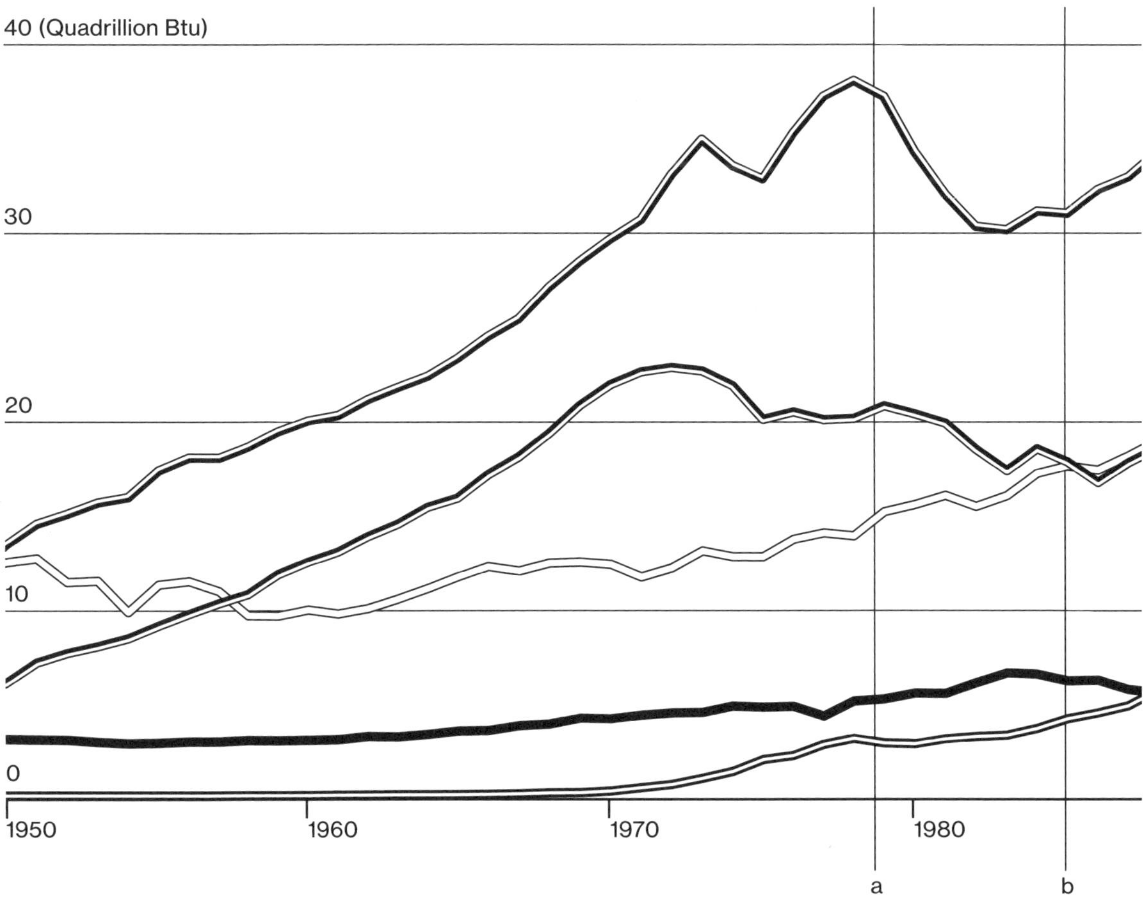

a Prizrenasja Hydro Power Plant Museum

b Pratt Street Power Plant

c Oregon Museum of Science & Industry

d Gasometer Oberhausen

e Centrale Montemartini

f Technopolis Gazi

g Tate Modern Museum

h Vienna Gasometers; Zollverein Coal Mine Industrial Complex

i Cultuurpark Westergasfabriek

j Santralistanbul

k CaixaForum Madrid; Contemporary Jewish Museum

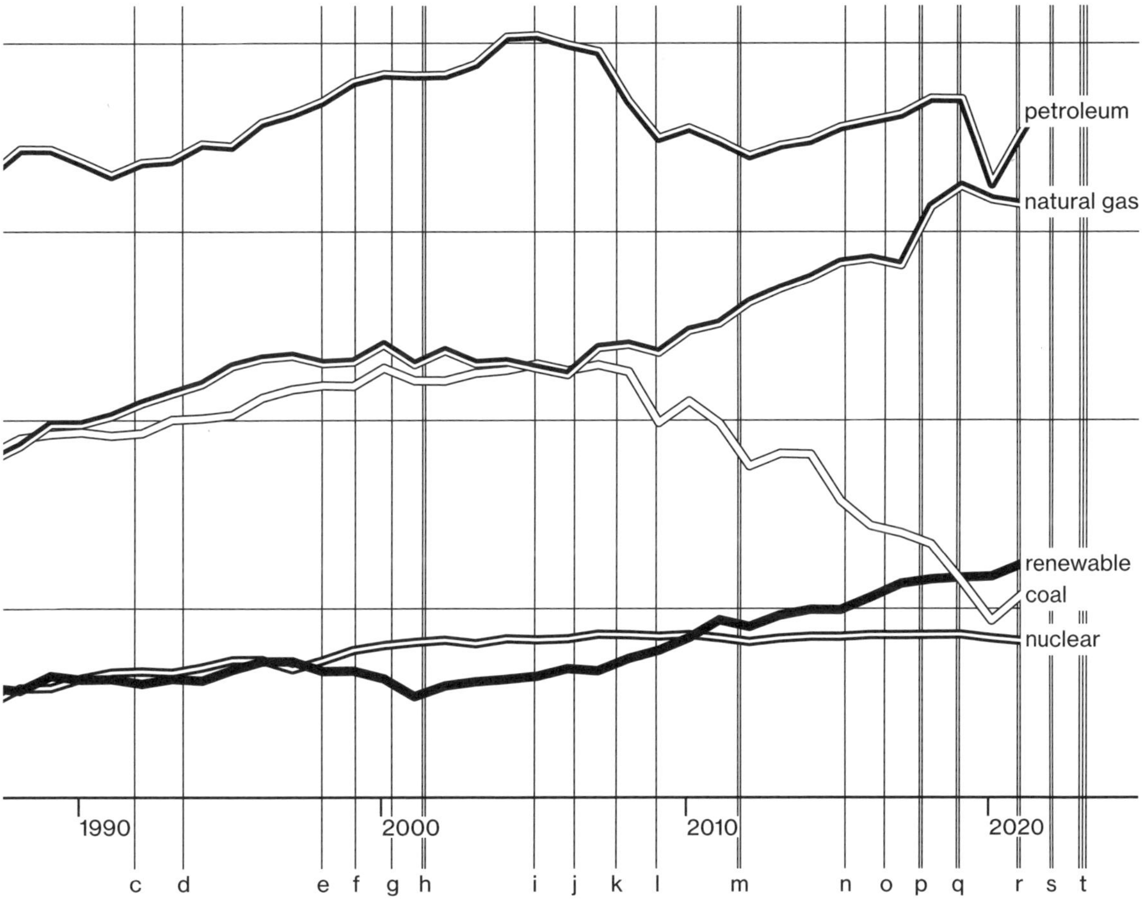

l	Powerhouse High School
m	City Hospital Power Plant Climbing Gym; Coal Mill
n	Muzeum Śląskie
o	Chain Bath in Queen Luiza Mine Complex
p	Carson Music & Campus Center; South Street Landing
q	Beloit College Power House; Coal Drops Yard; Gasholders
r	Base4Work; GES-2 Art Center
s	Kunsthalle Praha; Station A
t	Battersea Power Station Masterplan; West Heating Plant Condo; Yangshupu Power Plant; Gravatricity; Green Forests Work; Nature Conservancy conversions; Gasklockan

* Source: U.S. Energy Information Administration

"If you visit American city, you will find it very pretty. Just two things of which you must be aware, don't drink the water and don't breathe the air." These were the lyrics to the song "Pollution," recorded in 1965 by American satirist and songwriter Tom Lehrer. The song was prompted by a growing awareness of the impact of human actions on the environment that resulted from the convergence of different events in the 1960s. Anti-war sentiments, together with environmental consciousness, brought about a renewed interest in opposing nuclear technology and power. They manifested themselves in deeds such as the 1960 halting of radioactive waste dumping in France[1] and the 1963 Nuclear Test Ban Treaty between the US and USSR. The decades-long use of pesticides and their effect on the agricultural environment inspired *Silent Spring*, Rachel Carson's 1962 book. It raised widespread concern about the effects of pesticides, DDT in particular, on both the environment and on humans. Oil spills destroyed miles of coastlines such as from the 1967 Torrey Canyon oil tanker spill of 29 million gallons of oil on the French and English coastline and the 1969 Santa Barbara oil spill that "spewed an estimated 3-million gallons of crude oil into the ocean, creating an oil slick 35 miles long along California's coast and killing thousands of birds, fish and sea mammals."[2] In June 1969, the Cuyahoga River caught fire from oil and chemical pollution, prompting concern for clean water.

Awareness of Our Environment

In the wake of these environmental disasters, the first Earth Day took place on 22 April 1970. It consisted of college campus "teach-in" events through the efforts of US Senator Gaylord Nelson of Wisconsin.[3] With the intent to capitalize on the student anti-war protests, Senator Nelson hoped "to infuse the energy of student anti-war protests with an emerging public consciousness about air and water pollution."[4] These events "inspired 20 million Americans – at the time, 10% of the total population of the United States" to protest the impact of human activities on the environment. The movement prompted the adoption of a formal name: Earth Day. It brought heightened public awareness of air, land and water quality. This celebration of the Earth and its resources became an international event that takes place annually on 22 April. Nationally, this translated to the creation of the Environmental Protection Agency for oversight of the environment in 1970. Globally, the Human Environment was the focus of the 1972 United Nations conference in Stockholm. One result of the conference was the establishment of the United Nations Environmental Programme (UNEP). The UNEP would become "the coordinating body for the United Nations' environmental activities,"[5] placing the stewardship of the environment in a global arena. In 1975, American scientist Wallace S. Broecker published a paper in the journal *Science* titled "Climatic Change: Are We on the Brink of a Pronounced Global Warming?" It introduced the term "global warming" and signaled an end to earlier myths that sunlight-blocking air pollutants would cool the Earth.[6] It would take until the 1980s to recognize the reality of global warming and almost another ten years for the adoption of the Kyoto Protocol in 1997, the first of many global agreements to reduce greenhouse gases. It was not until the 2015 Paris Agreement that a global accord was reached to "substantially reduce global greenhouse gas emissions to limit the global temperature increase in this century to 2 degrees Celsius while pursuing efforts to limit the increase even further to 1.5 degrees."[7] The achievement of this goal by mid-century was the basis of the Glasgow Climate Pact, signed at the COP26 international climate conference in November 2021.

Safeguarding Our Resources

The late 1960s culminated in peak oil production for the United States and parts of Europe such as West Germany. Within this context, a different global event was unfolding in the early 1970s that, together with the conservation of the environment, would pave the way for the term "sustainability" and the embrace of its implications. In 1973, Egypt and Syria attacked Israel in what came to be known as the Yom Kippur War, a part of the ongoing Arab-Israeli conflict resulting from the 1948 creation of a Jewish state from Palestine. This conflict would have repercussions that would reverberate throughout the Western world. The US support for Israeli efforts prompted a retaliation by the Arab members of the Organization of Petroleum Exporting Countries (OPEC) that reduced petroleum production and

IMG 1 — National Capital Region Earth Day flag ceremony in Washington DC, April 22, 1970.
IMG 2 — Participants in the first Earth Day in New York City, April 22, 1970.

began an embargo of oil to the US and its allies, including Europe and Japan. This action severely impacted oil consumption, both in the US, where dependence on oil import had increased with the decline of domestic oil production in 1970, and in Europe, where dependence on imported oil in 1973 was 98%.[8]

The embargo led to fuel shortages, high prices and gas rationing. Long lines of cars at gasoline pumps remain an iconic image of what is termed the 1973–1974 energy crisis. The energy crisis of 1973 would be followed by a second energy crisis in 1979, triggered by the Iranian Revolution and the fall of the Shah.

One outcome of the energy crises was the recognition of a reliance on petroleum products. While the impact was temporarily held at bay with a short-term solution to increase domestic production, there was a reckoning with the American lifestyle of big vehicles and big homes – both of which consumed enormous quantities of petroleum products. US President Jimmy Carter warned that "the nation would begin to run short of energy supplies in the 1980's unless it changed its 'wasteful' use of fuels."[9] The struggle toward adopting a different lifestyle through energy-conscious decisions – such as smaller vehicles and homes – continues today. In Europe, the oil crisis took place at a critical time, before the European Community's commitment to a common energy policy. In 1973, a summit convened in Copenhagen resulting in the issuance of a general communiqué regarding energy measures. Outcomes included a request for the community to present proposals to address consumption but also to "adopt a comprehensive Community programme on alternative sources of energy."[10] It would require decades for the community to become the European Union and to establish a unified policy on energy in 2005. Amid the burgeoning awareness of the need for the conservation of our environment, the energy crisis brought about a critical focus on finding alternative sources of energy.

Investigating Renewable Sources

Replenishable sources of energy harness the power of nature and have been used throughout history: sun, wind, rivers, tides and hot springs. The urgency created by the energy crises resulted in renewed investigations of such sources. While notable experiments were added to the history of alternate energy production, such as Dr. Karl Böer's 1973 creation of Solar One, an experimental house with solar-generated heat and electricity,[11] the best efforts of the 1970s resulted in the creation of a governmental framework for the development of renewables.

Under the Energy Reorganization Act of 1974, a new federal entity was developed for the research and development of energy: the Energy Research and Development Administration (ERDA). The objective of ERDA was to study all forms of energy, conventional as well as renewable, including fossil, nuclear, solar, geothermal and advanced energy systems. It was an umbrella organization that encompassed resources, personnel and physical assets from the National Science Foundation, the Office of Coal

Research, the Atomic Energy Commission and the Environmental Protection Agency.[12] "Unlike many other government agencies that both develop and use new technology, ERDA held the responsibility for ensuring that appropriate technology development was carried out but with the expectation that it would be transferred to industry for use. In keeping with the urgency wrought by the energy crisis, a primary concern of ERDA was to develop technologies that would be acceptable in the marketplace."[13] In these circumstances, ERDA head Robert Seamans indicated that "a sixty-year lead time as in past energy transitions"[14] would need to be halved. Seamans' energy plan was titled, "Creating Energy Choices for the Future."[15] Instead of 2035, the target timeframe was 2005.

Within this expedited timeframe, solar energy held the most potential. There was public familiarity with such systems since the 1891 introduction of Climax, a commercial solar water heater system.[16] (By 1900, "over 1600 of these systems were installed" and, with continued development over the years, there were 60,000 solar heaters by 1941.[17]) With the ambition to supply "as much as twenty-five percent of the Nation's energy needs" by a target time of 2020, the goal was to develop, but more importantly to demonstrate, commercially attractive and environmentally acceptable applications of solar energy.[18] The Solar Research Institute was established in 1977 and continues today as the Renewable Energy Laboratory.[19] Efforts persisted throughout the decade to make solar energy affordable and accessible, especially with the second energy crisis of 1979. Despite these efforts, the introduction of solar energy as an alternative source and replacement for petroleum-based energy remained tentative. It would not be until the 21st century that the push for solar energy would reemerge at another time of rising oil imports and declining domestic oil production. The Energy Policy Act of 2005 and the American Recovery and Reinvestment Act of 2009 both provided stimulus and incentives for the use of solar energy. With the established urgent aims of climate change action in the 21st century, the solar industry soared in the midst of federal tax credits and an expanding market with falling prices of solar energy systems. Research data from the Solar Energy Industries Association indicates that in the first decade of the 21st century, "solar has experienced an average annual growth rate of 42%."[20]

Wind and geothermal energy were also studied as alternative sources. From 1974 to 1981, the NASA Glenn Research Center worked with US federal agencies such as the Environmental Protection Agency and the Department of Energy to lead the US Wind Energy Program. Prototypical wind-power systems were created in the mid-1970s. This research development established "the predominant systems used today to convert wind energy into mechanical energy."[21] The construction of the first wind farms of the early 1980s was followed by the National Wind Technology Center in 1993. In 2008, the US Department of Energy released a report titled "20% Wind Energy by 2030," addressing steps toward achieving such a goal. Progress in the following years include the 2011 announcement by the Department of Energy for a national offshore wind strategy and the installation of a first grid-connected offshore wind turbine in 2013.[22] In 2015, the Department of Energy released a new report, titled "Wind Vision: A New Era for Wind Power in the United States," that instead aimed for 35% wind energy by 2050.[23] The European Union has more ambitious targets as the global leader in offshore wind. The EU has "the largest floating wind energy capacity in the world – about 70% of the total."[24] Geothermal energy generation was concurrently explored. The Geothermal Steam Act of 1970 authorized the lease of public and federal land for geothermal exploration and the Geothermal Resources Council was formed. Various demonstration sites were created in the following decades, operating in Utah, Nevada, California and Hawaii. Incentives through legislation such as the Energy Policy Act of 2005 and the Energy Independence and Security Act of 2007 further advanced its development. In 2018, it accounted for approximately 1% of global power demand and 3% of heat demand.[25]

Toward the Next Half-Century

Many gains were made toward the exploration of alternative energy in the half-century since the energy crisis of 1973. While ERDA head Robert Seamans' ambitious 30-year expedited energy transition did not take place in that timeframe, the growth rates of solar, wind and geothermal energy use in the second decade of the 21st century allude to positive trends for a future transition. In such a transition, facilities and accessory structures related to fossil fuels would, over time, be replaced by their equivalent in renewable energy. This trend is already visible in aging power plants. With a specific lifecycle, aging power plants are renovated and updated with new systems, replaced or converted, where possible, for other types of renewable fuels. Eventually, these structures are decommissioned. Some are abandoned and fall into disrepair. From 2000 to 2021, for example, the US retired 132,951 coal-fired power plants.[26] But they are no longer being replaced. In fact, the number of new coal-fired plants in the US has dropped since 2010, when there were 5,879.[27] New plants have decreased yearly since, with 106 new facilities built in 2014, 50 in 2015 and 0 since 2016.[28] These developments have a ripple effect on coal-related structures for extraction, processing and transportation that would similarly fall out of use. In Europe, coal accounts for 20% of the European Union's electricity.[29] With the goal to become "the world's first climate-neutral bloc by 2050," the different countries have made commitments to coal phase-outs: Austria, Belgium, Sweden and Portugal by 2021, France in 2024, Italy and Hungary by 2025, Denmark and Spain by 2030 and Germany by 2038.[30] This has led to a 30% drop in coal production since 2021 and a decommissioning of mines and plants.[31] The reuse of decommissioned plants and other structures of fossil fuels for a new purpose is a relatively new phenomenon, beginning at the close of the 20th century. In the late 1990s, a thermoelectric plant in

IMG 3 — Gas stations closed during energy crisis.
IMG 4 — Gas lines at crowded gas stations.

Italy and a gas works in Austria were reused respectively for a museum and for housing. A coal mine in Germany was decommissioned and added to the UNESCO list of heritage sites in 2001 and then converted into a cultural site. A power station in the United Kingdom was awarded heritage status for its architectural features and, after being decommissioned, transformed into a museum. These were groundbreaking projects at the close of the 20th century and the turn of the 21st. Since then, many power structures have been decommissioned and transformed for new use. In 2021 and 2022, power structures from Bratislava to Moscow, Shanghai, London and San Francisco have been converted for different new purposes: co-working facility, art center, mixed-use complex, retail, hospitality. In 2022, construction began in Shanghai on the Yangshupu Power Plant, built in 1913 and "once the biggest thermal power plant in East Asia and Shanghai's tallest structure."[32] The complex will be preserved as industrial heritage and transformed into "a new industrial base for global headquarters of the energy and environmental sectors."[33] The reuse of this massive 290,000 m² industrial site for such a purpose is important in remediating the country's record as the "world's largest source of greenhouse gas emissions in recent years."[34] This project and many others are the fast-growing and tangible legacy of a series of events that began in the 1970s, events that served as a catalyst for a societal shift toward the choice of energy and its consumption in the stewardship of the environment.

A recent trend for the reuse of decommissioned coal mines is the production of renewable energy. Mine sites have particular architectural characteristics that can now be put to use for making clean energy. In the Appalachian Mountains of West Virginia, mine sites are characterized by vast tracts of flat areas exposed to sunlight. Some of these coal mines in the mountains are now being converted into solar farms where photovoltaic panels are optimized by the altitude and proximity to the sun. In the Silesian region of Czechia, the abandoned coal mines are instead valued for their many underground shafts. The Scottish start-up Gravitricity has developed a system whereby clean power is used "to raise a mass in a 150–1,500m shaft and discharges the electricity thus 'stored' by releasing the mass to rotate an electric generator."[35] The characteristic underground mine shafts render them ideal for such a gravity storage solution. The attraction at the abandoned coal mines of Hibburn Colliery, in Staffordshire, England, is the existence of the flooded mine shafts. Heat will be extracted from mine water as thermal energy. These different proposals offer unique reuse strategies for transforming sites of fossil fuel production into those of renewable energy. It is a circular trajectory for the structures of energy production.

However, these positive trends toward implementing renewable energy sources at the conclusion of this 50-year period have once again been affected by global affairs. At the conclusion of the half-century since the first oil crisis, the 2022 Russian attack on Ukraine has again brought the geopolitics of energy to the forefront, with a new energy crisis

IMG 5 — The Zollverein Coal Washing Plant, transformed.

for many parts of the world, especially Europe. The European Union's joint sanctions toward Russian oil imports brought attention to many EU members' continued dependence on oil. On a warm day in July 2022, the president of the European Commission, looking ahead, asked EU countries to reduce their consumption of natural gas by 15% until the spring of 2023, as part of a plan to negotiate these new circumstances. Even as the West struggles to cope with Russia's weaponizing of oil, there are hints of new geopolitical alliances with China, Iran and Saudi Arabia that are echoes of the 1970s. What are the short-term implications of this new energy crisis? Might it effect a reconsideration of coal phase-out schedules or, worse, a temporary return to coal use? Hopefully this will not be the case as the EU works to find both short- and long-term solutions to its energy dependence. Half a century later, however, there are graver implications for such decisions than the price of oil. With the full knowledge of the threat of climate change to the future of the planet, there is no time for policy reversals, even temporarily. But not all countries will adhere to climate-friendly action. Ironically, extreme heat and flooding in China caused by climate change have wreaked havoc, causing power outages in the summer of 2022. "Premier Li Keqiang said on Tuesday while touring a thermal power company that the country must increase coal production capacity to prevent power outages."[36] Will such action be reflected in the built environment in the future as a reverse trend in which decommissioned energy production facilities are reconverted to their original use? In the spirit of optimism for the future generations and our planet, hopefully not. These events do, however, demonstrate the vulnerability of intentions in the context of time.

• Base4Work	Bratislava, Slovakia, 2021
• Battersea Power Station Masterplan	London, UK, ongoing
• Beloit College Power House	Beloit, WI, USA, 2018
• CaixaForum Madrid	Madrid, Spain, 2008
• Carson Music & Campus Center	Concord, MA, USA, 2017
• Centrale Montemartini	Rome, Italy, 1997–2001
• Chain Bath in Queen Luiza Mine Complex	Zabrze, Poland, 2016
• City Hospital Power Plant Climbing Gym	St. Louis, MO, USA, 2012
• Coal Drops Yard	London, UK, 2018
• Coal Mill	Libčice nad Vltavou, Czech Republic, 2012
• Contemporary Jewish Museum	San Francisco, CA, USA, 2008
• Cultuurpark Westergasfabriek	Amsterdam, the Netherlands, 2006
• Gasholders	London, UK, 2018
• Gasklockan	Stockholm, Sweden, 2022–
• Gasometer Oberhausen	Oberhausen, Germany, 1994
• GES-2 Art Center	Moscow, Russia, 2021
• Gravitricity	Staříč, Czech Republic, 2022–
• Green Forests Work	Virginia, USA, 2022–
• Kunsthalle Praha	Prague, Czech Republic, 2022
• Muzeum Śląskie	Katowice, Poland, 2015
• Nature Conservancy Conversions	Virginia, USA, 2022–
• Powerhouse High School	Chicago, IL, USA, 2009
• Pratt Street Power Plant	Baltimore, MD, USA, 1985
• Prizrenasja Hydro Power Plant Museum	Prizren, Kosovo, 1979
• Oregon Museum of Science & Industry	Portland, OR, USA, 1992
• Santralistanbul	Istanbul, Turkey, 2007
• South Street Landing	Providence, RI, USA, 2017
• Station A	San Francisco, CA, USA, 2022
• Tate Modern Museum	London, UK, 2000
• Technopolis Gazi	Athens, Greece, 1999
• Vienna Gasometers	Vienna, Austria, 2001
• West Heating Plant Condo	Washington DC, USA, ongoing
• Yangshupu Power Plant	Shanghai, China, 2022
• Zollverein Coal Mine Industrial Complex	Essen, Germany, 2001

1 "France to Delay Atomic Disposal," *The New York Times, 13 October 1960.*

2 Christine Mai Duc, "The 1969 Santa Barbara Oil Spill that Changed Oil and Gas Exploration Forever," *Los Angeles Times*, 20 May 2015. https://www.latimes.com/local/lanow/la-me-ln-santa-barbara-oil-spill-1969-20150520-htmlstory.html, accessed 6 February 2022.

3 "The History of Earth Day," https://www.earthday.org/history/, accessed 6 February 2021.

4 Ibid.

5 "United Nations Environmental Programme (UNEP) Established," in the Environment and Society Portal. https://www.environmentandsociety.org/tools/keywords/united-nations-environmental-programme-unep-established, accessed 10 February 2022.

6 Michael Le Page, "Climate Myths: They Predicted Global Cooling in the 1970s," *NewScientist*, 16 May 2007. https://www.newscientist.com/article/dn11643-climate-myths-they-predicted-global-cooling-in-the-1970s/, accessed 10 February 2022.

7 "The Paris Agreement," *United Nations Climate Action*. https://www.un.org/en/climatechange/paris-agreement, accessed 14 February 2022.

8 Peter Stingelin, "Europe and the Oil Crisis," *Current History*, Vol. 68, No. 403, *The Nations of West Europe* (1975), p. 133.

9 Charles Mohr, "Carter Asks Strict Fuel Saving; Urges 'Moral Equivalent of War' to Bar a 'National Catastrophe,'" *The New York Times*, 19 April 1977.

10 Stingelin, "Europe and the Oil Crisis," op. cit., p. 132.

11 "In Memoriam: Karl W. Böer," UDaily of the University of Delaware website. https://www.udel.edu/udaily/2018/april/in-memoriam-karl-w-boer/, accessed 9 February 2022.

12 Alice Buck "A History of the Energy Research and Development Administration," US Department of Energy, March 1982, p. 2.

13 Ibid., p. 9.

14 Ibid., p. 5.

15 Ibid.

16 "Clarence Kemp," National Inventors Hall of Fame, https://www.invent.org/inductees/clarence-kemp, accessed 12 February 2022.

17 K. Butti and J. Perlin, "Solar Water Heaters in California, 1891–1930." *The Coevolution Quarterly*, United States Department of Energy. https://www.osti.gov/biblio/6772173-solar-water-heaters-california, accessed 12 February 2022.

18 Buck, "A History of the Energy Research," op. cit., p. 6.

19 Matthew Sabas, "History of Solar Power," IER Institute for Energy Research, 18 February 2016. https://www.instituteforenergyresearch.org/renewable/solar/history-of-solar-power/, accessed 10 February 2022.

20 "Solar Industry Research Data," from SEIA Solar Energy Industries Association. https://www.seia.org/solar-industry-research-data, accessed 10 February 2022.

21 "Glenn Responds to the 1970s Energy Crisis," National Aeronautics and Space Administration (NASA), 10 April 2008. https://www.nasa.gov/centers/glenn/about/history/70s_energy.html, accessed 11 February 2022.

22 "History of U.S. Wind Energy," US Department of Energy. https://www.energy.gov/eere/wind/history-us-wind-energy, accessed 13 February 2022.

23 "Wind Vision: A New Vision for Wind Power in the United States," Office of Efficiency and Renewable Energy, US Department of Energy, April 2015, p. xxiii.

24 "Why the EU Supports Wind Energy Research and Innovation," European Commission website, https://ec.europa.eu/info/research-and-innovation/research-area/energy-research-and-innovation/wind-energy_en, accessed 30 June 2022.

25 Marit Brommer, "Geothermal in the Future Energy Mix," *GeoExPro*, Vol. 15, No. 4, 2018, p. 30.

26 "Retired Coal-fired Power Capacity by Country-Global Coal Plant Tracker," *Global Energy Monitor*. https://globalenergymonitor.org/projects/global-coal-plant-tracker/, accessed 13 February 2022.

27 "New Coal-fired Power Capacity by Country – Global Coal Plant Tracker," *Global Energy Monitor*. https://globalenergymonitor.org/projects/global-coal-plant-tracker/, accessed 13 February 2022.

28 Ibid.

29 "Coal Regions in Transition," European Commission website https://energy.ec.europa.eu/topics/oil-gas-and-coal/eu-coal-regions/coal-regions-transition_en, accessed 23 June 2022.

30 Ibid.

31 Ibid.

32 Yang Jian, "Over Century-old Power Plant Gets a New Lease on Life," Shine, *Shanghai Daily*, 4 January 2022.

33 Ibid.

34 Lindsay Maizland, "China's Fight Against Climate Change and Environmental Degradation," Council on Foreign Relations, 19 May 2021. https://www.cfr.org/backgrounder/china-climate-change-policies-environmental-degradation, accessed 22 July 2022.

35 Emiliano Bellini, "Converting Coal Mines into Gravity-based Renewable Energy Storage Facilities," *pv magazine*, 26 October 2021.

36 Tiffany May, "Extreme Weather Hits China with Massive Floods and Scorching Heat," *The New York Times*, 23 June 2022.

		Project		Architect
E-1		CaixaForum Madrid Madrid, ES	2008	Herzog & de Meuron
E-2	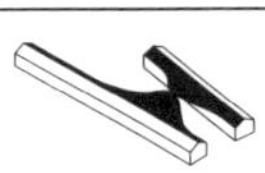	Coal Drops Yard London, UK	2018	Heatherwick Studio
E-3		Vienna Gasometers Vienna, AT	2001	Coop Himmelblau/ Jean Nouvel/Wilfred Holzbauer/ Manfred Wehdorn
E-4		GES-2 Art Center Moscow, RU	2021	RPBW Architects
E-5	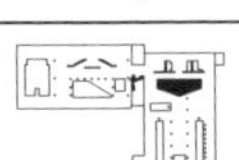	Centrale Montemartini Rome, IT	1997–2001	Paolo Nervi
E-6	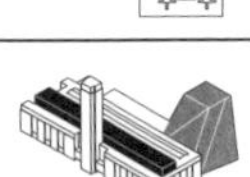	Tate Modern Museum London, UK	2000	Herzog & de Meuron

Energy

New Program

	Cultural	Education	Hospitality	Infrastructure	Office	Residential	Retail	Recreational	Memorial
	●								
							●		
						●	●		
	●								
	●								
	●								

E-1 CaixaForum Madrid

The CaixaForum Madrid, a cultural center facing one of the city's main boulevards, is reborn from the decommissioned Central Eléctrica Power Station. Built in the city's early industrial era, the power station with its brick facade and stone base was architecturally unremarkable. This lack of architectural heritage was the impetus for the unique interventions undertaken within this utilitarian host structure. The primary intervention to remove the stone base from the brick skin was the basis for the creation of what Herzog & de Meuron refer to as "two worlds": one above and an "underworld" below. The brick skin is left in situ, suspended above the void left by the stone base, which now serves as an entrance to the building on the newly created plaza. An auditorium is carved into the space below ground while an addition, in metal, above the top of the power station extends the height of the building with a new roof silhouette. New windows cut into the old brick facade, where the old window apertures have been filled in, reference the new spaces and activity inside. Visible from the Paseo de Prado, the remains of the unprepossessing electric station float – sandwiched – between the new interventions above and below, preserved in new time through reuse.

Location:	Madrid, Spain	
Year of Conversion:	2008	
Architects:	Herzog & de Meuron	
Original Use:	Power station	[energy]
New Use:	Art institution / cultural center	[culture]

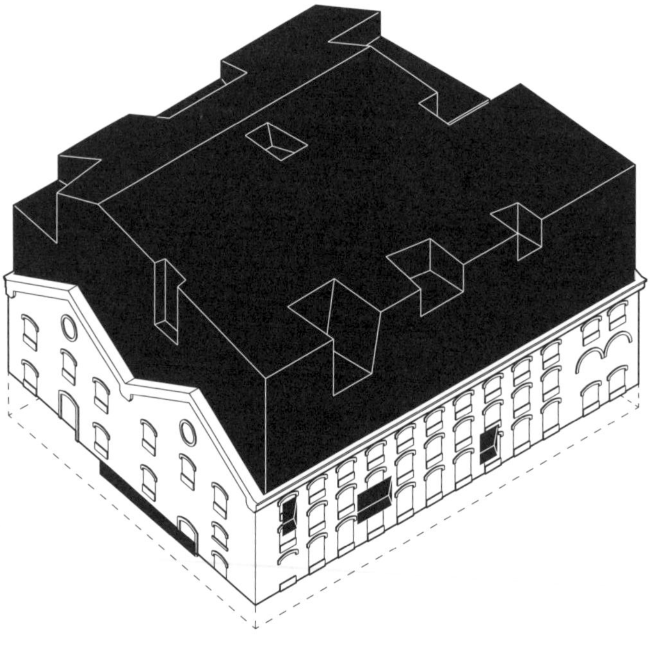

E-2 Coal Drops Yard

Coal Drops Yard is the 21st-century iteration of a pair of mid-18th-century viaduct sheds that were used to receive and transfer coal for the energy needs of Victorian London. With the advent of electricity, these brick structures became redundant and, subsequently, derelict. In the ensuing decades, these long and narrow sheds with repetitive bays were partially reused – for industrial purposes, warehouse storage and nightclubbing – before being abandoned at the close of the 20th century. In 2014, the King's Cross Central Limited Partnership proposed to rethink the industrial site and develop it as an upscale retail and market district. The placement of the two rectangular and almost parallel structures of different lengths located across from each other in the coal yard, once filled with the bustle of industrial activity, was an invitation to reuse this space for commercial activity. An intervention through an insertion of a fluid form lifting, rising, and stretching in the gabled roofs resulted in the formation of new and unusual function spaces. The sinewy roof additions concluded in a cantilever towards each other, merging over the outdoor space to create a single form from the two sheds. Coal Drops Yard is an example of the design intervention that unifies separate and sometimes disparate host structures to create a single project through adaptive reuse.

Location:	London, UK	
Year of Conversion:	2018	
Architects:	Heatherwick Studio	
Original Use:	Coal drop / warehouse / nightclub	[energy]
New Use:	Shopping center	[retail / recreation]

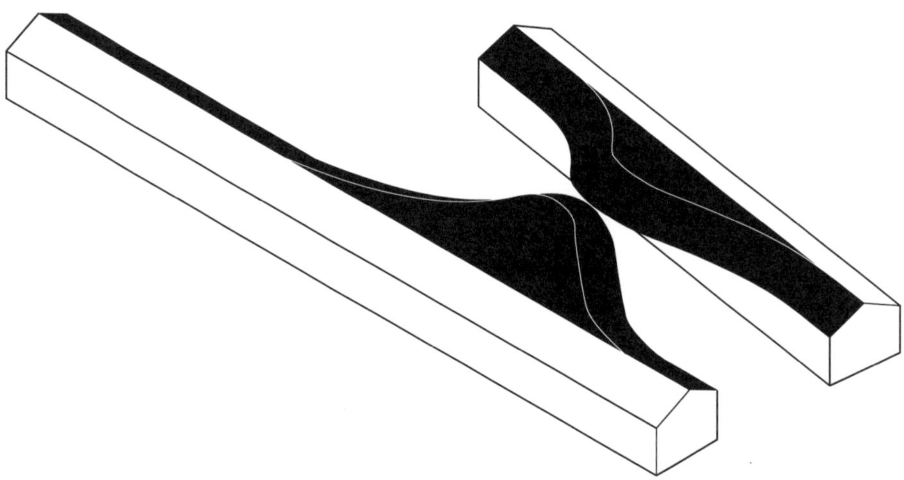

E-3 Vienna Gasometers

Begun in 1896, four gigantic gas holders were constructed as part of the municipal gasworks to supply the citizens of Vienna with town gas, a form of manufactured fuel and a byproduct of industrial processes. Located in Simmering, the 11th district, in Guglgasse Street, these structures of Gaswerk Simmering were a transition from previously privatized energy sources. The largest gasworks in Europe at the time, it received heritage designation in 1981 as an outstanding example of industrial architecture. From 1970 to 1978, however, the city converted to the use of natural gas and, in 1986, the gasometers were decommissioned due to obsolescence. Their location in the city prompted consideration of their reuse as housing in a plan for urban development.

In 1995, a competition brought forth proposals by four architectural firms. The proposals from Nouvel, Wehdorn and Holzbauer included different interventions for inserting housing units within the 55-m-high brick skin of the gasometer. Coop Himmelblau, along with the conversion, proposed the addition of a new glass and steel volume attached to Gasometer B. In total, the converted gasometers provided more than 600 units of apartments, shops and offices. Known as Vienna Gasometers, the reuse of these structures retains the monumental brick cylinders, protected through heritage designation, while transforming them for vibrant new use. Completed in 2001, the project was groundbreaking in the reuse of industrial infrastructure.

Location:	Vienna, Austria	
Year of Conversion:	2001	
Architects:	Coop Himmelblau / Jean Nouvel / Manfred Wehdorn / Wilhelm Holzbauer	
Original Use:	Gas tank	[energy / heritage]
New Use:	Housing and retail	[residence / retail]

E-4 GES-2 Art Center

The GES-2, originally named the Tramvaynaya in 1907 and the second major power station in Moscow, provided electric power for the city's tramline. The station had a second life thrust upon it in the 1917 Revolution when its clock tower, later dismantled, was used as a machine gun tower. Over the next century, it was refurbished including a conversion to natural gas. Despite maintenance, the power station was closed in 2006. In 2009, the GES-2 was listed as a structure of cultural heritage and, in 2014, it was acquired as a permanent home for the V-A-C Foundation to rethink the model of the "house of culture." Located on Bolotny Island, the GES-2 is part of a destination site that includes the Strelka Institute, the Red October chocolate factory and the historic Udarnik Cinema. The reuse of the GES-2 consists of diametric types of interventions. On the exterior, the structure was returned to its original form through the removal of later additions and the restoration of four iconic chimneys that had been removed. The interior, conceived as a "cathedral of light," has been gutted to create a large airy atrium, with exposed structure, a glass roof, and circulation in the form of connecting walkways and bridges – all painted white.

Location:	Moscow, Russia	
Year of Conversion:	2021	
Architects:	Renzo Piano Building Workshop	
Original Use:	Power station	[energy]
New Use:	Art center	[culture]

E-5 Museum of the Centrale Montemartini

The Museum of the Centrale Montemartini is housed in Rome's first plant for the production of electricity, inaugurated in 1912. Maintained and upgraded throughout WWII, the plant on the left bank of the Tiber was decommissioned in the mid-1960s when it was no longer useful. ACEA, Rome's municipal electric company, chose to reuse the facilities for various purposes: an art and multimedia center, offices, laboratories and warehouses. At the same time, Rome's Capitoline Museums were in need of additional space for their vast collections. Staging an exhibition of classical sculpture within the surviving machinery of the electric plant was an experiment in museography. The show, "Machines and Gods," opened in 1997, a contrast between "archaeology and industrial archaeology."[1] The show received much public acclaim confirming the success of the industrial setting as a museum. In 2001, the electric plant officially became a permanent part of the Capitoline Museums as the Museum of the Centrale Montemartini. It is an example of adaptive reuse with minimal intervention where the presence of the past is a salient part of the new design. In this case, its industrial character is the driver of adaptive reuse. Different from other projects of adaptive reuse, the past and the present co-exist in a new use.

Location:	Rome, Italy	
Year of Conversion:	1997–2001	
Architects:	Paolo Nervi	
Original Use:	Power station	[energy]
New Use:	Museum	[culture]

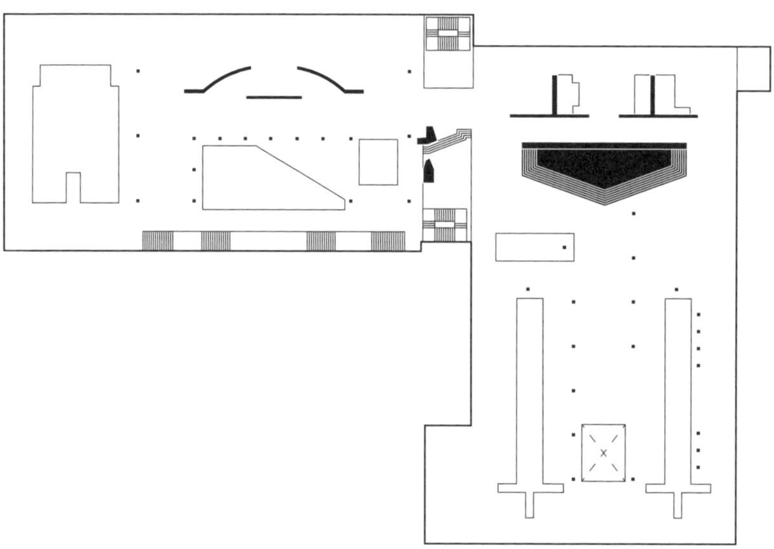

1 From the website of the Capitoline Museum. https://www.centralemontemartini.org/en/il_museo/storia_del_museo

E-6 Tate Modern Museum

Tate Modern, one of the four branches of the Tate network of galleries, is located in the former Bankside B Power Station that generated electricity for the City of London from 1947–1981. Designed by Sir Giles Gilbert Scott, Bankside B was oil-fired. It produced an annual output of more than 6 million kWh/day in 1970 but the oil crisis of 1973 made such production uneconomical. The station became redundant and was decommissioned in 1981. Efforts were made to list Bankside B as a heritage site but applications were denied. In 1994, the Tate Trustees selected the former power station for their new gallery and Herzog & de Meuron as the architects of the conversion because of their unique proposal to retain the building's character. While the machinery was removed, the interventions to the station were minimal. Spaces that once accommodated huge generators the width and height of the entire building were retained for their scale, such as in the reuse of the massive turbine hall as a place of congregation. An understated aesthetic was applied to the galleries, in keeping with the industrial character of the Scott structure. The only visible exterior alteration is the addition of a translucent linear volume on the roof. The success of the project led to the reuse of the oil tanks as additional galleries in 2012 and an extension to the museum in 2016. Tate Modern set a precedent for the reuse of power plants at the start of the 21st century.

Location:	London, UK	
Year of Conversion:	2000	
Architects:	Herzog & de Meuron	
Original Use:	Power plant	[energy]
New Use:	Museum	[culture]

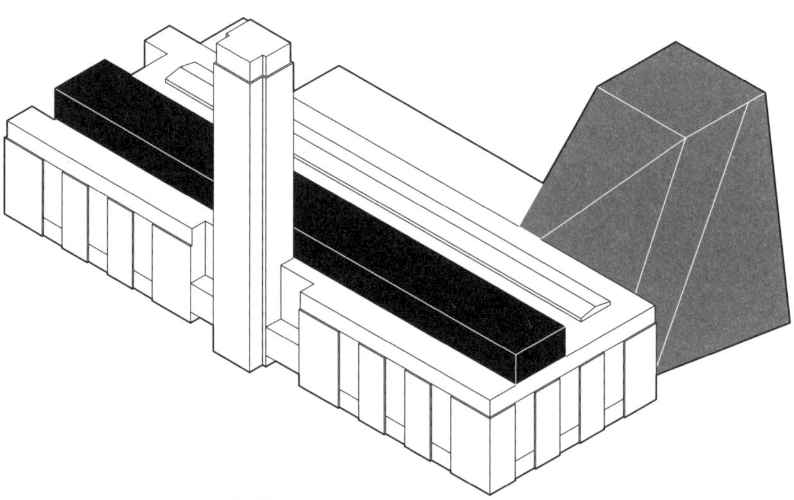

Manufacturing

Reuse of Manufacturing Structures
+ Manufacturing Employment vs. Output 1939–2019*

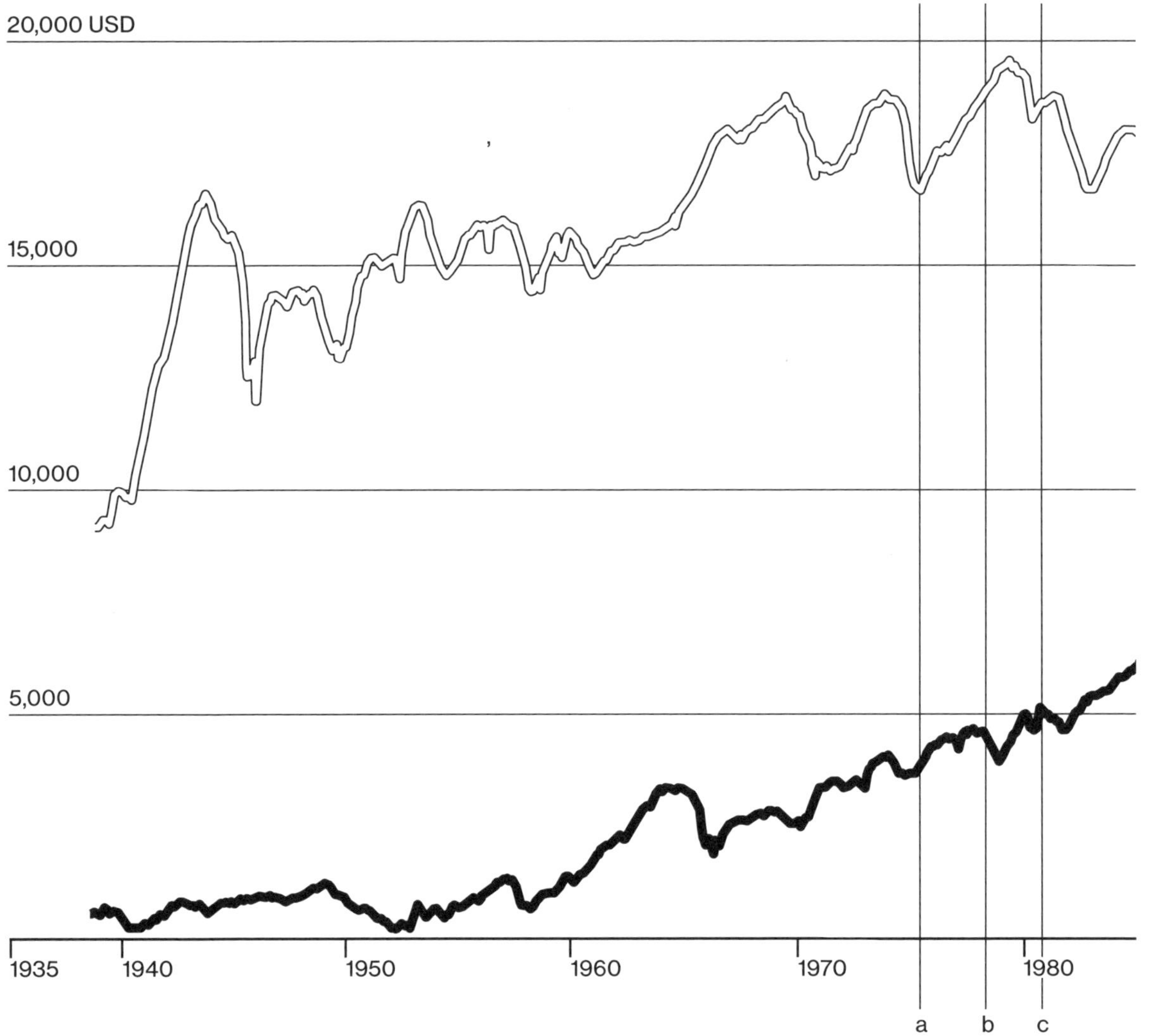

a La Fábrica

b Granville Island

c WUK Werkstätten- und Kulturhaus

d SESC Pompéia

e Clocktower Building

f Temporary Contemporary

g 798 Art Zone

h Parque Fundidora

i MASS MoCA

j ExRotaprint; M50 (50 Moganshan Road)

k Distillery District; Leipziger Baumwollspinnerei

l CaixaForum Barcelona; Rog Centre of Contemporary Art

m Mill City Museum

n Huashan 1914 Creative Park; Proekt Fabrika

o Manufaktura and Andel's Hotel; San Francisco Armory

p Inujima Art Project; LX Factory

q RCA Sackler Building; St. Nicholas Eastern Orthodox Church

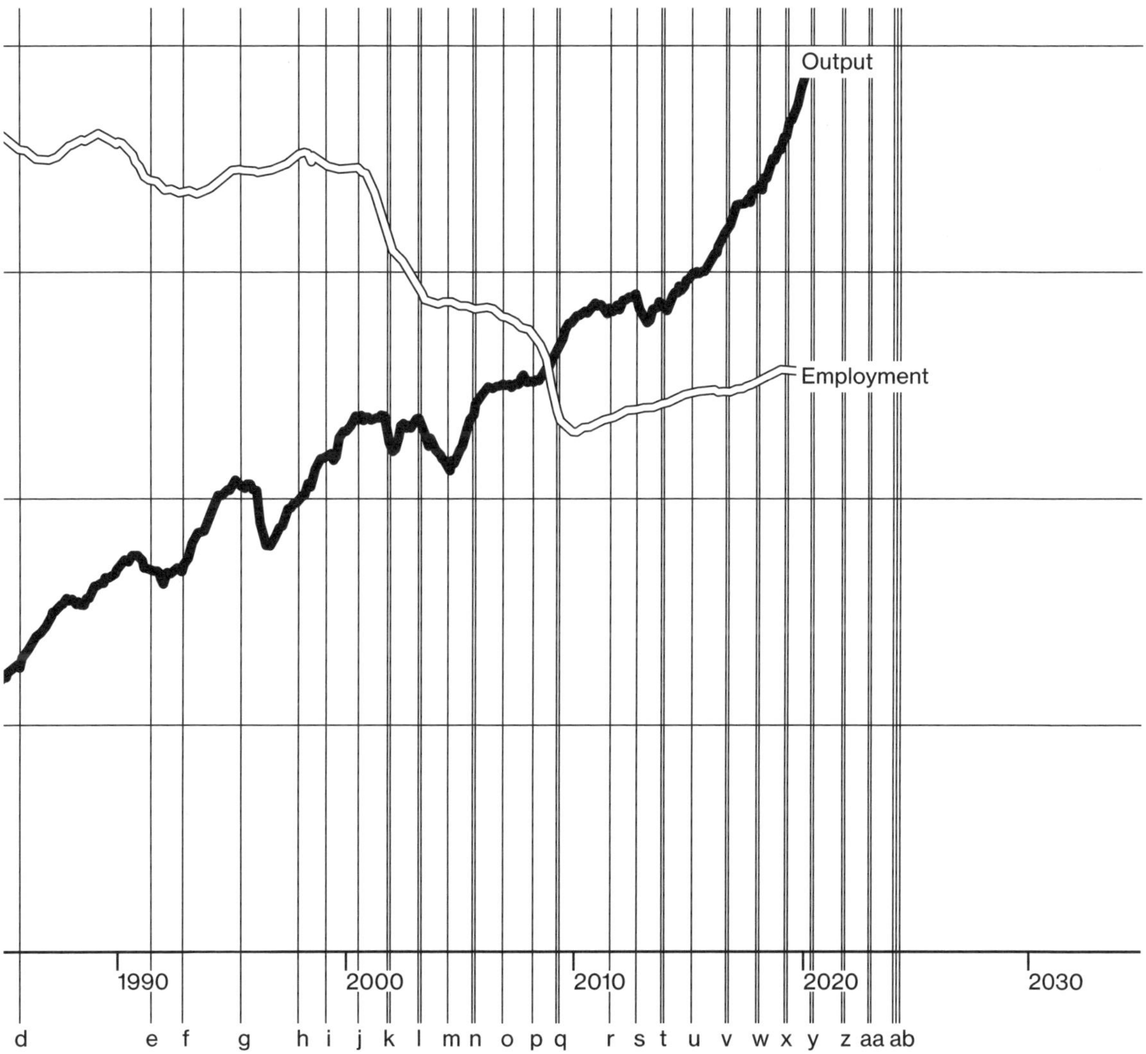

r 178 Townsend

s FRAC Grand Large

t Klan KOSOVA TV Station; Launchlabs; Market One

u Transformer Fitzroy

v Elbphilharmonie; Fondaco dei Tedeschi

w Kanaal Antwerp; Tsingpu Yangzhou Retreat; WaterFire Arts Center

x Fondazione Prada; Plant Seven (Congdon Yards); Streetmekka Viborg

y Alembic Industrial Heritage & Redevelopment

z Alte Mälze Lauterhofen Renovation; Baoshan Exhibition Center; MUHBA Oliva Artés

aa Cau Dat Tea Museum; The Plant

ab Bob Dylan Center; Lantern Art Factory; Ennaire Foundation

* Sources: Bureau of Labor Statistics/Macrotrends

In 1973, American sociologist Daniel Bell published *The Coming of Post-Industrial Society: A Venture in Social Forecasting.* A central theme was the evolution of society from agrarian to industrial to the then transformation to post-industrial. He further contrasted the mass-production mindset of the industrial "goods-producing societies" to that of a "services"-based society. Comparing data from the 1950s, when "half of all workers were engaged in production of goods, and almost 34 percent directly in manufacturing," to the metrics of the 1970s, when "65 out of every hundred workers is engaged in services," he predicted that in the year 2000 "only 10 percent of the labor force will be in manufacturing."[1] His prediction was prescient, as in 2021 "manufacturers in the United States account for 10.94% of the total output in the economy, employing 8.58% of the workforce."[2] As a forecaster, Bell cautioned that "a post-industrial society does not displace an industrial society," but that "these goods will be produced by fewer and fewer persons."[3] In addition, he conjectured that "a post-industrial society is, preeminently, a high technology economy."[4] Viewing his work from a half-century later, these two aspects have proven true with far-reaching implications for the built environment.

Ping-Pong Diplomacy

Bell penned his book in a Cold War era when the world was divided into three sections; the West and their allies were grouped in the First World, the Communist bloc in the Second, and all others in the Third.[5] He referenced historian Arnold Toynbee's term "external proletariat" in forecasting that "the divisions within the world ... the Third World (and Fourth and Fifth) against the Industrial First World (and even the Communist Second) – will become the central fact of world politics."[6] The Second included China, whose limited relationship with the United States dated back to 1949 when the US backed Chiang Kai-shek and the Nationalist government in Taiwan. In the context of decades of fraught Sino-US relations with little diplomacy or trade, an unexpected encounter took place between a member of the US team and a member of the Chinese team at the 1971 World Table Tennis Championship in Nagoya, Japan. This led to an invitation from China's ping-pong team to the US team. Those nine players became the first Americans to enter China since the formation of the People's Republic of China in 1949. This event led to an opening of Sino-US relations and, a few months later, the lifting of the trade embargo against China. The following year, a US president made a groundbreaking visit to China, touring the country and meeting Chairman Mao. In 1979, the US granted China full diplomatic recognition. What took place in April of 1971 was termed ping-pong diplomacy as it paved the way for shifting alliances in world politics and the development of a new world order for the next half-century. US President Nixon said of the trip, it was "the week that changed the world."[7]

The opening of China after 1972 propelled the country into the global spotlight on many levels. In 1978, under the leadership of Deng Xiaoping, China embraced a new policy that allowed it to break out of its isolation and catapult into the global economy. "Cheap labor rates and proximal access to quickly growing consumer populations in Southeast Asia made one of the most lucrative business hubs in the world. It quickly overtook the United States in 2011 to become the world's largest manufacturer driving growth in the nation's GDP by 40%."[8] In 2019, it produced 25.72 million vehicles[9] and 53.3% of the world crude steel production.[10] From cars

IMG 1 — President Richard Nixon attending a ping pong tournament, Beijing 1972.
IMG 2 — The Intel 4004 chip.

to steel, four decades later, China ranks as the "largest manufacturer in the world."[11] In contrast, manufacturing jobs in the US, "which had been relatively stable at 17 million since 1965, declined by one third in that decade, falling by 5.8 million to below 12 million in 2010 (returning to just 12.3 million in 2016)."[12] In 2020, the US workforce was made up of 59.8% professionals[13] while only 7.9% was employed in manufacturing.[14] In Europe, employment in both manufacturing and agriculture decreased in a 20-year study from 1996 to 2016.[15] The term "outsourcing" emerged in 1979 to explain the phenomenon of procuring goods and services from outside and foreign sources.[16] Other countries, especially in Asia, were part of the outsourcing of manufacturing, but "in the decades following the Nixon-Mao meeting, China became the world's manufacturing hub, filling Walmart shelves, Amazon boxes, and the welcome arms of American consumers."[17] Manufactured goods remained in demand, but these demands were now met in great part by workers of other countries. A half-century after ping-pong diplomacy, the legacy of the dramatic shift in the Western workforce from manufacturing to services since the 1970s is visible in the underused, unused or decommissioned factory buildings in many developed (and even undeveloped) nations.

The Chip that Changed the World

Seven months after the US table tennis team traveled to China, an obscure California start-up called Intel announced the launch of the 4004, the first commercially available microprocessor. The advertisement stated: "Announcing a New Era of Integrated Electronics – A micro-programmable computer on a chip!"[18] Following decades of developments in integrated circuitry, the Intel 4004 was a breakthrough that was termed "the chip that changed the world."[19] The size of a fingernail, "with 2,300 transistors, it could process what must have seemed like an astounding 60,000 instructions a second."[20] This seemingly modest invention in 1971 changed the world as it was known, beginning with the office, where paper, typewriters, erasing typing tapes and files became relics of the past. The advent of the 4004 microchip processor heralded the modern computing era and was critical to the transformation of the workforce not only in the US, but across the world. Microprocessing computing is described as "the brains" that make nearly every modern technology, from the cloud to the edge, possible. "Microprocessors enable the convergence of the technology superpowers – ubiquitous computing, pervasive connectivity, cloud-to-edge infrastructure and artificial intelligence – and create a pace of innovation that is moving faster today than ever."[21] The digital revolution created countless new jobs for knowledge workers, further increasing the service versus manufacturing divide. The invention of this chip and its subsequent effect on the

IMG 3 – Spencer Finch's installation "Cosmic Latte" at MASS MoCA Museum, transformed from the Arnold Print Works.
IMG 4 – The Geffen Contemporary at MOCA (formerly the Temporary Contemporary) was a former police car warehouse.

workforce corroborated Bell's prediction of a technology economy. The swerve toward technology would triply affect the built environment. First, office spaces would be redefined from tight, rectangular boxes to those without physical walls and, recently, during the Covid-19 pandemic, to virtual rooms. Second, the digital revolution outmoded many of the existing manufacturing processes. Those factories and structures for which there was no economically feasible update were decommissioned, unused and abandoned. Finally, the shift toward a high-tech economy increased the services industry manyfold. While there was a plethora of new items to manufacture related to the digital revolution, the majority of these items were once again manufactured outside the US. In 2021, for example, TSMC of Taiwan was the largest manufacturer of semiconductors at 54% of the market share, followed by South Korea's Samsung at 17% and the US's Global Foundries at 7%.[22] The Sprague Electric Company in North Adams, Massachusetts, exemplifies the impact of these shifts on a historical industrial structure. A mill in the 18th century, a printworks in the 19th century and an electronics plant in the 20th century, it was also a successful research and development center whose products were used in space-launch systems as well as the atomic bomb. It closed in 1985 when it could no longer compete with the prices of components produced outside the US.[23] The Sprague Electric Company has since been converted to the Massachusetts Museum of Contemporary Art (MASS MoCA).

While outsourcing and new technological processes were factors contributing to the closure of factories, there were also others. Environmental policies following the first Earth Day also contributed inadvertently to the demise of certain factories. One of the objectives of the Clean Air Act of 1970 was to raise awareness of pollution and the importance of pollution control. Many, however, believed that environmental protection would harm economic growth. A mayor of a small American town was purported to have said: "If you want this town to grow, it has got to stink,"[24] advocating for the development of the industrial sector. Despite such opposition, developed countries formed policies targeting air pollution. After the 1972 UN Conference on Human Environment, the EU adopted its first Environment Action Programme, promoting ideas such as that of "polluter pays."[25] One consequence of these actions in the industrial sector was the closing of factories that were non-compliant. A cement factory built during the industrialization of Catalonia is one such example. The factory was abandoned after the Second World War due to outmoded methods as well as those contributing to pollution.[26] It was adapted over decades and used as the office and residence of architect Ricardo Bofill, who purchased the property in 1973.

Inhabiting the Post-Industrial

Together, ping-pong diplomacy and the advent of the microprocessing chip, two events of the 1970s that "changed the world," created a set of conditions that, over time, fulfilled Daniel Bell's prediction of the post-industrial society. These shifts in labor over a half-century resulted in defunct factories that became the sites of adaptive reuse. While there are a few projects from the 1970s and early 1980s, such as La Fábrica and Frank Gehry's project, The Temporary Contemporary, the conversion of a hardware factory into a museum in Los Angeles, notable reuse projects of manufacturing sites only emerged toward the end of the 20th century. Initially, these were sites in developed countries where the differentiated labor force statistics between 1969 and 2016 were evidence of a shift – in some cases up to 30% – toward the service industries. (The labor force in 1969: the US with 5.2% agriculture, 33.7% industry, 61.1% service; the UK with 3.1% agriculture, 47.1% industry, 49.7% service; West Germany with 10.6% agriculture, 48% industry, 41.4% service.[27] The labor force in 2016: the US with 1.43% agriculture, 19.78% industry, 78.79% service,[28] the UK with 1.3% agriculture, 15.2% industry, 83.5% service; Germany with 1.4% agriculture, 24.2% industry, 74.3% service.[29]) These sites include factories for textiles, electronic parts, alcohol distillation, munitions, flour, rubber and hosiery, and are located from the United States to Portugal, France, Spain and Germany. But countries whose labor forces benefitted from the manufacturing shift have themselves evolved in time toward a service industry, albeit in lower percentages (in 1960, Southeast Asia with 75% agriculture, 8% industry, 17% service and East Asia (mainland) with 75% agriculture, 10% industry, 15% service; in 2016, India with 47% agriculture, 22% industry, 31% services and China with 27.7% agriculture, 28.8% industry, 43.5% service).[30] There are now a few notable projects of industrial reuse from those countries as well.

Manufacturing plants are large and simple structures, defined by column bay sizes to accommodate various types of machinery. Most manufacturing structures are open, rectangular spaces with a grid of columns. With few limitations other than the column grid spacing, they are adaptable for many new programs of use. Such structures were initially reused by artists for housing and studios, establishing the concept of the loft with its high ceilings and open plan. This concept originated in New York City, where an abundance of industrial structures in New York's garment district were in disrepair or derelict. The Factory, one of Andy Warhol's studios from the 1960s, is an example of the occupation of such sites by artists; leaders in appropriating industrial space. This trend continues today as countries outside the West contend with the remnants of post-industrialization. In China, it came about at the turn of the 21st century in Shanghai and Beijing with the reuse of factories by artists at M50 and the 798 Art Zone. In India, the 2018 project of repurposing the Alembic factory as exhibition space and art studios focuses on maintaining the spirit of the 116-year-old brick structure. The 1973 purchase by architect Ricardo Bofill of a massive cement factory in Barcelona for his personal use speaks to the allure of the industrial past. As relatively "empty" boxes embedded with vestiges of our history, this type of structure has since been adapted for many types of new use besides the artist studio. They have become museums, hotels, offices, radio stations, centers of retail, schools, television stations and even churches, with their industrial past often referenced in the new use. The Plant in Chicago, its name alluding to its past as a meatpacking facility, is now an indoor vertical farm, beer business incubator and sustainable food research/education space. Funded in part by an economic-opportunity grant, the 8,640m^2 factory is now host to a closed-loop aquaponic growing system to grow produce, farm fish, brew beer and generate electricity through a recycling of biomass. This self-sustaining business is in itself a new form of manufacturing.

IMG 5 — Factories for storage battery assemblage would become prime real estate for modern lofts.
IMG 6 — The Bau-Xi Gallery located in a former textile factory is representative of the open characteristics of manufacturing structures that allow for many different types of reuse.
IMG 7 — A sign above the entrance to Tabakfabrik in Linz, Austria, a technology and creative industries hub located in the former plant of the Austria Tabak – a cigarette factory designed by Peter Behrens – says "Open Due to Reconstruction."

Based on the innovation and developments of the past four decades, it would seem that manufacturing plants are structures of the past. But recent trends are shifting once again. In the United States, one outcome of the post-industrial society is the creation of inequality in the workforce. The decline in manufacturing has resulted in an economic imbalance between the working class and the professional sector. This change in the economy now threatens to be a social disruptor as "the median income of men without a secondary school diploma fell by 20% between 1990 and 2013; for men with secondary school diplomas or some college, median income fell by 13%."[31] This income inequality was addressed by US President Obama in his "Blueprint for an America Built to Last" at his 2012 State of the Union address. His plan laid out measures and incentives to bring overseas jobs back to the US and to create a positive environment for creating manufacturing jobs at home. Similar sentiments are taking place outside of the US for reasons that range from intellectual property rights to tariffs and, of course, the Covid-19 pandemic and the supply chain. "The Garner survey of supply chain leaders showed that 33% have plans to move at least a portion of their manufacturing out of China by 2023."[32]

New manufacturing plants in the United States that have opened since 2022 include Tesla's Texas Gigafactory, which will manufacture the Tesla Model Y and the future Cybertruck, Intel's expanded D1X semiconductor facility in Oregon, Thermo-Fisher Scientific's bioprocessing plant in Utah, Serta Simmons' bed construction plant in Wisconsin and Steel Dynamics's solar tracking production plant in Texas.[33] VinFast, a new factory in North Carolina that manufactures electric vehicles, is the first US facility of a Vietnam-based company. With the expectation of producing 150,000 electric SUVs annually, it will create 7,500 jobs for American workers.[34] Is this the beginning of a reversal in outsourcing? At the close of the half-century since Bell's forecast, there might well be the beginning of a new trend for manufacturing in a post-industrial society. What it portends for adaptive reuse is not readily apparent.

IMG 8 — Growing beds in The Plant, a converted vertical farm.

• 178 Townsend	San Francisco, CA, USA, 2012
• 798 Art Zone	Beijing, China, 1995
• Alembic Industrial Heritage & Redevelopment	Vaododara, India, 2019
• Alte Mälze Lauterhofen Renovation	Lauterhofen, Germany, 2020
• Baoshan Exhibition Center	Shanghai, China, 2020
• Bob Dylan Center	Tulsa, OK, USA, 2022
• Cau Dat Tea Museum	Thành Phó Lat, Vietnam, 2021
• CaixaForum Barcelona	Barcelona, Spain, 2002
• Clocktower Building	San Francisco, CA, USA, 1992
• Cukrarna	Llubljana, Slovenia, 2022
• Distillery District	Toronto, Canada, 2001
• Elbphilharmonie	Hamburg, Germany, 2016
• Enaire Foundation	Santander, Spain, 2022–
• ExRotaprint	Berlin, Germany, 2000
• Fondaco dei Tedeschi	Venice, Italy, 2016
• Fondazione Prada	Milan, Italy, 2008–2018
• FRAC Grand Large	Dunkirk, France, 2013
• Granville Island	Vancouver, Canada, 1979
• Huashan 1914 Creative Park	Taipei, Taiwan, 2005
• Inujima Art Project	Inujima, Japan, 2008
• Kanaal	Antwerp, Belgium, 2017
• Klan KOSOVA TV Station	Pristina, Kosovo, 2014
• La Fábrica,	Sant Just Desvern, Spain, 1975
• Lantern Art Factory	Detroit, MI, USA, 2022
• Lao Ding Feng	Beijing, China, 2022
• Launchlabs	Basel, Switzerland, 2014
• Leipziger Baumwollspinnerei	Leipzig, Germany, 2001
• LX Factory	Lisbon, Portugal, 2008
• M50 (50 Moganshan Road)	Shanghai, China, 2000
• Manufaktura and Andel's Hotel	Łódź, Poland, 2006
• Market One	Des Moines, IA, USA, 2014
• MASS MoCA	North Adams, MA, USA, 1999
• Mill City Museum	Minneapolis, MN, USA, 2003
• Mineral Water Factory	Copenhagen, Denmark, 2021
• MUHBA Oliva Artés	Barcelona, Spain, 2020
• Parque Fundidora	Monterrey, Mexico, 1998
• Plant Seven (Congdon Yards)	High Point, NC, USA, 2018
• Proekt Fabrika	Moscow, Russia, 2005
• RCA Sackler Building	London, UK, 2009
• Rog Centre Creative Hub	Ljubljana, Slovenia, 2002

• San Francisco Armory	San Francisco, CA, USA, 2006
• SESC Pompéia	São Paulo, Brazil, 1986
• St. Nicholas Eastern Orthodox Church	Springdale, AR, USA, 2009
• Streetmekka Viborg	Viborg, Denmark, 2018
• Temporary Contemporary	Los Angeles, CA, USA, 1983
• The Plant	Chicago, IL, USA, 2021
• Transformer Fitzroy	Fitzroy, Australia, 2015
• Tsingpu Yangzhou Retreat	Yangzhou, China, 2017
• WaterFire Arts Center	Providence, RI, USA, 2017
• WUK Werkstätten- und Kulturhaus	Vienna, Austria, 1980

Notes and Sources

1 Daniel Bell, "The Coming of Post-Industrial Society," *The Educational Forum*, Vol. 40, No. 4, pp. 574–579, DOI: 10.1080/00131727609336501 (1976), p. 577.

2 "2021 United States Manufacturing Facts," National Association of Manufacturers. https://www.nam.org/state-manufacturing-data/2021-united-states-manufacturing-facts/, accessed 16 February 2022.

3 Bell, "The Coming of Post-Industrial Society," op. cit., p. 578.

4 Ibid., p. 579.

5 This terminology was based on French anthropologist Alfred Sauvy's coining of the term "third world" in a 1952 article for the French magazine *L'Observateur*.

6 Ibid.

7 "'The Week that Changed the World': The 40th Anniversary of President Nixon's China Trip," The Wilson Center, 17 February 2012. https://www.wilsoncenter.org/article/the-week-changed-the-world-the-40th-anniversary-president-nixons-china-trip, accessed 17 February 2022.

8 Prince Ghosh, "The Exodus of Chinese Manufacturing: Shutting Down 'The World's Factory,'" *Forbes*, 18 September 2020.

9 According to the International Organization of Motor Vehicle Manufacturers (OICA), in 2019, China produced 25.72 million vehicles, followed by the United States (10.88 million), Japan (9.68 million), Germany (4.66 million) and India (4.51 million). "Car Production by Country 2022," *World Population Review*. https://worldpopulationreview.com/country-rankings/car-production-by-country, accessed 18 February 2022.

10 The statistics of the World Steel Association indicates that China produced 53.3% of the world's crude steel production, followed by India at 5.9%, Japan at 5.3% and the US at 4.7%. "Global Crude Steel Output Increases by 3.4% in 2019," Press Release of the World Steel Association, 27 January 2020. https://worldsteel.org/media-centre/press-releases/2020/global-crude-steel-output-increases-by-3-4-in-2019/, accessed 18 February 2022.

11 "World Manufacturing Production in December 2020 Report," United Nations Industrial Development Organization (UNIDO), 16 March 2021, p. 2.

12 William Bonvillian, "US Manufacturing Decline and the Rise of New Production Innovation Paradigms," OECD Organization for Economic Cooperation and Development, 2017. https://www.oecd.org/unitedstates/us-manufacturing-decline-andthe-rise-of-new-production-innovationparadigms.htm, accessed 18 February

13 "The Professional and Technical Workforce: By the Numbers – Fact Sheet 2021," Department for Professional Employees, 27 September 2021. https://www.dpeaflcio.org/factsheets/the-professional-and-technical-workforce-by-the-numbers, accessed 18 February 2022.

14 "Table 2.1: Employment by Major Industry Sector," US Bureau of Labor Statistics. https://www.bls.gov/emp/tables/employment-by-major-industry-sector.htm, accessed 18 February 2022.

15 "Which Sector is the Main Employer in the EU Member States?" Eurostat, October 24, 2017, ahttps://ec.europa.eu/eurostat/web/products-eurostat-news/-/DDN-20171024-1, accessed 23 June 2022.

16 The first known use of "outsource" was in 1979, according to the *Merriam-Webster Dictionary*. https://www.merriam-webster.com/dictionary/outsource, accessed 17 February 2022.

17 Derrick Shearer, "Fifty Years After the Nixon-Mao China Opening, U.S. – Chinese Relations Are Getting Worse," *Washington Monthly*, 11 February 2022. https://washingtonmonthly.com/2022/02/11/fifty-years-after-the-nixon-mao-china-opening-u-s-chinese-relations-are-getting-worse/, accessed 17 February 2022.

18 From a two-page spread in *Electronic News*, November 1971.

19 Elizabeth Jones, "The Chip that Changed the World," Intel, 15 November 2021. https://www.intel.com/content/www/us/en/newsroom/opinion/chip-thatchanged-world.html#gs.py88r2, accessed 17 February 2022.

20 Wilson Da Silva, "The Microchip that Changed the World Turns 50," *Medium*, 14 November 2021. https://medium.com/predict/the-microchip-turns-50-a-revolution-in-progress-93c45d7c9624, accessed 17 February 2022.

21 "Intel Marks 50th Anniversary of the Intel 4004," Intel, 15 November 2021. https://www.intel.com/content/www/us/en/newsroom/news/intel-marks-50th-anniversary-4004.html#gs.q2we7z, accessed 18 February 2022.

22 Govind Bhutada, "The Top 10 Semiconductor Companies by Market Share," *Visual Capitalist*, 14 December 2021. https://www.visualcapitalist.com/top-10-semiconductor-companies-by-market-share/, accessed 21 February 2022.

23 "History," Massachusetts Museum of Contemporary Art (MASS MoCA). https://massmoca.org/about/history/, accessed 18 February 2022.

24 Paul G. Rogers, "EPA History: The Clean Air Act of 1970," EPA – US Environmental Protection Agency web archive. https://archive.epa.gov/epa/aboutepa/epa-history-clean-air-act-1970.html, accessed 18 February 2022.

25 "Celebrating Europe and its Environment – 1970s," European Environmental Agency. https://www.eea.europa.eu/environmental-time-line/1970s, accessed 18 February 2022.

26 "Architect Turns Cement Factory into Castle," *Paintsquare*, 3 March 2017. https://www.paintsquare.com/news/view/?16306, accessed 27 May 2022.

27 Daniel Bell, *The Coming of Post-Industrial Society*, New York: Basic Books, 1973, p. 17.

28 "Distribution of the Workforce across Economic Sectors in the United States from 2009 to 2019," Statista. https://www.statista.com/statistics/270072/distribution-of-the-workforce-across-economic-sectors-in-the-united-states/, accessed February 22, 2022.

29 Bell, *The Coming of Post-Industrial Society*, op. cit., p. 17.

30 Ibid.

31 Bonvillian, "US Manufacturing Decline," op. cit.

32 Doug Donahue, "Subcontracting Manufacturing in China: The Risks and Alternative Options," *Forbes*, June 2021. https://www.forbes.com/sites/forbesbusinesscouncil/2021/06/18/subcontract-manufacturing-in-china-the-risks-and-alternative-options/?sh=6bfee9117de7, accessed 22 February 2022.

33 "New U.S. Manufacturing Plants Announced in April 2022," IndustrySelect, 27 April 2022. https://www.industryselect.com/blog/new-us-manufacturing-companies-for-april-2022, accessed 23 July 2022.

34 Ibid.

		Project		Architect
M-1		Pace Gallery – 798 Art Zone Beijing, CN	2008	Gluckman Maynard
M-2	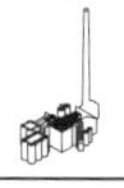	La Fábrica Sant Just Desvern, ES	1975–	Ricardo Bofill
M-3		RCA Sackler Building London, UK	2009	Haworth Tompkins
M-4	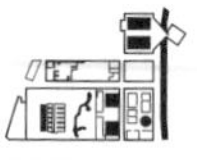	SESC Pompéia São Paulo, BR	1977–1986	Lina Bo Bardi
M-5	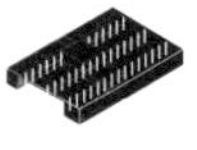	Streetmekka Viborg Viborg, DK	2018	EFFEKT
M-6		Tsingpu Yangzhou Retreat Yangzhou, CN	2017	Neri & Hu

Manufacturing

New Program

Cultural	Education	Hospitality	Infrastructure	Office	Residential	Retail	Recreational	Memorial
●								
				●	●			
	●							
●							●	
							●	
		●						

M-1 Pace Gallery—798 Art Zone

The 798 Art Zone, also known as the Dashanzi Art District, is a group of galleries and artists' studios occupying the complex of a former manufacturing plant. Part of a military-industrial cooperation between the Soviet Union and its allies, the Dashanzi factory, or Project #157, was a collaboration between East Germany and the People's Republic of China.[1] Designed by the University of Architecture and Civil Engineering (now Bauhaus University) in Weimar, the project incorporating a Bauhausian sensibility broke ground in 1954. Renamed Factory #718, the complex served as a model factory of the communist regime. It was decommissioned in the wake of China's "Open Door Policy" in the 1970s and subsequently abandoned. In the late 1990s, the Central Academy of Fine Arts, in need of space, set up a studio in one of the factory buildings. In an organic fashion, other artists followed suit and repurposed the complex as galleries and workshops. The Pace Gallery occupies part of this complex. Its renovation was minimal, exposing the beauty of the concrete structure and its repetitive saw-toothed skylights. Through adaptive reuse, a particular geopolitical moment in time is preserved through its architecture.

Location:	Beijing, China	
Year of Conversion:	2008 (complex in 1995)	
Architects:	Gluckman Maynard	
Original Use:	Weapons factory	[manufacturing]
New Use:	Gallery & artist studios	[culture]

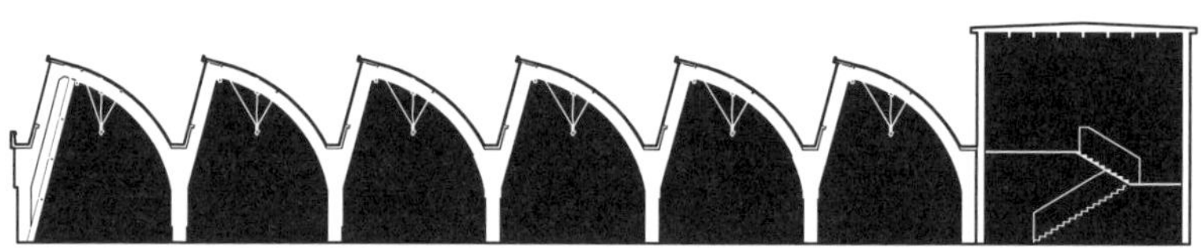

1 Marja Sarvimäki, "Reverse Cultural Revolution – Preserving Bauhausian Architecture in Beijing," *The Int|AR Journal*, Vol. 2, 2010, p. 68.

毛主
伟大的统帅 伟大的舵手

M-2 La Fábrica

La Fábrica is an early precedent in the conversion of a manufacturing plant for new use. It was constructed in 1924 as a cement factory for La Auxiliar de la Construcción, located in a western suburb of Barcelona. A sprawling enterprise of 31,000 m² with 30 massive silos, chimneys and interconnected underground tunnels, the factory employed hundreds of employees and commanded its own railway line for transportation of goods until the mid-1950s. At issue with the community due to the pollution the factory generated, the company relocated in 1968. Architect Ricardo Bofill purchased the abandoned factory in 1973 for his personal use as a residence and office. In today's environment where adaptive reuse projects are more commonplace, the conversion of a vast factory for a residence and office made little fiscal or spatial sense. But as the first conversion of a factory, the structure held an allure as a relic of industrialization in Catalonia. Without heritage designation or client concerns, the adaptation was not about function but about the beauty of the industrial forms. The project is ongoing over five decades as different areas of the factory continue to be transformed, providing a continuum between an industrial past and the present.

Location:	Sant Just Desvern, Spain	
Year of Conversion:	1975–	
Architects:	Ricardo Bofill	
Original Use:	Concrete factory	[manufacturing]
New Use:	Residence & office	[residence/office]

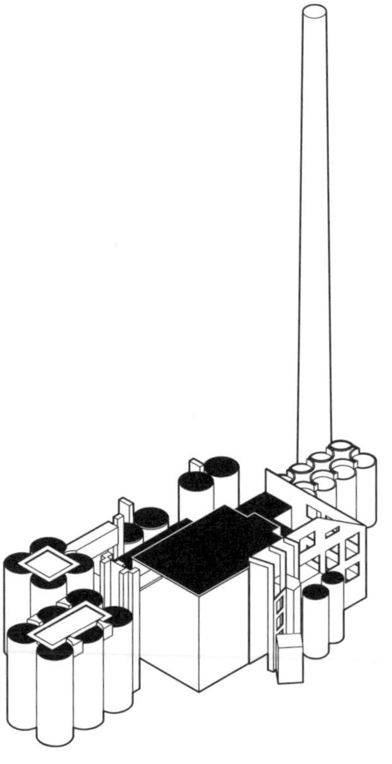

M-3 RCA Sackler Building

The Sackler Building is part of the Royal College of Art's new campus to house the Schools of Fine Art and Applied Art. Intended to house RCA's painting studios, the Sackler Building is converted from a former factory in Battersea. Developed during the Industrial Revolution, the area around Battersea has a long history in manufacturing that concluded in the 1970s with the decline of industry. The Sackler Building is transformed from a nondescript single-story building through the insertion of a new roof structure within the brick skin of the factory. This steel insertion serves a dual purpose. As a series of skylights, it provides daylighting and additional height to the painting studios below. In a unique sawtooth form, these skylights are north-facing to provide the ideal lighting conditions for painting. A corridor divides the open space into top-lit studios: six double-height 7-m-high and a number of smaller 3.5-m-high ones on an upper floor. As an independent structure, the roof insertion also provides bracing for the brick skin of the existing building, allowing for free spans in the studios. The removal of the roof and the introduction of a new structure within an existing enclosure is a classic intervention of adaptive reuse, demonstrated here in an industrial context.

Location:	London, UK	
Year of Conversion:	2009	
Architects:	Haworth Tompkins	
Original Use:	Factory	[manufacturing]
New Use:	College building	[education]

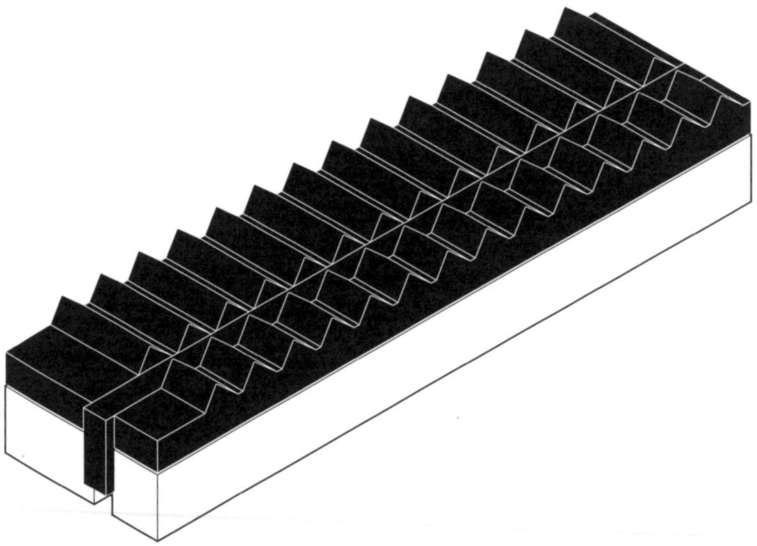

M-4 SESC Pompéia

A SESC (Serviço Social do Comércio) is a non-governmental organization created to provide employees with benefits: health, leisure and culture. In the early 1980s, SESC Pompéia was introduced to São Paulo as the Centro de Lazer Fábrica da Pompéia (Pompéia Factory Leisure Centre), a conversion of a barrel factory – a brick shed – for leisure, cultural and educational purposes. The brick shed was transformed into a large open community space and furnished with tables and chairs designed by Bo Bardi. Begun in 1977, it was the first in a complex of reused structures completed over a decade for the working-class district of Pompéia that included exhibition spaces, a library, workshops, a theater and a pub. Two new concrete buildings for sports activities were later added. The reuse of a manufacturing structure was unique at that time, especially in a country emerging from a 20-year military dictatorship. Dating to the 1920s, the barrel factory was not listed as heritage but Bo Bardi advocated for the preservation of its functional beauty. The work of Bo Bardi, an Italian-born architect who studied under Gustavo Giovannoni, holds a common thread in its interest in existing structures. SESC Pompéia broke new ground in its recognition of the value of a factory, corroborating the Venice Charter's extension of the term monument to modest works that acquired significance with the passage of time.

Location:	São Paulo, Brazil	
Year of Conversion:	1977–1986	
Architects:	Lina Bo Bardi	
Original Use:	Factory	[manufacturing]
New Use:	Cultural center	[culture/recreaction]

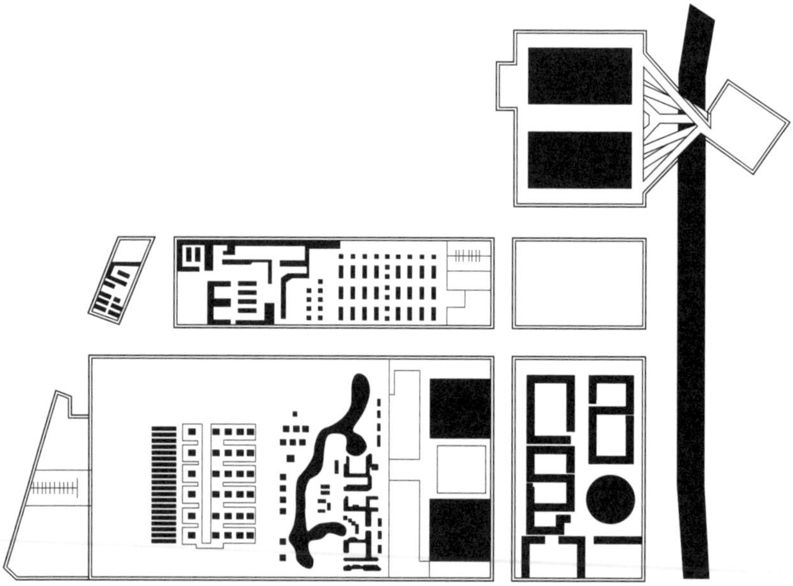

M-5 Streetmekka Viborg

The ubiquitous rectangular structure produced windmills but is emblematic of many such identical factory buildings from the 1960s–1970s that are remnants of industrialization in the West. The reuse of the structure incorporated the aims of GAME, an NGO working for social change through youth-led street sports and culture. This objective translates to programmatic elements such as spaces for parkour, basketball, skating and rock climbing as well as for DJ'ing, music production, dance, animation and art. These spatial requirements were well matched for the large, high-ceilinged volume of the factory where infinite open floor space was limited only by the dimensions of the column grid. In accommodating the GAME program, the interior of the factory was transformed to a covered streetscape in which the open floor was used for different sports activities. Programs that required enclosure were accommodated through volumes inserted between the columns. On the exterior, the prefabricated concrete panel facade was wrapped in a performative translucent polycarbonate skin that revitalized the structure and expressed the new life within. An adaptive reuse project of relative low cost, Streetmekka serves dual positive purposes: preserving the legacy of manufacturing through reusing the industrial structure while empowering the future of a new generation through innovative programs.

Location:	Viborg, Denmark	
Year of Conversion:	2018	
Architects:	EFFEKT	
Original Use:	Factory	[manufacturing]
New Use:	Street sports and arts center	[recreation / culture]

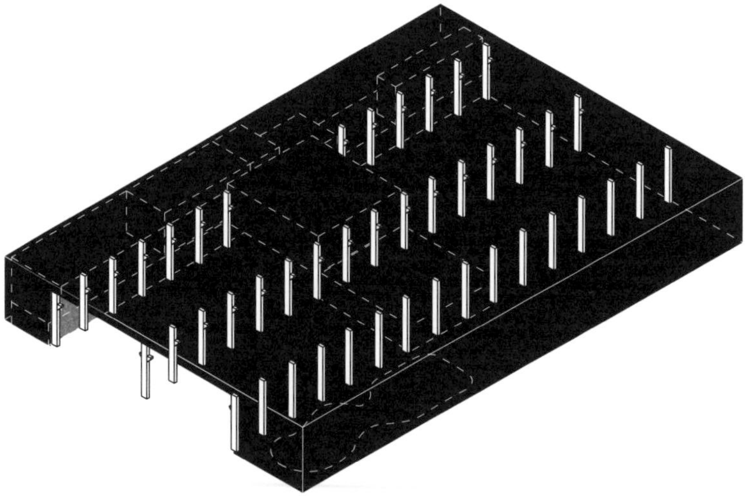

M-6 Tsingpu Yangzhou Retreat

An ancient economic and cultural center with a Grand Canal connecting to the Yangtze River, Yangzhou is today a transportation and market city in which tourism plays a role. The Tsingpu Yangzhou Retreat, a boutique hotel, is part of the Tsingpu Cultural Travel Group's experiential hospitality concept that combines culture and nature. It is located near Slender West Lake, a scenic tourist destination on the western limits of the city. The site, characterized by small bodies of water, included a series of derelict structures and warehouses. While they had few historic features, they harkened to a different time. These outbuildings had a particular relationship neither to each other nor to the site. In adapting these disparate structures for an experience of culture and nature, Neri & Hu sought to unite them through the imposition of a new grid created by the insertion of reclaimed brick walls. As an act of organization derived from vernacular Chinese courtyard house typology, this grid subdivided the existing structures while defining the placements of new structures. This intervention creates a hierarchy of open and enclosed spaces that frame the Yangzhou landscape and sky through a modern architectural language. The Yangzhou Retreat demonstrates the use of the design intervention for unifying existing structures in adaptive reuse.

Location:	Yangzhou, China	
Year of Conversion:	2017	
Architects:	Neri & Hu Design and Research Office	
Original Use:	Warehouse buildings	[manufacturing]
New Use:	Hotel and cultural event space	[hospitality/culture]

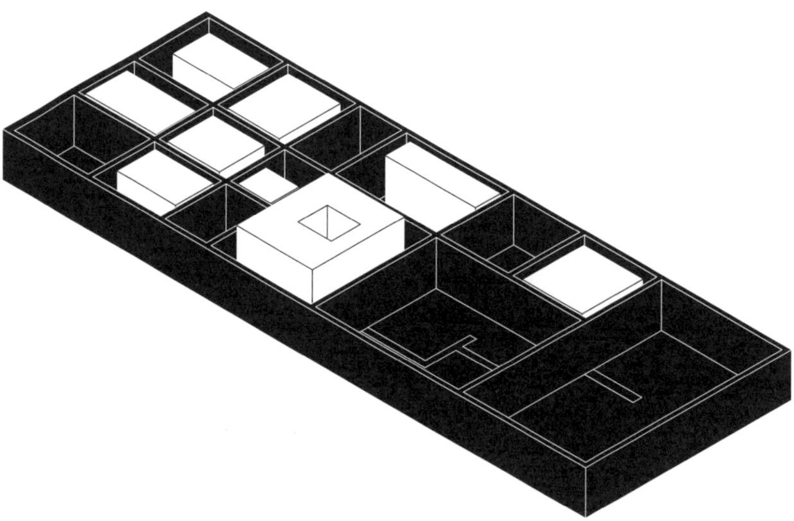

Agriculture

Reuse of Agricultural Structures + Number of People Employed in Agriculture 1945–2019*

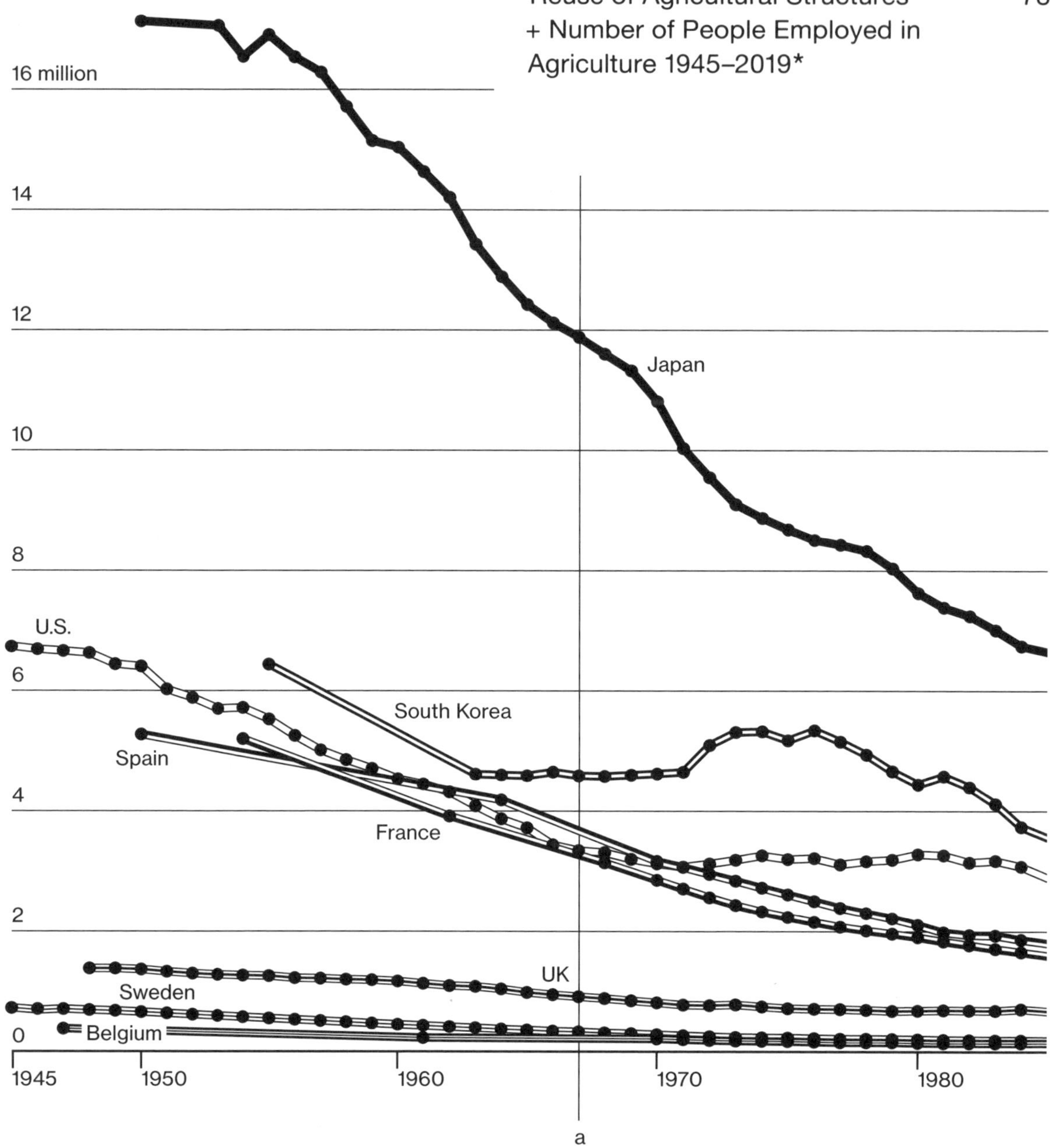

a Hedmark Museum

b Yellow House

c MKM Museum Küppersmühle

d Frøsilo/Gemini Residence; Unser S(ch)austall (Pigsty Showroom)

e Matadero Madrid

f 1933 Old Millfun

g Dovecote Studio

h Cineteca Matadero; Professional Cooking School; The Singular

i Allez UP Rock Climbing Gym; University of Rome Testaccio

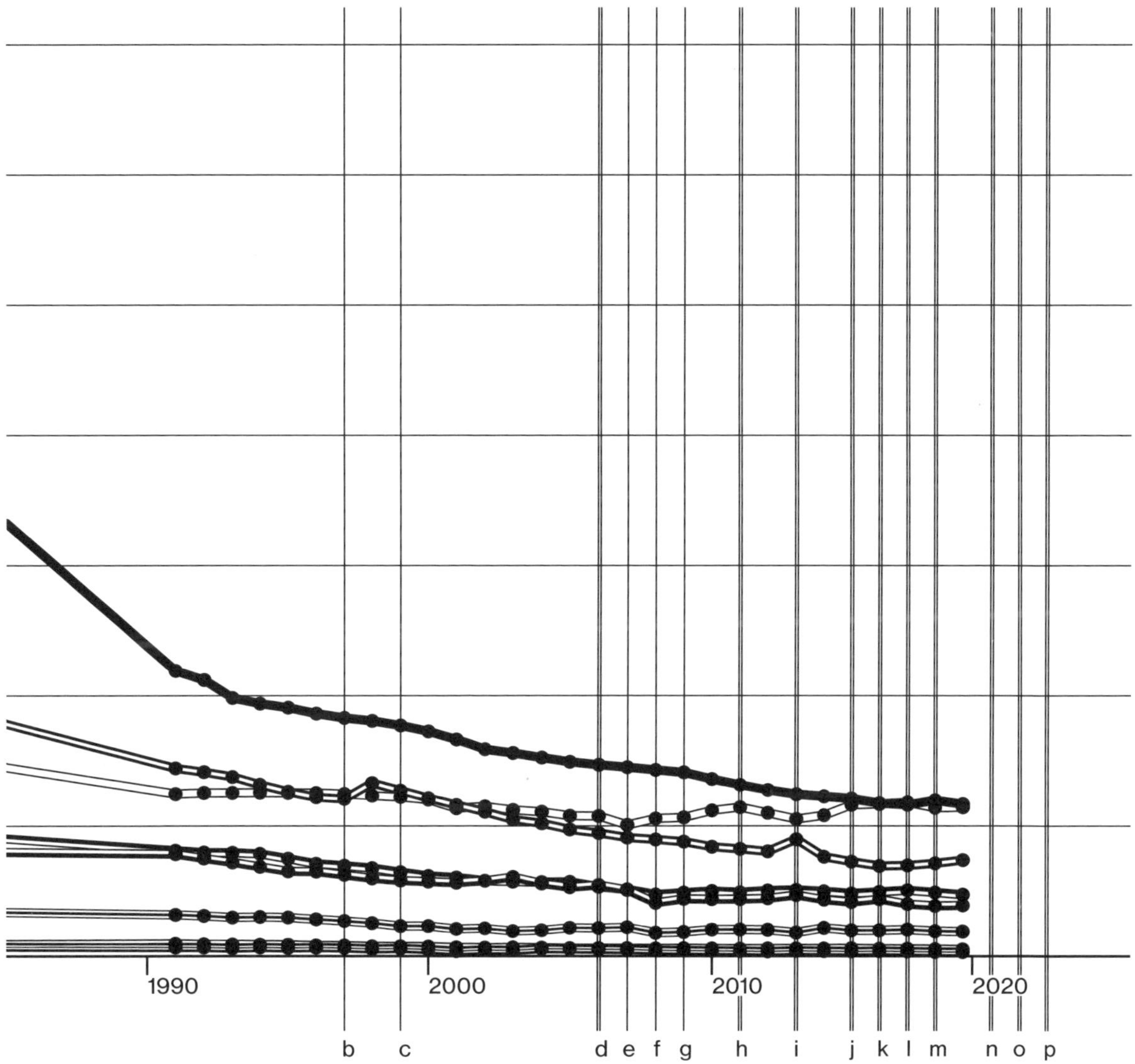

j Artist Studio; BOMEL Slaughterhouse

k Kanaal Wijnegem; Zwarte Silo

l Alila Yangshuo Hotel; Tervahovi Silos; The Silo; Zeitz MOCAA

m After Image; MACRO

n Conversion of Slaughterhouse; Egg Shed Heritage & Community Centre

o Buda Mill and Grain Co.; Monuments Project; TaoCang Art Centre

p Aaltosilo; Silo City; Kunstsilo; Porto Slaughterhouse Cultural Centre; Bourse de Commerce — Pinault Collection

* Source: WorldInData based on International Labor Organization

The town of Brim, population 171, was one of many small wheatbelt towns in Western Australia converted for agricultural use in the mid-19th century with the arrival of the Europeans. Today, the region and its livelihood, like many others, have been affected by climate change. Farmers claim a loss of 20% of the typical growing season rainfall while experiencing more severe frost.[1] Brim was on the decline, its school closed in 2000, its hotels in 2013 and in 2018.[2] In 2015, artist Guido van Helten painted its decommissioned silos with images "representative of the farming generation the Wimmera region is noted for."[3] This was the beginning of a trend of silo painting across Australia (and even in the US) that has spawned what is known as the silo art trails in which silo facades are reused as canvases. With different artists painting the local farmers, but also the animals, flora and fauna, this reuse of silos has transformed these agricultural structures into outdoor galleries. As massive works of art, these painted silos have simultaneously generated a tourist economy that has invigorated these blighted towns and raised awareness of the plight of farming communities around the world.

IMG 1 — Brim silo mural by artist Guido van Helten.
IMG 2 — Concentrated animal feeding operation at a pig farm.
IMG 3 — Silage bags replace the need for silos on many farms.

The global rural population peaked in 1971 at 63.4%, but has since declined to 43.8% in 2020.[4] In Western countries, the transition from agrarian societies has been steady since the Industrial Revolution. By the start of the 1970s, only 4% of the American workforce was employed in agriculture,[5] accounting for 2.3% of the total GDP.[6] Half a century later, only 1.4% of the American workforce[7] contributes to the agricultural output, totaling 0.6% of the total GDP.[8] Similar trends are found in European countries.[9] These trends were directly reflected in the farms themselves. "After peaking at 6.8 million farms in 1935, the number of U.S. farms fell sharply until the early 1970s,"[10] and then continued to slowly decline. Since the turn of the 20th century, the number of farms has decreased by 63%, the average farm size has increased by 67%, harvesting was mechanized, and the average farm commodity has dropped from five to one per farm.[11] Small family farms became increasingly redundant as agriculture evolved into an automated business. These changes were reflected in agricultural buildings that fell out of use, from the farmstead to the outbuildings and the related structures of agricultural production.

Various farm bills were passed in the 1970s to support rural life and agricultural endeavors. The Rural Development Act of 1972 was passed with the intent to "revitalize and develop rural areas and to help foster a balance between rural and urban America."[12] The 92nd US Congress believed that this balance was "essential to the peace, prosperity, and welfare of all our citizens" and "that the highest priority must be given to the revitalization and development of rural areas."[13] The Agricultural Act of 1970, the Rural Development Act of 1972, the Agriculture and Consumer Protection Act of 1973, and the Food and Agriculture Act of 1977 were different pieces of legislation for supporting American agriculture as the country evolved from agricultural to industrial and service industries. Loosely termed "farm bills," these national policies were formulated to lend a hand in the "age-old scourge of farm price and income stability."[14] Although well intended, many benefits were based on production amounts and therefore often benefitted larger farms.[15] For example, according to ActionAid USA, a non-profit for social justice, the American state of Iowa, which produces 7.1% of the nation's food,[16] "lost almost a third of its farms since the late 1970s," which equates to approximately 40,000 families.[17] Some of these small farms were sold and/or abandoned. Some were subsumed by large farms. As small wooden structures on acres of arable land, their reuse is limited. The scale of the farmhouse and its outbuildings, together with the nature of materials used for that purpose, renders the type less conducive to reuse. Those historical farmsteads of exceptional traditional character are preserved for their architectural heritage, although funding for their maintenance must be procured. Historic England, the UK's public body for the historical environment, provides a national planning policy framework for preserving and adapting historical farmsteads as part of the English countryside. Other structures of this nature are often used in agritourism – from olive farms in Italy to cranberry bogs in Massachusetts in the United States. Those historical farm homesteads that are part of a distinctive rural setting are sometimes preserved as part of a unique landscape.

Despite the trends of decline in agricultural land use and the number of farms, total farm output in the United States "nearly tripled between 1948–2019."[18] This production was achieved with fewer farms and laborers, but aided by technology. While 89% of all US farms are small and family owned, they accounted for "less than $350,000 in gross cash farm income (GCFI)."[19] Large-scale farms that make up approximately 3% of all farms instead accounted for 46% of the income at $1 million in GCFI.[20] This phenomenon, which gave rise to the term agribusiness, began in the 1970s under Earl Butz. The Secretary of Agriculture under US President Richard Nixon, Butz was reputed to have said of farming to "get big or get out."[21] Butz's advocacy for efficiency and increased production led to larger and more efficient farms and a prosperous farm economy. This efficiency was fueled by the introduction of concentrated animal feeding operations (CAFO), what the Environmental Protection Agency (EPA) defined in 1976 as a "specific type of large-scale industrial agricultural facility that raises animals, usually at high-density, for the consumption of meat, eggs, or milk."[22] "CAFOs are only a minority of U.S. farms [but] they dominate animal production and have an outsize influence on crop growing."[23] Under Butz's policies, farm income increased from $14 billion in 1970 to $26 billion in six years.[24] Small-scale farmers voiced their concern that it was an enterprise in which "a few multinational corporations control a vast majority of the livestock."[25] In the 21st century, the divide between small and large farms has widened as mechanized processes are further augmented by autonomous ones. Satellite-based guidance systems for GPS-enabled field machinery have introduced the concept of self-steering tractors, grain carts and tractor-trailers. These systems have also impacted grain handling with automated receiving, grading, sampling and transfers.[26]

These developments signified a death knell for small farms but they led to a surge of US agricultural exports that more than quadrupled from $6.7 billion in 1970 to $27.3 billion in 1978.[27] In the 1970s "the U.S. accounted for more than 80 percent of the total worldwide increase in grain exports."[28] A robust system of storage, transportation and handling was required to facilitate this scale of production. At the heart of the system was the grain elevator. Critical to the success of export, it emerged in the mid-19th century as an agricultural building type to facilitate the storage and transportation of bulk grains. They comprised vast vertical silos for storage and the attendant equipment for the transfer and conveyance of the grain. Domestic grain transportation was serviced by trains and, eventually with the development of a highway system, trucks. Exports were serviced primarily from major cities by rail and waterways. This resulted in the siting of early grain elevators within the industrial zones of cities, near railroad tracks and harbor docks. As infrastructure aged and transportation systems were upgraded and relocated, these grain elevators fell out of use. In addition, these sites that had once been underutilized, fringe industrial and waterfront land became, with the growth of cities, prime real estate for development. An example of this can be seen in Copenhagen, Denmark, where various grain structures, one from 1909, were situated on an undeveloped industrial harbor. As the city transitioned from "an ailing manufacturing city to one of the wealthiest cities in the world,"[29] these industrial areas were transformed in plans of urban regeneration. The silos and elevators were successfully adapted into housing as these industrial areas became part of new and vibrant waterfront districts. The transformation of Copenhagen's grain structures is an example of the redevelopment potential for many such sites from

IMG 4 — The abandoned Silo No. 5 in Point-du-Moulin, Montreal.
IMG 5 — Circulation paths used by animals are now used by shoppers at Shanghai's 1933, a former slaughterhouse.

Europe to Canada. Silo No. 5 along the Pointe-du-Moulin in Montreal's Old Port is one such potential site. Completed in stages from 1906 to 1958, the silo was part of the Grand Trunk Railway and the grain export through the Port of Montreal, the world's leading grain port by 1928.[30] It fell out of use and was eventually abandoned in 1996. Although it has been recognized as architectural heritage, the complex awaits plans and funding for its reuse. The complexity of adapting silos leaves many similar structures waiting for reuse.

Changes to peri-urban sites over time contributed to the loss of grain storage complexes. But there were other factors inherent in the business of farming. By 1970, the U.S. was the top exporter of corn and wheat,[31] accounting for two fifths of the world's trade in wheat and rice, 50% of the trade in feed grains and 90% of soybeans.[32] Over the next half-century, these trends would fluctuate with shifting geopolitics and global trade patterns. In 1970, Canada and Russia were the third and fourth leading purchasers of American agricultural products,[33] but a half-century later, both countries had become part of the top five grain producers in the world.[34] These frequent fluctuations impacted the price of grain, farm income and cost of storage. Grain elevators, as places of negotiations, were duly affected. Global distribution companies who purchased grain did so based on market futures and "have traditionally locked in prices for grain they've bought or contracted from farmers by hedging in the futures market."[35] Prices negotiated before planting were subject to factors ranging from the weather to world events, price of fuel, grasshoppers, etc., any of which would cause a ripple effect on the price of grain. The uncertainty and risk of commodity futures resulted in frequent margin calls. Such volatility is thought to be responsible for the financial difficulties that have closed many grain elevators. Shrinking farmlands, too, have lessened the demands for storage, as evidenced by the recent closure of Perdue Agribusiness's largest grain elevator in Maryland.[36] The gravity of such closures inspired the creation of a specific law[37] to provide "a review process to ensure that [Hoosier] farmers are further protected during grain elevator closures."[38] In the meantime, grain elevator closures have led to a new type of agricultural host building for adaptation and reuse.

The half-century of change in agriculture equally affected livestock producers. With an increase in world population and in wealth, meat became a source of nutrition as the number of people who can afford to eat meat increased.[39] In the past 50 years, meat production has tripled.[40] In the spirit of the 1960s protests, the Wholesome Meat Act of 1967 was passed to protect the consumer. It is a US federal law that "requires that states have inspection programs 'equal to' that of the federal government which are administered by the Food Safety and Inspection Service (FSIS) of the United States Department of Agriculture (USDA)."[41] The law prohibited the sale of meat that has not been inspected by a USDA inspector. It effected the closure of many local slaughterhouse structures that were not USDA-approved. To meet these requirements, small farmers had to ship their animals to slaughter to a USDA-approved facility, many of which were distant and even out of state. "In 1967 there were nearly 10,000 slaughterhouses in the country; today there are less than 3000."[42] The closure of

IMG 6 — The Ex-Mattatoio slaughterhouse in the Testaccio neighborhood of Rome before its conversion to MACRO Museum of Contemporary Art of Rome.
IMG 7 — The abandoned silo was reclad in its transformation into harborfront apartments in Nordhavn, Copenhagen.

slaughterhouses increased with the passage of the Humane Methods of Slaughter Act of 1978, championed by animal advocacy groups for the prevention of animal suffering. Slaughterhouses using earlier non-compliant methods were decommissioned. Finally, urbanization and urban regeneration affected the closure of older slaughterhouses that, like the grain elevators, had also been built in what was once a city's industrial zone. With the growth of highways and the development of refrigerated trucks, meat packing houses no longer needed to be built within cities.[43] Their relocation outside of the urban areas also removed the gruesome sounds and smells from the cities.

The decommissioning and abandonment of urban slaughterhouses were similar in many major cities around the world. Notable adaptations of this type of unused structure corroborate this trend: the 1933 Old Millfun in Shanghai, China, an Art Deco concrete structure, was adapted into a retail complex; Matadero Madrid in Madrid, Spain, was transformed into a center for contemporary culture; Sütlüce Slaughterhouse in Istanbul, Turkey, was converted into a congress center; Les Abattoirs in Toulouse, France, became a museum for modern and contemporary art; the Alter Schlachthof in Dresden, Germany, is now a concert venue. Some decommissioned slaughterhouses have been transformed more than once. The Ex-Mattatoio in the Testaccio neighborhood of Rome, Italy, was a slaughterhouse complex from the late 19th century. Closed in 1975 after new slaughterhouses were built outside the city, the Ex-Mattatoio sat vacant for two decades while the city considered plans for this industrial area of the city. In the 1990s, it was taken over by squatters and activists. At the turn of the 21st century, the buildings were used by the architecture school of the University of Rome Tre. Since 2017, it is part of Rome's art museums as the Museum of Contemporary Art of Rome (MACRO). The different types of new uses over more than four decades reflect the cycle of time involved in urban regeneration and the time required for the gentrification process. From its abandonment in the mid-1970s, the transformation of the Testaccio neighborhood is an example of the social context of change in the built environment. Other current examples can be found in the Ex Macello project in Lugano, Switzerland, where the slaughterhouse complex will become part of the university, as well as in Copenhagen, Denmark, where the the Kødbyen (or Meat District), once an industrial part of the Vesterbro district, is now in the midst of transitioning to a creative economy.

As agriculture changed over time and agrarian societies dwindled, they left behind structures, many of which are of humble construction and have not withstood the test of time for reuse. Grain elevators and slaughterhouses are two exceptions. Solidly constructed, they are building types of a larger scale, sharing similar histories of agricultural societies as they collided with the Industrial Revolution, services industry and the tech economy. Grain elevators, with their specialized volumes, are less conducive to adaptation and new programs of use. Creative architectural interventions are required, such as in Heatherwick Architects' cutting of the massive concrete cylinders in the Zeitz Modern Museum of Contemporary Art Africa (MOCAA), or Cobe's inventive reskinning of the Copenhagen Silo. Slaughterhouses, on the other hand, are large vacuous spaces allowing for a large array of new uses, from classroom to museum and concert hall. The exception is the slaughterhouse with a built-in system of herding paths such as the Art Deco slaughterhouse in Beijing, China, built in 1933, that is defined by Escher-like winding ramps in concrete. Both grain elevators and slaughterhouses are agricultural heritage with architectural authenticity and a capacity to assume new uses and new values.

But reuse of agricultural structures is no longer limited to the buildings. With abundant land, small farms are piloting programs for hosting energy production among their crops. Agrivoltaics make use of farm land for solar power generation with photovoltaic panels placed in alternating rows with the plants. Some fields are flooded to host floating photovoltaics. Where agriculture will be in another half-century provides for interesting conjectures. Some future possibilities for farming lie in the adaptive reuse of building types within our built urban environment rather than those in a rural setting. Vertical farms in vacant office buildings, parking garages and warehouses have led to “agritecture”– new models of urban agriculture or farming without soil.

• 1933 Old Millfun	Shanghai, China, 2008
• Aaltosilo	Oulu, Finland, 2021
• After Image	Groningen, the Netherlands, 2018
• Alila Yangshuo Hotel	Guilin, China, 2017
• Allez UP Rock Climbing Gym	Montreal, Canada, 2013
• Artist Studio	Sizun, France, 2014
• BOMEL Slaughterhouse	Namur, Belgium, 2014
• Bourse de Commerce – Pinault Collection	Paris, France, 2021
• Buda Mill and Grain Co.	Buda, TX, USA, 2020
• Cineteca Matadero	Madrid, Spain, 2011
• Conversion of Slaughterhouse	Pauillac, France, 2019
• Dovecote Studio	Snape Maltings, Suffolk, UK, 2009
• Egg Shed Heritage & Community Centre	Ardrishaig, Scotland, UK, 2019
• Frøsilo/Gemini Residence	Copenhagen, Denmark, 2005
• Guido van Helten Silo Murals,	Brim, Australia, 2016
• Hedmark Museum	Hamar, Norway, 1967–2005
• Kanaal	Wijnegem, Belgium, 2015
• Kunstsilo	Kristiansand, Norway, 2022–
• Matadero Madrid	Madrid, Spain, 2006
• MKM Museum Küppersmühle	Duisburg, Germany, 1999
• Monuments Project	Mankato, MN, USA, 2020
• Museum of Contemporary Art of Rome (MACRO; Ex-Mattatoio)	Rome, Italy, 2018
• Porto Slaughterhouse Cultural Centre	Porto, Portugal, 2022–
• Professional Cooking School	Medina, Spain, 2011
• Silo City	Buffalo, NY, USA, 2023
• University of Rome Testaccio	Rome, Italy, 2013
• TaoCang Art Centre	Jiaxing, China, 2020
• Tervahovi Silos	Oulu, Finland, 2017
• The Silo	Copenhagen, Denmark, 2017
• The Singular	Puerto Bories, Chile, 2011
• Unser S(ch)austall (Pigsty Showroom)	Ramsen, Germany, 2005
• Yellow House	Flims, Switzerland, 1999
• Zeitz MOCAA	Cape Town, South Africa, 2017
• Zwarte Silo	Deventer, the Netherlands, 2015

1 Robert Baird, "'Living Climate Change Now': How WA Farmers are Trying to Turn the Tide," *The Guardian*, 24 May 2021.

2 "Brim, VIC," Aussie Towns. https://www.aussietowns.com.au/town/brim-vic, accessed 5 June 2022.

3 "Brim Silo Project," Guido van Helten. https://www.guidovanhelten.com/projects/brim-victoria, accessed 5 June 2022.

4 "Rural Population Growth," The World Bank online data, https://data.worldbank.org/indicator/SP.RUR.TOTL.ZG?end=2020&start=1961&view=chart, accessed 29 March 2022.

5 Max Roser (2013), "Employment in Agriculture." Published online at OurWorldInData.org. https://ourworldindata.org/employment-in-agriculture, accessed 29 March 2022.

6 C. Dimitri, A. Effland and N. Conklin, "The 20th Century Transformation of U.S. Agriculture and Farm Policy," United States Department of Agriculture, Economic Research Service, *Economic Information Bulletin* No. 3. June 2005, p. 2.

7 "Ag and Food Sectors of the Economy," USDA Economic Research Service. https://www.ers.usda.gov/data-products/ag-and-food-statistics-charting-the-essentials/ag-and-food-sectors-and-the-economy/, accessed 5 April 2022.

8 "What is Agriculture's Share of the Overall U.S. Economy?" US Department of Agriculture Economic Research Service. https://www.ers.usda.gov/data-products/chart-gallery/gallery/chartdetail/?chartId=58270, accessed 30 March 2022.

9 Roser, "Employment in Agriculture," op. cit. In 1970: Germany (1.7%), UK (3.1%), Denmark (10.6%), France (13.6%) and by 2015, Germany (1.2%), UK, (2.0%), Denmark (2.8%), France (3.3%).

10 "The Number of U.S. Farms Continues to Decline Slowly," US Department of Agriculture Economic Research Service. https://www.ers.usda.gov/data-products/chart-gallery/gallery/chart-detail/?chartId=58268, accessed 30 March 2022.

11 Dimitri, Effland and Conklin, "The 20th Century Transformation," op. cit., p. 2.

12 "41 CFR § 102-83.50 – What is the Rural Development Act of 1972?" Legal Information Institute – Cornell Law School. https://www.law.cornell.edu/cfr/text/41/102-83.50, accessed 30 March 2021.

13 "42 U.S.C.3122 Rural Development Act of 1972," US General Services Administration. https://www.gsa.gov/reference/statutes/42-usc-3122, accessed 30 March 2022.

14 R. G. F. Spitze, "The Food and Agriculture Act of 1977: Issues and Decisions," *American Journal of Agricultural Economics*, Vol. 60, No. 2, May 1978, p. 226.

15 T. Stucker and W. Boehm, "A Guide to Understanding the 1977 Food and Agricultural Legislation," US Department of Agriculture, Washington, DC, Agricultural Economic Report No. 411, p. 4.

16 "Valued Added Agriculture," Iowa Area Development Group. https://www.iadg.com/iowa-advantages/value-added-agriculture/, accessed 5 April 2022.

17 "Agribusiness is Devastating to Family Farmers, Rural Communities, and the Environment," ActionAid USA. https://www.actionaidusa.org/work/agribusiness-family-farmers/, accessed 3 April 2022.

18 "Farming and Farm Income," US Department of Agriculture Economic Research Service. https://www.ers.usda.gov/data-products/ag-and-food-statistics-charting-the-essentials/farming-and-farm-income/, accessed 30 March 2022.

19 Ibid.

20 Ibid.

21 Roger Johnson, "We Must Reject the 'Go Big or Go Home' Mentality of Modern Agriculture." *The Hill*. https://thehill.com/opinion/finance/464856-we-must-reject-the-go-big-or-go-home-mentality-of-modern-agriculture, accessed 30 March 2022.

22 Carrie Hribar, *Understanding Concentrated Animal Feeding Operations and Their Impact on Communities*. National Association of Local Boards of Health, Bowling Green, 2010, p. 1.

23 Chris McGreal, "How America's Food Giants Swallowed the Family Farms," The *Guardian*, 9 March 2019.

24 J. Risser and G. Anthan, "Why They Love Earl Butz," *The New York Times*, 13 June 1976.

25 McGreal, "How America's Food Giants," op. cit.

26 Dirk Maier, "Grain Ops: Grain Elevator of the Future," World-Grain, 8 August 2019. https://www.world-grain.com/articles/12433-grain-ops-grain-elevator-of-the-future, accessed 2 April 2022.

27 R. Abrams and E. Harshbarger, "U.S. Agricultural Trade in the 1970s: Progress and Problems," *Economic Review*, May 1979, p. 3.

28 Ibid., p. 4.

29 Bruce Katz and Luise Noring, "The Copenhagen City and Port Development Corporation: A Model for Regenerating Cities," Centennial Scholar Initiative – The Brookings Institute, Washington, DC, 1 June 2017, p. 4.

30 "Silo No. 5," Archives from Memento, Héritage Montreal. https://memento.heritagemontreal.org/en/site/silo-no-5/, accessed 6 April 2022.

31 Karen Braun, "How the 19th Century Boosted America to the Top of the World Corn Market: A History of U.S. Grain Trade," Thomson Reuters, 12 June 2020.

32 Harry D. Fornari, "U.S. Grain Exports: A Bicentennial Overview," *Agricultural History*, Vol. 50, No. 1, January 1976, p. 149.

33 Abrams and Harshbarger, "U.S. Agricultural Trade in the 1970s," op. cit., p. 5.

34 "Wheat Production by Country 2022," World Population Review. https://worldpopulationreview.com, accessed 14 August 2022.

35 Todd Neeley, "Grain Elevator Closures, Institute for Agriculture & Trade Policy," 14 May 2008. https://www.iatp.org/news/grain-elevator-closures, accessed 3 April 2022.

36 Krista Pfunder, "Closing of Grain Elevator Leave Framers in a Lurch," Bay Weekly. https://bayweekly.com/closing-of-grain-elevator-leaves-farmers-in-a-lurch/, accessed 3 April 2022.

37 House Enrolled Act 1483 of the Indian legislature, from April 2021.

38 "Indiana Farm Bureau Supports Hoosier Framers Impacted by Grain Elevator Closure," Indian Farm Bureau, 15 April 2020. https://hoosieragtoday.com/indiana-farm-bureau-supports-hoosier-farmers-impacted-by-grain-elevator-closures/, accessed 4 April 2022.

39 Hannah Ritchie, "Which Countries Eat the Most Meat?" BBC News, 4 February 2019. https://www.bbc.com/news/health-47057341, accessed 4 April 2022.

40 H. Ritchie and M. Roser, "Meat and Dairy Production." Published online at OurWorldInData.org (2017). https://ourworldindata.org/meat-production, accessed 4 April 2022.

41 "H. R. 12144 (90th): An Act to Clarify and Otherwise Amend the Meat Inspection Act, to Provide for Cooperation with Appropriate State Agencies with Respect to State Meat Inspection Programs, and for Other Purposes," GovTrack, 2018. https://www.govtrack.us/congress/bills/90/hr12144/summary, accessed 4 April 2022.

42 Pete Kennedy, "The Wholesome Meat Act of 1967: Disaster for Small Slaughterhouses from the Start," Farm-To-Consumer Legal Defense Fund, 10 September 2015. https://www.farmtoconsumer.org/blog/author/pete/page/5/, accessed 4 April 2022.

43 "Our History," USDA Food Safety and Inspection Service, U.S. Department of Agriculture. https://www.fsis.usda.gov/about-fsis/history, accessed 4 April 2022.

		Project		Architect
A-1		Bourse de Commerce– Pinault Collection Paris, FR	2021	Tadao Ando
A-2	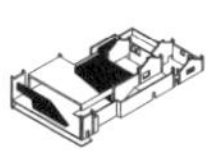	Cineteca Matadero Madrid, ES	2011	ch+qs arquitectos
A-3	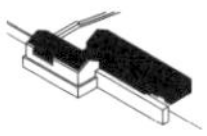	Egg Shed Heritage & Community Centre Ardrishaig, UK	2019	Oliver Chapman Architects
A-4		Frøsilo/Gemini Residence Copenhagen, DK	2005	MVRDV
A-5		Hedmark Museum Hamar, NO	1967–2005	Sverre Fehn
A-6		Yellow House Flims, CH	1999	Valerio Olgiati
A-7		Zeitz MOCAA Cape Town, ZA	2017	Heatherwick Studio

Agriculture

New Program

Cultural	Education	Hospitality	Infrastructure	Office	Residential	Retail	Recreational	Memorial
●								
●								
●	●							
					●			
●								
●								
●		●						

A-1 Bourse de Commerce – Pinault Collection

The Bourse de Commerce – Pinault Collection is located within a site with a rich and complex history. Placed on the demolished 16th-century residence of Catherine de Medici, a circular corn storage and exchange building was built in the mid-18th century and renovated in 1885 by Henri Blondel. Symbolic murals were added below the glass dome in 1889, the year of the Exposition Universelle. The Commodities Exchange was created in the mid-19th century for the commerce of wheat, rye, oats and flour among other things and was expanded to international trading post-WWII. The function of the building became obsolete with the digitization of the futures market and activities at the Bourse ceased in 1998. The murals (1,400 m^2) and the dome were classified as French historic monuments in 1975. In 2013, François Pinault, a businessman and art collector, was offered a 50-year lease on the building. In 2021, the building was transformed into a museum without altering its existing structure. The new use comprises ten exhibition spaces, a sound studio, an auditorium, reception space and restaurant. The primary intervention is the insertion of 29-m-wide and 9-m-tall concrete cylindrical walls into the rotunda. These curved walls form a large exhibition space on one side and contain stairs on the other that give closer access to the murals and the dome. The Bourse de Commerce is a grand-scale example of the co-existence of heritage structures and new forms.

Location:	Paris, France	
Year of Conversion:	2021	
Architects:	Tadao Ando	
Original Use:	Grain exchange	[agriculture/heritage]
New Use:	Museum	[culture]

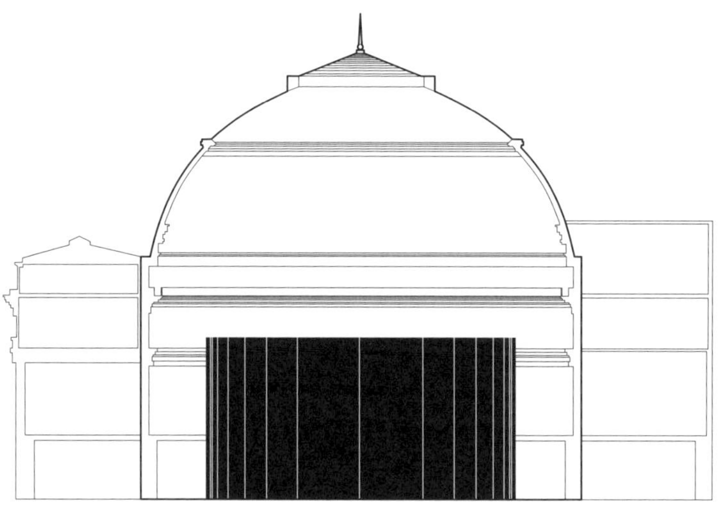

A-2 Cineteca Matadero

The Cineteca Matadero is part of Matadero Madrid, a contemporary art center converted from Madrid's former slaughterhouse and cattle market. Built in the early 20th century, the abattoir ceased operations in the late 1990s. In 2006, the Madrid City Council converted the complex into two independently managed centers for public art, one of which is the Cineteca Madrid. A vast brick structure, the slaughterhouse was designed to accommodate large numbers of animals, the butchering process, meat storage and their attendant structures. Cineteca Matadero, comprising two cinemas, a film archive, film studios and office space, resides in the former abattoir's refrigerators and boiler houses. Within the large stretches of unadorned industrial space, a low and continuous wooden layer, painted grey, over the existing brick walls and floor presents itself as a new intervention over the vestiges of an agricultural past. With the wood insertion serving as a new datum, in the film rooms, a second intervention is introduced above: a fantastical volume of woven steel and straw. Recalling the early days of the abattoir and the basketry craft of that bygone era but realized in today's tectonics, these volumes are illuminated basket-walls that transform the internal spaces. These glowing permeable partitions create an unforgettable experience to rival that of the films, demonstrating the power of invention in the remaking of existing structures.

Location:	Madrid, Spain	
Year of Conversion:	2011	
Architects:	Churtichaga + Quadra-Salcedo	
Original Use:	Slaughterhouse	[agriculture]
New Use:	Cinema, film archive, studio	[culture]

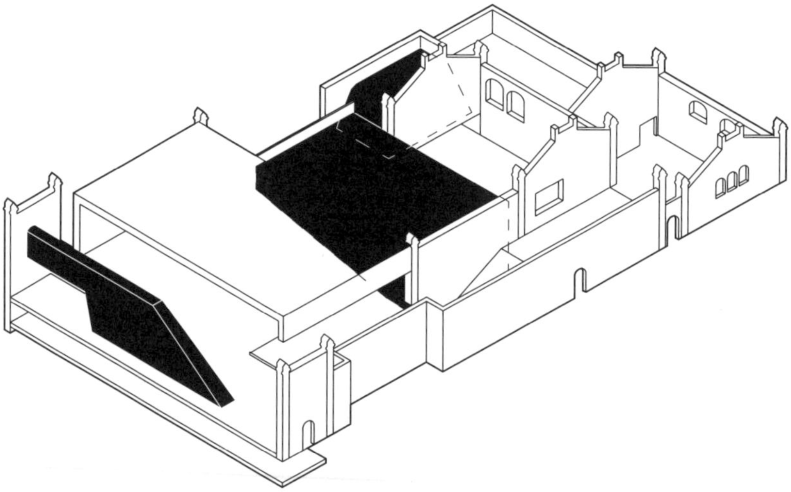

B01
B03
B05
B07
B09
C01
C03
C05
C07
C09
C11

A-3 Egg Shed Heritage & Community Centre

Sited at the Crinan Canal, which served commercial freight between Glasgow and the West Highland villages, the Egg Shed once serviced the transit storage of eggs at the harbor of Ardrishaig. A thriving 19th-century harbor and fishing community, Ardrishaig experienced changes in the 20th century that brought the closure of passenger traffic on the canal and economic decline. No longer in service to agricultural commerce, the Egg Shed was used as an oil storage depot that was eventually decommissioned and abandoned. In the 21st century, the Egg Shed has been transformed into a learning center for local history and natural heritage, and a multipurpose community space. A metal pitched-roof insertion completes the stone walls of the remaining original structure. This simple shed structure inspired the addition of a linear, metal volume to house the new programs. On the interior, a new 1-m concrete plinth, used in the reclamation of the site from its industrial contamination and also to protect it from rising seas, is visible as a new internal datum line connecting the old and new structures.

Location:	Ardrishaig, Scotland, UK
Year of Conversion:	2019
Architects:	Oliver Chapman Architects
Original Use:	Transit storage for eggs/oil storage [agriculture]
New Use:	Exhibition and interpretation center [culture/education]

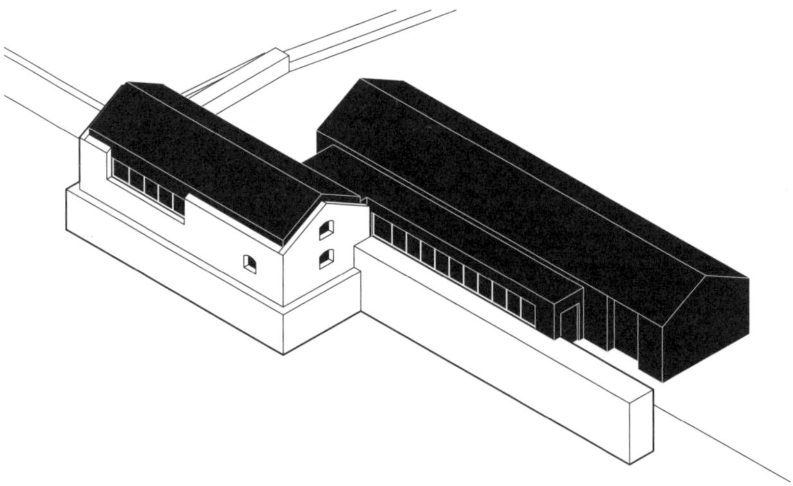

A-4 Frøsilo/Gemini Residence

Frøsilo, or the Gemini Residence, is located on Islands Brygge, today a residential neighborhood of Copenhagen's harbor front. Created in the late 19th century through land reclamation, this area served various industrial activities of the Port of Copenhagen. The Gemini Residence was a former double silo serving the Dansk Sojakagefabrik, a facility built in 1909 that processed soybean for animal feed. The closure of these and other industrial structures in the third quarter of the 20th century left the area in decline. In the 1990s, investors, attracted by the waterfront, fueled a large-scale redevelopment of the area in which the transformation of a double silo to housing units was one of the early examples of agricultural adaptive reuse. Taking into consideration the nature of the silo both as a concrete ring that would not permit many new openings and as a structure created around a void, the intervention consisted of hanging a three-dimensional skin, eight stories high, of housing units on the outside of the silo. Eighty-four apartments with terraces and harbor views transform the silos with a new glass and steel facade from the second floor. The void of the silo is covered with a glass roof that allows it to serve as circulation and a core for connecting the apartments. The original structure is exposed on the ground floor, a testament to its agricultural roots.

Location:	Copenhagen, Denmark	
Year of Conversion:	2005	
Architects:	MVRDV	
Original Use:	Silo	[agriculture]
New Use:	Housing	[residence]

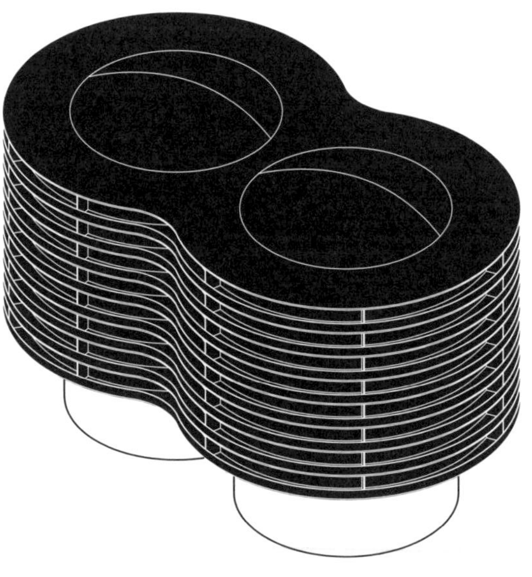

A-5 Hedmark Museum

The Hedmark Museum is part of a site near Lake Mjøsa that serves as an open-air museum of structures from different eras of Norwegian history. Originally named Storhamarlåven, the Hedmark Museum began as a barn, built in the early 18th century above the ruins of a bishop's manor. A restoration of the barn and its transformation into a museum are achieved with the completion of walls, roof and openings in new materials. The ground below the barn is excavated and the addition of a concrete ramp raises the visitor above the ruins. These additions are completed with the introduction of four materials: concrete, glass, timber and iron. The implementation of these materials in the particular forms they take suggests a coexistence with the existing structures, one without hierarchy. Old and new occupy the same space in layered time. Designed by Pritzker Prize winner Sverre Fehn, this project is considered one of the most important works of post-war Norwegian architecture. As a project of adaptive reuse, it is a precedent for giving form to transformative and timeless interventions. Fehn wrote in one of his notebooks from 1973 that "[w]hat matters is to give form to what is already in us."

Location:	Hamar, Norway	
Year of Conversion:	1967–2005	
Architects:	Sverre Fehn	
Original Use:	Barn	[agriculture / heritage]
New Use:	Museum	[culture]

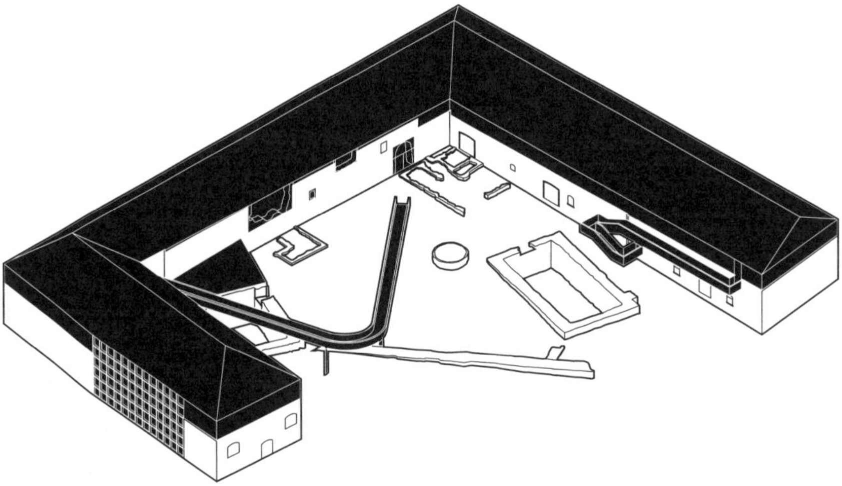

A-6 Yellow House

The Yellow House is a cultural center transformed from an old farmhouse located in the middle of Flims. With a population of approximately 2,900, Flims is a municipality in which a third of its land was devoted to agricultural purposes. The yellow farmhouse was located at the curve of a road and in full view of passersby from both directions. It was vacant for decades and used for various purposes including a grocer and as apartments. The Swiss architect Rudolf Olgiati lived and practiced in the village. In 1995, Olgiati bequeathed part of his collection of cultural objects to the municipality with the proviso that the Yellow House be rebuilt according to his wishes – the primary condition being to paint the house white. Olgiati's son, Valerio, was commissioned to transform the house after his father's death. In the process of doing so, the house was gutted, the roof was redesigned and the entrance was moved. The interiors are abstract, a complete departure from its agricultural past. The building now serves as an exhibition space and a conference venue. And, of course, it was painted white from top to bottom. In the whitewashing, the skin of the old farmhouse has changed. The plaster that characterized 19th-century buildings was chipped off and the rough material is exposed in its new persona. The Yellow House is the physical personification of the societal trend away from agriculture – this past is now in name only.

Location:	Flims, Switzerland	
Year of Conversion:	1999	
Architects:	Valerio Olgiati	
Original Use:	Farmhouse	[agriculture]
New Use:	Cultural center	[culture]

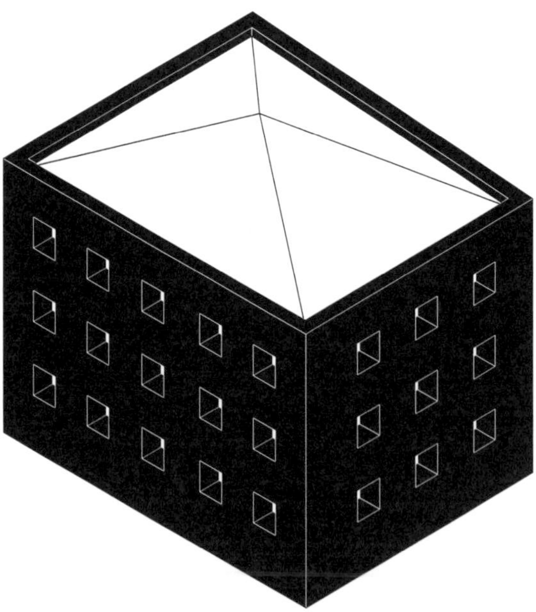

A-7 Zeitz MOCAA

Sited at the Victoria & Alfred Waterfront in South Africa's oldest working harbor, Cape Town's Grain Silo was used to store and grade maize from all over South Africa. Built in the 1920s and at one time the tallest building in sub-Saharan Africa, it held 100-foot-tall bins with 30,000-ton storage capacity. With the advent of shipping containers there was no longer any need for grain transfer. The silo was decommissioned and eventually closed in 2001. In 2011, the building was purchased with the intent to transform it into a museum of contemporary art and a hotel. As the silo building is divided into two parts – the grading tower and 42 grouped storage silos – the transformation consisted of different interventions. In the silos, a 4,600 m^3 atrium was achieved through carving into the center of the existing storage bins while the perimeter bins were converted into five floors of galleries. On the upper floors, new "pillow" skylights were inserted into the existing concrete frame. These transformations comprised 70 triangular glass panes and 3,518 tons of concrete, glass and steel.[1] Additions are commonly used in adaptive reuse projects. Subtraction as an intervention is a powerful tool for reuse in which a massive existing structure is sized to the needs of a new program through the creation of large and, in this case, unique volumes.

Location:	Cape Town, South Africa	
Year of Conversion:	2017	
Architects:	Heatherwick Architects	
Original Use:	Grain silo	[agriculture]
New Use:	Museum and hotel	[culture/hospitality]

1 "Reimagining a redundant industrial building into an iconic gallery," https://www.arup.com/projects/grain-silo-complex.

Transportation

Reuse of Structures for Transportation + Development of Operational Speed for Major Transport Modes (1750–2020)*

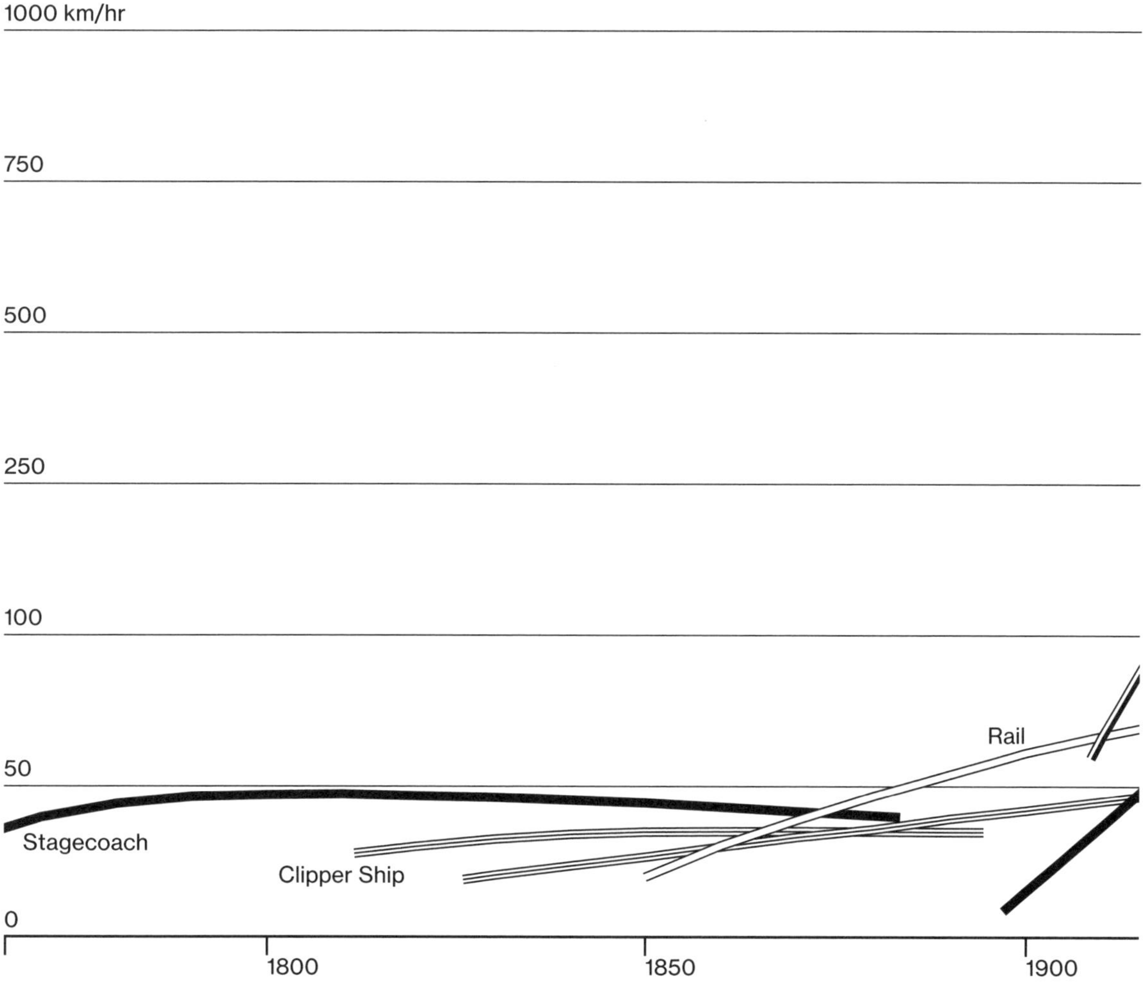

a	Museé d'Orsay
b	Coulée Verte René-Dumont
c	Kraanspoor
d	Tempelhof Airport; The High Line
e	House of Air; Im Viadukt Arches
f	Gas Station (Mies van der Rohe)
g	Baana; Casa Mediterráneo; Superkilen
h	Danish Maritime Museum; The Exploratorium at Pier 15
i	House of Vans; Long Museum West Bund

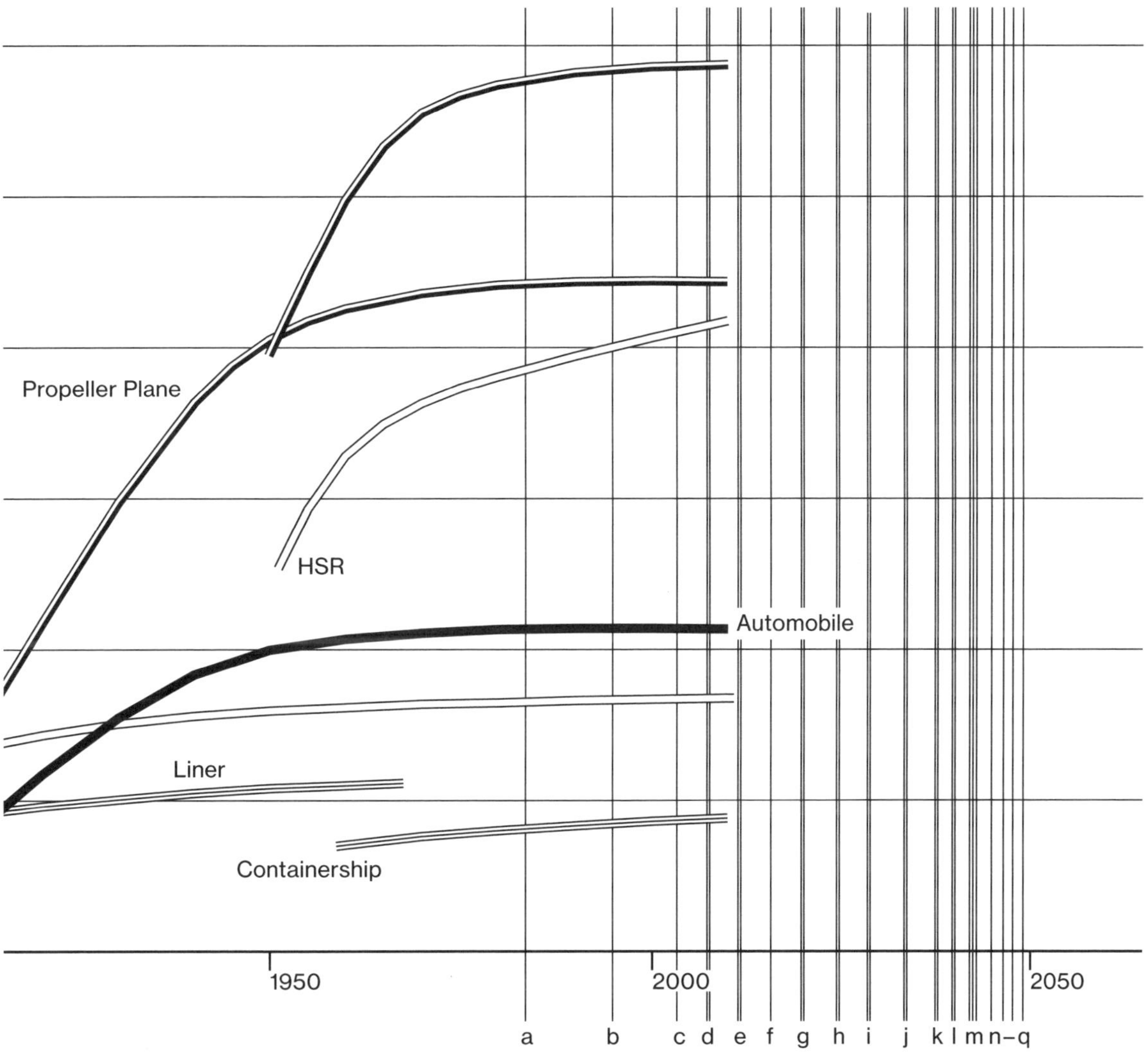

j 606; Garage Museum of Contemporary Art; The Goods Line

k Bay Bridge Steel Program; Federal Shipyard

l Seoullo 7017 Skygarden

m Bicycle Parking Main Station Karlsruhe; Google Spruce Goose Hangar; Marine-doc Estates; Seattle Central Waterfront; Shipyard 1862

n Chemin des Carrières

o Floating Church

p Castlefield Viaduct

q Extension of Garage Museum; Karstadt Re-Parked

* Source: Rodrigue, J.-P., *The Geography of Transport Systems*, 5th ed., New York: Routledge

The Gare d'Orsay in Paris, a terminus station for Compagnie Paris-Orléans' railways to the south and west, opened in 1900 as the first train station with electrified rails. Operated without steam and smoke, the Beaux Arts station, outfitted with ramps, luggage lifts and elevators, was enclosed. Despite the state-of-the-art innovations of the time, the station fell out of use by 1939 because it could not accommodate the new, longer trains. After decades of uncertainty, its demolition was stayed and, in 1973, it was placed on France's Supplementary Inventory of Historic Monuments. Plans to transform it into a museum formed shortly after, with the introduction of a competition. In 1986, it was inaugurated as the Musée d'Orsay, a groundbreaking transformation of an industrial infrastructure into a significant art museum.

The history of the Gare d'Orsay and its journey to becoming the Musée d'Orsay exemplifies the history of the reuse of transportation infrastructure. As transportation is premised on invention and technology, the infrastructure of transportation is characterized by the limitations of that invention and technology. Transportation structures related to land, water and air all face similar threats posed by obsolescence – extinction spurred by the advent of newer and more technologically advanced invention. While all structures – agricultural, religious, manufacturing – face eventual obsolescence from age and/or a paradigm shift, the speed and certainty with which technology renders transportation infrastructure obsolete sets this category of host structures apart. In addition to technological advancements, the variable nature of the systems that govern transportation and the users themselves further contribute to the fate of this group of structures.

Rail

Railroads originated in the Industrial Revolution with the introduction of the steam engine in the mid-18th century. In the centuries since, many developments and innovations have taken place: new modes of power, high-speed operations, passenger amenities, specialized accommodations for freight, safer traffic control, service networks. Each advancement had its impact although many did not cause the systemic upheaval as in the case of the Gare d'Orsay. The station's inability to accommodate trains, albeit longer and larger ones, is an example of pivotal change, critical developments resulting from technological and design advancements that outmode previous methods. Advancement in materials technology is a different catalyst for pivotal change. An example of such change can be found at Paris' Coulée Verte René-Dumont, a 3-mile (4.5-km) elevated promenade adapted from the tracks of the 1859 Vincennes Line. At the period of the construction of Paris' Vincennes line, as in many railways of that age, the portions that traversed steep ground were supported on viaducts. With the advent of modern concrete and steel supports, rails on viaducts were abandoned or demolished for reasons of structural safety. The sections of the Coulée Verte supported by arches have now been repurposed to accommodate enclosed art spaces, aptly named the Viaduc des Arts. While pivotal change was often derived from technological progress, it was not the sole instigator of change in structures of transportation. As systems embedded in urban environments, transportation structures were subject to changes wrought by urban (and social) developments over time, often unrelated to transportation. The eventual abandonment of the Vincennes Line after 110 years of use resulted from the reorganization of the rail lines to accommodate the construction of the new Paris opera house in the place of the existing rail station. Such a substitution of use speaks to a century of urban growth in Paris. The transformation of the Vincennes Line into the Coulée Verte, completed in 1993, provided a lush greenway for recreation directly over the old tracks. Demonstrating a successful adaptation of rail infrastructure, it was a precedent for New York City's High Line project 16 years later, and for Zurich's Im Viadukt shopping area 17 years later.

By the latter half of the 20th century, rail lines were facing other threats, such as competition from automobiles (cars, trucks, buses) for both travel and haulage. This competition led to lower rail use and reduced profitability in both the United States and in parts of Europe. The Beeching cuts (or Beeching axe) in the UK resulted from a two-part report from the 1960s, titled "The Reshaping of British Railways," to address such loss in usership and profits. Authored by Richard Beeching, Chairman of British Railways in the 1960s, the reports proposed the reorganization of

IMG 1 — The Coulée Verte passes between two buildings at Rue Montgallet.

British railways and included "statistics that would decide the fate of the 2,363 stations and 5,000 miles of track earmarked for closure."[1] Railroads in the US were facing similar challenges when three major railroads combined in 1968 as Penn Central. By 1970, the company filed for bankruptcy.

In succession, "nine Class I railroads, representing almost one-quarter of the industry's trackage, file for bankruptcy protection"[2] from 1970 to 1975. By the last quarter of the 20th century, centuries after the first operational railroads came into being, the rail industry was in crisis. In the 1970s, the focus on profitability through deregulation brought about American legislation such as the Railroad Revitalization and Regulatory Reform Act of 1976 and the Staggers Rail Act of 1980. The actions of the late 1960s and the 1970s led to both new and upgraded stations and lines and also the abandonment and decommissioning of other outdated railway stations and their accessory structures. The Gare d'Orsay and the Coulée Verte were early examples of a trend for reusing transportation infrastructure that would, in the 21st century, become the norm from South Korea to Finland and Australia.

Water

Other means of transportation followed similar trajectories of development and decline. As with railways, some of these advancements created a ripple effect on their attendant structures. One particular development in waterborne transport demonstrates the unique and direct relationship between technological advancements and the outmoding of infrastructure. Through history and even pre-history, mobility has been associated with maritime travels. Boats, especially as instruments of trade, have a history dating back to the Neolithic routes of the Austronesian peoples. Water vessels as a means of travel have evolved in size, materials and sophistication. Today, "74% of the world's trade is carried by ship, 99% of the US international trade is transported by boat and 60% of the US energy is imported by ship."[3] This level of maritime industry required not only boats, but also their support infrastructure, including ports, docks, service and maintenance equipment, craneways, etc. Over the centuries, these various structures developed in size and complexity in tandem with the growth of the industry. But, modern freight transportation by sea was revolutionized by a single event in 1956: Malcolm McLean's invention of the shipping container. The loading and transferring of items from vehicles to boats in maritime industry was standard practice since the beginning of trade. This practice was memorialized by J.M.W. Turner in his 1835 painting *Keelmen Heaving in Coals by Moonlight*, which attests to this practice at the town of Shields, on the River Tyne, downriver from the vast coal mines of Newcastle, England. Inspired by such inefficiencies, McLean proposed the use of a container that would transfer directly as a unit from vehicle to boat, thereby eliminating a time-consuming and cumbersome task. A converted Second World War tanker carrying 58 metal containers served as his first prototype.[4] In the 1960s, the labor of loading loose cargo was estimated to cost $5.83 per ton.

Using McLean's prototype, experts calculated the cost of loading metal containers to be 15.7 cents per ton.[5] This enormous cost differential changed the face of cargo handling and consequently the maritime industry worldwide. Based on such economics, McLean created Sea-Land Service, a container service that began with port cities in the US, but by the 1970s branched out to include Europe and the Far East. The success of this endeavor, and at such a scale, led to the exponential growth in the size of the vessels and the number of containers they carried. Today, the *Ever Ace*, which set sail for the first time in July 2021, has a capacity of 23,992 TEUs.[6] With a TEU as one 20-foot-long container, this is more than a 40,000% increase on the storage capacity of McLean's prototype. The establishment of international

IMG 2 — J. M. W. Turner's 1835 painting *Keelmen Heaving in Coals by Moonlight* illustrates the long tradition of loading and unloading at ports that was made obsolete by the invention of the container ship.
IMG 3 — The container ship *MSC Isabella*.

container service in 1970 and the resultant increase in the number of containers per ship necessitated larger (and deeper) ships. In turn, the causal effect of these changes on related infrastructure led to upgraded or new facilities to accommodate the ever-increasing vessel sizes. In the built environment, the domino effect of this change brought a plethora of decommissioned docks, craneways and boat maintenance facilities.

As structures of maritime industry, this category of host building has unique characteristics. Such buildings are typically open to the exterior, sited near the water, sized for high structural loads and are of a massive scale. Differentiated from other host structures by these attributes, the abandoned infrastructure related to maritime trade has spawned creative and novel proposals for reuse. Kraanspoor, a 260-m concrete craneway of a former shipyard in the harbor of Amsterdam, the Netherlands, is a lengthy and repetitive structure. In its new use, it serves as structural support for a three-story, lightweight office building that is constructed directly above it. Its new use as a building foundation is an example of reuse as material. This reuse, as in the spolia of the Romans, is of significance for the reduction of construction costs, with foundations estimated at a minimum of 10% of total construction costs. The Maritime Museum in Helsingør, Denmark, offers a different use of the host structure, the massive void that once serviced ships at a decommissioned drydock. The multi-storied void is the focus of the architectural intervention, providing a vast empty container for connector bridges and the outdoor activities of the new Maritime Museum. It is a novel case of the reuse of negative space.

Air

Transportation by air is the most recently developed type of transportation with the oldest continually operating airport dating to 1909, in College Park, Maryland. The College Park Airport was established as the military demonstration site for the Wright Brothers,[7] the inventors and operators of the first motor-operated airplane. Of the various structures related to transportation, the airport with its accessory buildings is also the largest, with its accommodation of vast numbers of passengers, enormous machines and the related personnel serving both. Airports face obsolescence primarily due to pivotal changes related to the workings of the airplane. Due to the complex nature of the airplane as a massive and complicated machine, technological advancements that would affect the airport have not been frequent. In 1970, the advent of the first Boeing 747, nicknamed "Queen of the Skies," was one such change. With dimensions of 231ft (70.6m) nose to tail and a wingspan of 195 ft (59m), it was too large to build in Boeing's existing facilities.[8] The introduction of the Jumbo Jet impacted existing airports in various ways, ranging from the length of runways and the size of aircraft

IMG 4 — A gas station designed by Mies van der Rohe, a designated Canadian heritage site, is now a community center.

hangars, to the design of the classic "hub-and-spoke" system of planes and the accommodation of the needs of increasingly large numbers of passengers. While updating existing airports to accommodate these changes was possible for larger airports, it was not the case for smaller ones. In time, Jumbo Jets would fly only between large hubs, bypassing smaller airports, which faced abandonment if they were unable to survive by servicing only smaller planes. Eero Saarinen's TWA terminal in Queens, New York, built in

1962, was closed in 2001 because it could not accommodate larger planes. It was placed on the National Register of Historic Places in 2005 and reopened in 2019 as the TWA Hotel. The history of the TWA terminal captures a moment in modern commercial aviation and the changes wrought in a half-century that led to the abandonment and subsequent reuse of a type of aviation infrastructure.

Airlines require substantial financial undertakings as both national and international commerce. Since the 1930s, American domestic air transport was regulated as a public utility and characterized by fare regulations. By the early 1970s, the introduction of the Boeing 747 and the energy crisis created a perfect storm of escalating prices. The Airline Deregulation Act of 1978 introduced competition to the business of transportation services through a plan for ending domestic fare regulation by 1983. Over decades, the competition enabled by deregulation resulted in the creation of new airlines, but also in the loss of some major carriers. Deregulation also lifted restrictions on flight routes. Airlines streamlined their services by adopting the hub system in which "using a few major airports as central connecting points ... maximized aircraft use, increased passenger loads, and kept more aircraft flying."[9] This resulted in the expansion of certain airports and the contraction of those found to be redundant. Financial issues and shifting operations led to the abandonment of airports around the world; Ciudad Real Central Airport in Madrid, Spain, Stapleton International Airport in Denver, Colorado, and Jaisalmer Airport in Rajasthan, India, are examples of airports abandoned due to financial instability.

Airports and structures related to air transport are also the victims of circumstances outside the immediate operations of transportation. As critical infrastructure, airfields and airports are important targets in armed conflicts. Airports have been abandoned due to damage from war and war-related circumstances. After the Turkish invasion of Cyprus in 1974, the Nicosia International Airport in Cyprus, declared a United Nations Protected Area during the conflict, was closed with the ceasefire and subsequently abandoned. Similarly, the civil war of the 1990s left the Sukhumi Babushara Airport in Abkhazia damaged and filled with landmines.

As large, complex structures sited on long stretches of land outside of urban centers, these airport structures create a particular set of challenges for reuse. The reuse of a single terminal, such as Saarinen's TWA terminal, represents only a fraction of that size. Size and scale present financial challenges, as few single programs are large enough for such a structure. Outdoor recreation is one, such as the conversion of the old Mariscal Sucre International Airport at Quito, Ecuador, into the Parque Bicentenario de Quito, a vast urban park. Park spaces provide enormous value as recreation for citizens, but the potential revenue inherent in these vast tracts of land and buildings is ever-present. Due to the sheer volume of space, the reuse of airports is typically achieved by a combination of different revenue-generating uses. The Stapleton International Airport that was replaced by the Denver International Airport is an example; the airfields were demolished and the structures, including the tower, will serve as a 3,000m^2 "eatertainment" district that includes sports/entertainment facilities, indoor/outdoor dining, bars and gambling.[10] Berlin's Tempelhof Airport, with its history as part of Albert Speer's design of the Nazi vision, closed in 2008 and was transformed into a creative district with a park and event space, hosting concerts and fashion shows. In 2015, it was used as a refugee camp. In addition, many airports are located by water and are valuable as waterfront property. At Hong Kong's Tai Kak Airport, this proximity to water led to the reuse of the decommissioned site as a new cruise ship terminal. In Athens, Greece, when the Ellinikon International Airport was closed in 2001, part of it was converted into sports facilities related to the 2004 Olympics. It has, to the dismay of nationals, since been developed by a foreign conglomerate as a luxury seaside complex of homes, hotels, offices and a casino. The size of airports and the investments required for their reuse bring this new dimension of global financial politics to adaptive reuse. The future of airports on the water and their new uses are already threatened by climate change. Sea level rise may well change the future direction of the reuse of abandoned airport infrastructure.

Automobiles

Americans' so-called "love affair with the car" was coined from an episode of the *DuPont Show*, a 1961 television program.[11] In the six decades since then, the automobile remains at the heart of American life with "91.55% of households reported having access to at least one vehicle in 2020, up from 90.82% in 2015."[12] Even in European cities, where bike infrastructure and public transportation support non-vehicular mobility, the car remains the dominant means of transportation. A global consumer survey of how one commutes to work resulted in findings that a majority of countries used automobiles, including the US, France, Australia, Spain, Mainland China, Germany, the UK, the Netherlands and Brazil.[13] The use of bicycles is increasing; the Netherlands has the highest share of bike commuters at 38% and the US the lowest at 6%.[14] With the Paris Agreement for limiting global temperature rise by reducing greenhouse gas emissions by 2030, the emission by a typical passenger vehicle of 4.6 metric tons of carbon dioxide per year[15] is unsustainable. In the near future, reliance on the automobile will have to change. This might lead to an embrace of other means of transportation or a change in the makeup of the vehicle itself. In the former, bicycle use is poised to increase to balance a decrease in car use. Such a transition would affect current accessory structures related to the automobile such as parking garages, gas stations and even bridges. Fewer cars portend fewer parking garages. The transformation in Karlsruhe of a parking garage into a bike garage is a prediction of what the very near future will bring. With fewer cars, or with a transition to cars that do not utilize gasoline, gas stations would eventually be abandoned. On a global scale, this would be a

IMG 5 — A proposal for adding bicycle access to the Pell Bridge in Rhode Island through a 3-D printed pathway suspended below the original structure by graduate students of adaptive reuse at the Rhode Island School of Design, Department of Interior Architecture.
IMG 6 — The architecture of the Long Museum West Bund in Shanghai is designed around a remnant of a coal hopper bridge.

daunting number of decommissioned gas stations. Estimates made in 2020 place 21,750 stations in Italy, 14,459 in Germany, 13,000 in Turkey and 3,000 in Belgium.[16] In the US, it is estimated that there are currently 145,000 fueling stations.[17] As electric cars become mainstream, electric charging stations will perhaps take up some of the defunct gasoline stations. Finally, infrastructure such as highways and bridges that are now inhospitable to bicycles and pedestrians will all need to be adapted for a different future.

The longevity of transportation-related infrastructure is inextricably tied to a particular technological life span. With the exponential speed of change in technology, transportation-related infrastructure is subject to quicker decline. At the end of the 20th century, the growing numbers of adaptive reuse projects of these types of structures parallel the speed of technological change. While it is said that nostalgia is an indulgence, nostalgia for these structures of transportation have prompted some one-off examples of reuse. The Marine-doc Estates company in the Netherlands offers retrofitted boats as luxury residences to be sited on land. The Long Museum West Bund in Shanghai, located at the edge of the Huangpu River where a coal-hopper bridge once facilitated the loading of waterborne freight, holds onto a vestige of this rapidly disappearing past by incorporating a remnant of the bridge into the design of the new museum. These are backward glances at the way people and things were moved, made tangible by adaptive reuse.

• 11th Street Bridge Park	Washington, DC, USA, 2023–
• 606	Chicago, IL, USA, 2015
• Baana	Helsinki, Finland, 2012
• Bay Bridge Steel Program	San Francisco, CA, USA, 2016
• Bicycle Parking Main Station	Karlsruhe, Germany, 2018
• Casa Mediterráneo	Alicante, Spain, 2012
• Castlefield Viaduct	Manchester, UK, 2021
• Chemin des Carrières	Rosheim, France, 2019
• Coulée Verte René-Dumont	Paris, France, 1993
• Danish Maritime Museum	Helsingør, Denmark, 2013
• Extension of Garage Museum	Moscow, Russia, 2022–
• Federal Shipyard	New Jersey, USA, 2016
• Floating Church	London, UK, 2020
• Garage Museum of Contemporary Art	Moscow, Russia, 2015
• Gas Station (Mies van der Rohe)	Montreal, Canada, 2011
• Google Spruce Goose Hangar	Los Angeles, CA, USA, 2018
• House of Air	San Francisco, CA, USA, 2010
• House of Vans	London, UK, 2014
• Im Viadukt Arches	Zurich, Switzerland, 2010
• Kraanspoor	Amsterdam, the Netherlands, 2007
• Long Museum West Bund	Shanghai, China, 2014
• Marine-doc Estates	USA, Europe, South America, Russia, China, Australia, 2018–
• Museé d'Orsay	Paris, France, 1986
• Seattle Central Waterfront	Seattle, WA, USA, 2018
• Seoullo 7017 Skygarden	Seoul, South Korea, 2017
• Shipyard 1862	Shanghai, China, 2018
• Superkilen	Copenhagen, Denmark, 2012
• Tempelhof Airport	Berlin, Germany, 2009
• The Exploratorium at Pier 15	San Francisco, CA, USA, 2013
• The Goods Line	Sydney, Australia, 2015
• The High Line	New York, NY, USA, 2009
• The Rail Park	Philadelphia, PA, USA, 2022–

1 "Dr. Beeching's Axe," NetworkRail. https://www.networkrail.co.uk/who-we-are/our-history/making-the-connection/dr-beechings-axe/, accessed 2 May 2022.

2 "Chronology of America's Freight Railroads," Association of American Railroads. https://www.aar.org/chronology-of-americas-freight-railroads/, accessed 2 May 2022.

3 "What is the Maritime Industry?" Northeast Maritime Institute, 24 March 2020. https://www.northeastmaritime.com/blog/what-is-the-maritime-industry/, accessed 4 May 2022.

4 "The History of the Maritime Industry: How Container Shipping Changed the World," Nordic IT. https://nordic-it.com/the-history-of-the-maritime-industry-how-container-shipping-changed-the-world/, accessed 3 May 2022.

5 "The Story of Malcom McLean," *The Maritime Executive*, 28 December 2016. https://www.maritime-executive.com/article/the-story-of-malcolm-mclean, accessed 3 May 2022.

6 "Top 10 World's Largest Container Ships in 2022," Marine Insight News Network, 23 February 2022. https://www.marineinsight.com/know-more/top-10-worlds-largest-container-ships-in-2019/, accessed 5 May 2022.

7 Website of College Park Airport, https://collegeparkairport.aero, accessed 24 July 2022.

8 Dowling, Stephen. "The Boeing 747: The Plane that Shrank the World," BBC, 19 June 2020. https://www.bbc.com/future/article/20180927-the-boeing-747-the-plane-that-shrank-the-world, accessed 8 May 2022.

9 "Airline Deregulation: When Everything Changed," Smithsonian National Air and Space Museum, 17 December 2021. https://airandspace.si.edu/stories/editorial/airline-deregulation-when-everything-changed, accessed 9 May 2022.

10 Harriet Baskas, "Defunct Airports Take Flight with Creative New Uses," *USA Today*, 30 November 2017.

11 Emily Badger, "The Myth of America's Love Affair with Cars," *The Washington Post*, 27 January 2015.

12 Matt Timmons, "Car Ownership Statistics in the U.S.," ValuePenguin, 17 April 2022. https://www.valuepenguin.com/auto-insurance/car-ownership-statistics, accessed 10 May 2022.

13 Martin Armstrong, "How the World Commutes," Statista, 29 June 2021.

14 Ibid.

15 "Greenhouse Gas Emissions from a Typical Passenger Vehicle," US Environmental Protection Agency. https://www.epa.gov/greenvehicles/greenhouse-gas-emissions-typical-passenger-vehicle, accessed 10 May 2022.

16 N. Sonnichsen, "Number of Petrol Stations in Selected European Countries at the End of 2020," Statista, 14 September 2021. https://www.statista.com/statistics/525523/number-of-petrol-fuel-filling-station-in-europe-by-country/, accessed 10 May 2022.

17 "Service Station FAQs," American Petroleum Institute. https://www.api.org/oil-and-natural-gas/consumer-information/consumer-resources/service-station-faqs, accessed 10 May 2022.

		Project		Architect
T-1	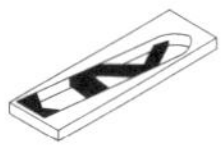	Danish Maritime Museum Helsingør, DK	2013	BIG
T-2	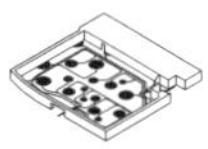	Bicycle Parking Main Station Karlsruhe, DE	2018	JOHNNY architecture
T-3		FRAC Grand Large Dunkirk, FR	2013	Lacaton & Vassal
T-4		The High Line New York, US	2009	Diller Scofidio + Renfro
T-5		Im Viadukt Arches Zurich, CH	2010	EM2N
T-6		Kraanspoor Amsterdam, NL	2007	OTH Architecten
T-7		Musée d'Orsay Paris, FR	1986	Gae Aulenti & ACT Architecture
T-8		Karstadt Re-Parked Berlin, DE	2025	Lendager

Transportation

New Program

	Cultural	Education	Hospitality	Infrastructure	Office	Residential	Retail	Recreational	Memorial
	●								
				●					
	●								
								●	
							●		
					●				
	●								
					●		●		

T-1 Danish Maritime Museum

The Danish Maritime Museum located in the medieval harbor city of Helsingør demonstrates the ever-shifting relationship of adaptive reuse to history and context. The museum was once part of the Kronberg Castle, an icon of the city and the setting for Shakespeare's *Hamlet*, until heritage designation requirements forced its relocation. Its new placement within a decommissioned drydock recalls Helsingør's industrial past when the shipyard and the Wiibroe brewery of Carlsberg beer were prominent 19th-century landmarks of industrialization. Their closure in the late 20th century required the city to rebrand itself through arts and culture. Today's Kulturhavn Kronberg (culture harbor) includes Kronberg Castle, the Culture Yard, a public library, and the Danish Maritime Museum. The reuse of the drydock to accommodate the museum program is simultaneously a spatial and contextual strategy that embraces both Helsingør's past and present. The exhibition galleries are arranged below ground surrounding three sides of the drydock, which is reused as an outdoor area and café. The intervention of enclosed bridges and walkways within the dock provides connections within the museum itself and between the public harbor sites. The museum's placement within the underground dock establishes an unobtrusive but distinct modern identity in deference to a setting crowned by the nearby UNESCO World Heritage Kronberg Castle.

Location:	Helsingør, Denmark	
Year of Conversion:	2013	
Architects:	Bjarke Ingels Group	
Original Use:	Drydock	[transportation]
New Use:	Museum	[culture]

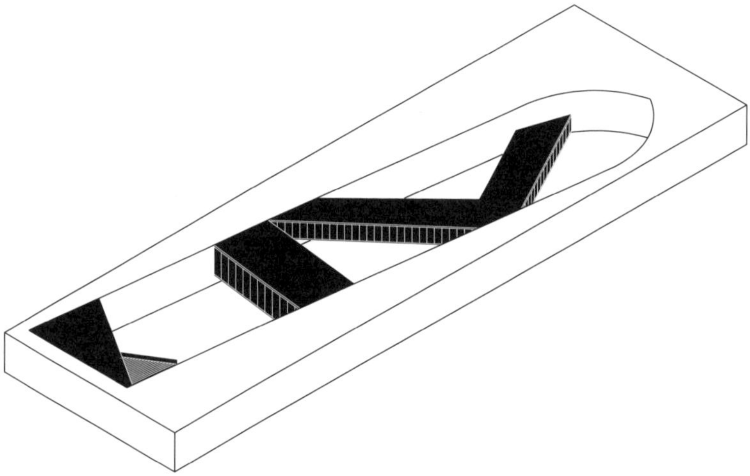

Studiecenter / Study Centre

T-2 Bicycle Parking Main Station Karlsruhe

The abundance of parking infrastructure near major train stations is a ubiquitous urban condition. The area around the main station of Karlsruhe was no different. For decades, it was filled with parking garages that accommodated cars and buses. In 2017, parking was demolished in the construction of a new development. This was a catalyst for change, in light of a city objective for 30% bicycles in its total traffic count. To that end, the city chose to renovate a parking garage and transform it for bicycle parking. The renovated garage is divided into five zones, mapped by colorful graphics. It will fit up to 670 bikes of different kinds, from cargo bikes to bikes with trailers and electric bikes. Accessory spaces include a changing room with lockers and a workshop with tools for maintaining the bicycles. Each year, the General German Bicycle Club compares cities of similar sizes and Karlsruhe was placed in the top among cities with between 200,000 and 500,000 inhabitants for its bicycle accessibility. With the reuse of a car park for bicycle parking, the city is embarking on a strategy that embraces the future of transportation, particularly in this time of limited energy supplies. This project of adaptive reuse is a glimpse of what is to come as we stand on the edge of change.

Location:	Karlsruhe, Germany	
Year of Conversion:	2018	
Architects:	JOHNNY architecture	
Original Use:	Garage	[transportation]
New Use:	Bike parking	[infrastructure]

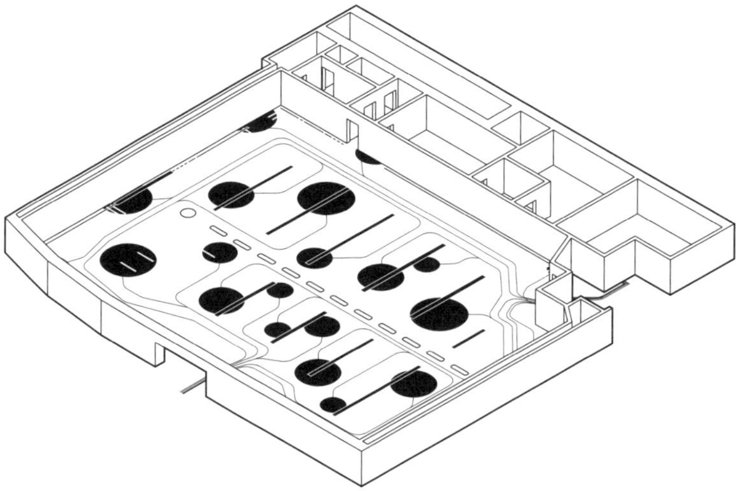

T-3 FRAC Grand Large

FRAC (Fond Régional d'Art Contemporain) is a public collection of contemporary art. Its regional branch in the north is located in the port of Dunkirk at Halle AP2 (Atelier de Préfabrication no.2), the site of an old boat warehouse. Built in 1947 and nicknamed "'The Cathedral' and the cradle of the nation's biggest ships,"[1] Halle AP2 was a prefabrication workshop in a former national shipyard, decommissioned with the collapse of the shipbuilding industry. True to its nickname, the interior of the boat warehouse was an exceptionally vast and light-filled volume. A subdivision of the space would have been necessary to house the program of a museum with its many spaces for exhibition as well as support spaces. Lacaton & Vassal chose to preserve Halle AP2 and duplicate it with an adjacent twin volume constructed from a light and bioclimatic envelope. Halle AP2 would remain and be used for flexible space including art installations, while the new volume with its transparent skin would be designed with six levels to accommodate the required programmatic elements. The old and new structures are connected by an interior street that is an extension of the Grand Large footbridge. FRAC Grand Large is a complex project of reuse that probes issues of preservation and fit while embarking on an intervention of duplication.

Location:	Dunkirk, France	
Year of Conversion:	2013	
Architects:	Lacaton & Vassal	
Original Use:	Boat storage/shipyard	[transportation]
New Use:	Museum	[culture]

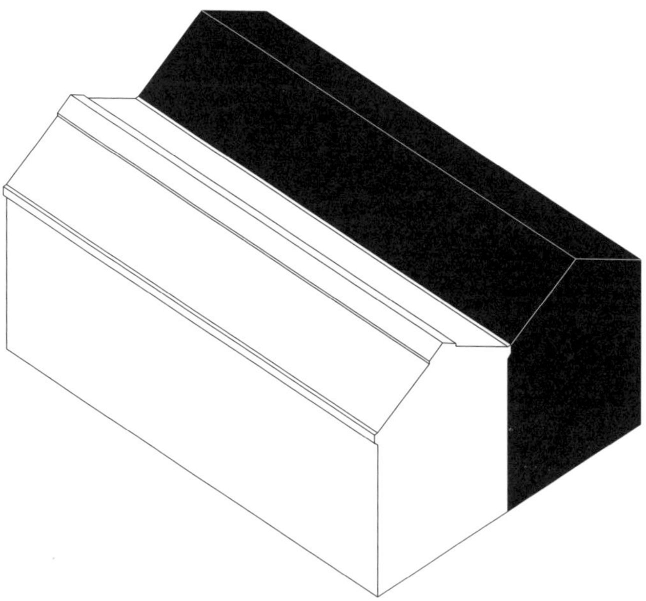

1 Website of FRAC Grand Large. https://www.fracgrandlarge-hdf.fr/en/architecture/

L'ART EST SIMPLEMENT
LA PREUVE D'UNE VIE
PLEINEMENT VÉCUE

T-4 The High Line

The High Line is a 1.5-mile-long public park built on an abandoned section of the New York Central Railroad's West Side Line. This elevated viaduct section connecting the Meatpacking District and the Hudson Rail Yards was constructed in 1934 for shipping coal, dairy and beef. With the growth of interstate trucking, this section experienced a drop in use that was compounded by the construction of the Jacob K. Javits Covention Center that required the demolition of a part of the elevated rail. In 1980, it was shut down and disconnected from the rail line. Failed efforts to use it as light rail or to preserve it led to plans for its demolition in 1992. In 2003, a competition for its reuse led to the transfer of the structure for reuse as a park, inspired by Paris' Coulée Verte. The strategy for its reuse is referred to as 'agri-tecture' by the architects in reference to the design's combination of built and planted sections. The park is created by a paving system of pre-cast concrete planks with open joints through which vegetation grows. The reuse of the rail as public space has become a tourist attraction in New York City with pre-pandemic visitor numbers of 8 million per year. The success of this reuse of abandoned infrastructure has inspired similar transformations in many cities around the world.

Location:	New York, NY, USA	
Year of Conversion:	2009	
Architects:	Diller Scofidio + Renfro in collaboration with James Corner Field Operations and Piet Oudolf	
Original Use:	Highway	[transportation]
New Use:	Park	[recreation]

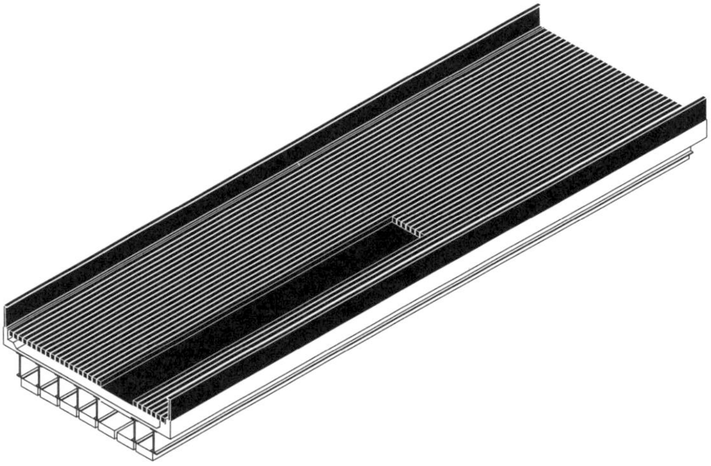

T-5 Im Viadukt Arches

In Zurich's industrial quarter the presence of railways impacted urban development until their replacement by viaducts in 1894. The work of stone masons, the viaduct lifted the rails several stories above ground level. Since their construction in the late 19th century, local vendors have set up business within the different stone arches. In the 1980s, proposals were made to expand the viaduct eastward despite the limitations of the existing infrastructure, especially the size of the connecting tunnel. The project did not materialize due to lack of funding. Public outrage against an outmoded expansion that would not have served its needs grew, culminating in a cantonal initiative for a proper underground station. The initiative resulted in the construction of the underground station Löwenstrasse and the Weinbergtunnel. Protests broke out again with the plans to transform the decommissioned viaduct into an upper-class shopping district. Im Viadukt instead repurposes the arches to mitigate the spatial barrier created by railways that bisect areas of the cities they traverse. A new covered market is introduced, occupied by merchants rooted in the district, continuing a centuries-long tradition. Passages are created within the arches that connect the levels and the two sides of the city. In an architectural vocabulary of restraint, the new use of the viaducts draws attention to the work of the stonemasons of long ago.

Location:	Zurich, Switzerland	
Year of Conversion:	2010	
Architects:	EM2N	
Original Use:	Railroad viaduct	[transportation]
New Use:	Market	[retail]

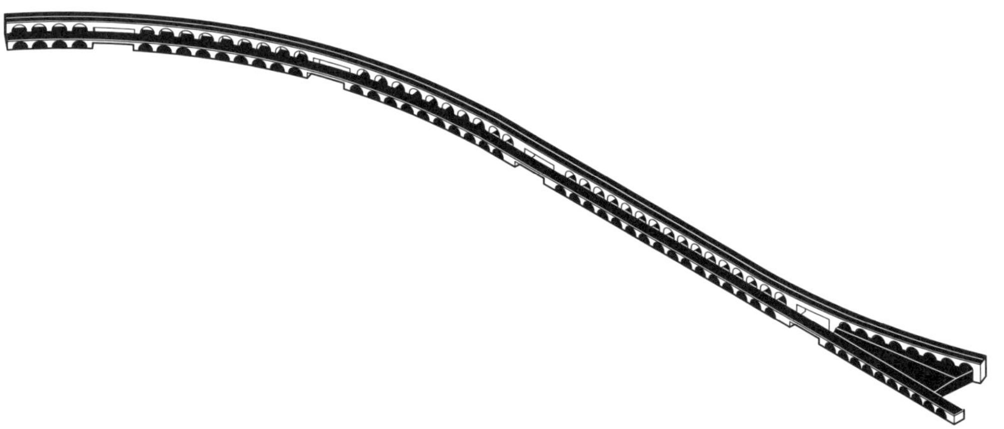

VOM FISCHER & SYNER FRU
...52
Delikatessen Metzgerei Wipkingen
...50

T-6 Kraanspoor

Kraanspoor is an office building located in Amsterdam's harbor at the former shipyard NDSM (Nederlandsche Dok en Scheepsbouw Maatschappij). Dutch naval power reached its height from the 15th to the 17th centuries, placing an emphasis on their superior shipbuilding industry. In the 20th century, shipbuilding reached a post-war peak by the end of the 1960s and fell into decline from the 1970s. The NDSM, part of the industry of the Port of Amsterdam, came into existence as the result of a merger in 1946 that lasted until 1979 when the company became defunct. The craneway – 270 m × 8.7 m – was built in 1952 and stands at a height of 13.5m above the IJ River. In this transformation, the craneway is used as the foundation and structural support for the three-story light-weight glass and steel office building. The new building seemingly floats above the top of the craneway, an illusion made possible by slender 3-m-high steel columns that transfer the weight to the concrete below. The features of the craneway – four stairwells and the catwalks – are reused as part of the circulation of the new building. The regulating lines of the old structure are reflected in the new in a transformation of this vestige of the industrial past.

Location:	Amsterdam, the Netherlands	
Year of Conversion:	2007	
Architects:	OTH Architecten	
Original Use:	Craneway	[transportation]
New Use:	Office	[office]

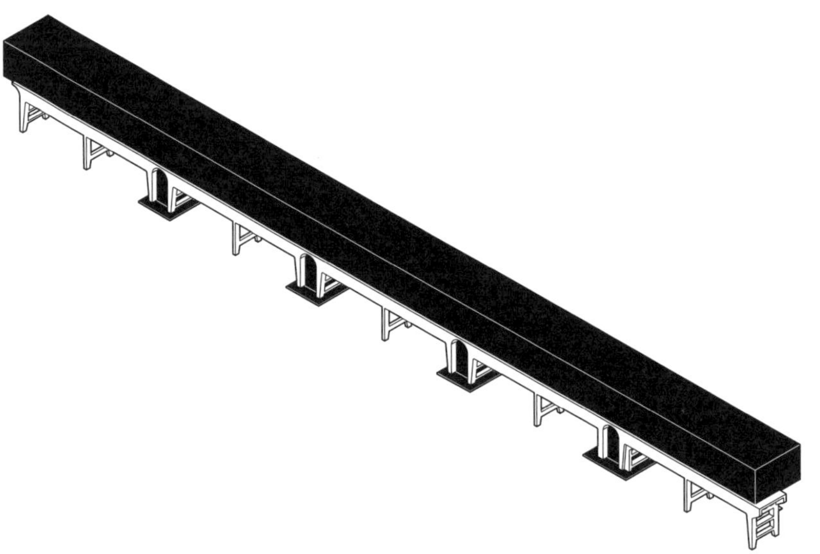

T-7 Musée d'Orsay

The Musée d'Orsay, housing France's largest collection of Impressionist paintings, is adapted from the former Gare d'Orsay, a railway station terminus built in 1900 for the Paris–Orléans Railway. Designed in the Beaux-Arts style, the station was equipped with state-of-the-art electrified rails. By 1939, the station was decommissioned as its platforms were not long enough to service newer and longer trains. After decades in which the abandoned station was temporarily used for different purposes, including reception for liberated WWII prisoners, a car park, film set, etc., there was discussion of its demolition in 1970. In 1977, the French government decided to convert it into a museum and, in 1978, the structure was designated a French monument. Its transformation into a museum was completed through the establishment of three levels, all part of an atrium created within the train's grand skylit hall. Circulation within the museum followed that of the former train platforms. These interior interventions, while accommodating the new needs, retained the spirit of the train station. The reuse of the Gare d'Orsay as a museum broke new ground for adaptive reuse in general and certainly set a precedent for the reuse of transportation structures. The collection has grown since 1986 and there are plans for another renovation of the museum, slated for completion in 2026.

Location:	Paris, France	
Year of Conversion:	1986	
Architects:	Gae Aulenti & ACT Architecture	
Original Use:	Train station	[transportation/heritage]
New Use:	Museum	[culture]

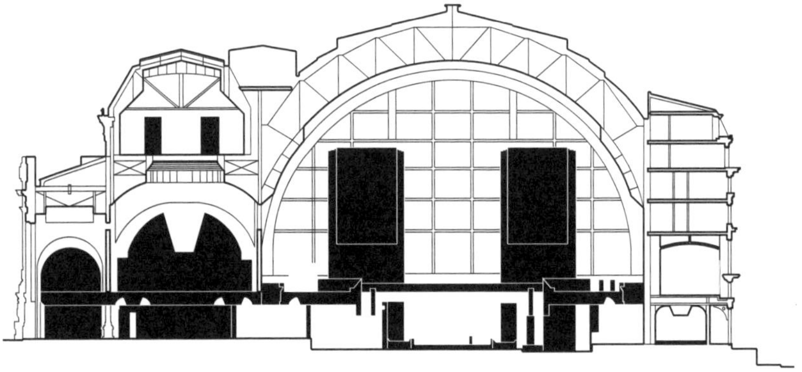

T-8 Karstadt Re-Parked

The Karstadt department stores are part of a historic chain of retail establishments first opened in 1881 by Rudolph Karstadt. Its success as a retail concept led to the opening of many such stores in different German cities. In 1929, a Karstadt opened in Hermannplatz in Berlin-Kreuzberg, a nine-story building with two monumental towers. One of the largest department stores of its time, it was destroyed by the Nazis and rebuilt in the post-war era but on a smaller scale. The structure is registered as heritage in the Berlin Monuments Office. Since the beginning of the 21st century, the parent company has struggled to remain relevant with the introduction of other types of retail. Insolvency and the Covid-19 pandemic have led to the closing of many of its stores. Plans were made by its current owner Signa Holding in 2019 to "reconstruct" and rebuild the old Karstadt. The current design by Lendager proposes a novel project of reuse within the existing store and parking structure in which all materials on site will be "recirculated and 'reparked' in new aesthetic configurations."[1] The facade, roof, interior materials and the car park will be dismantled but reused as new facades and structural floor slabs, in combination with a wood structure. This unique strategy, if fulfilled, will push the limits of reuse. Lendager claims that they will create the most sustainable retail and office building in the world.

Location:	Berlin, Germany	
Year of Conversion:	2025	
Architects:	Lendager	
Original Use:	Retail and parking	[retail/transportation/heritage]
New Use:	Retail and office	[retail/office]

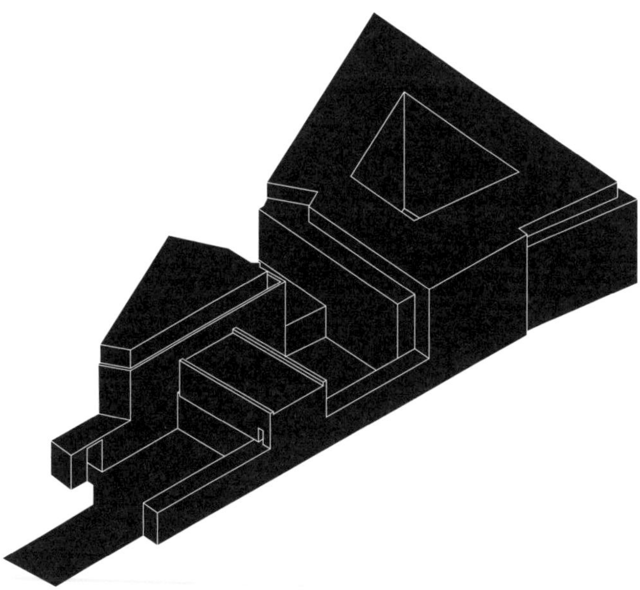

1 https://lendager.com/project/karstadt/

Bücher

Religion

Reuse of Religious Structures + Rise of the Religious Nones (1955–2021)*

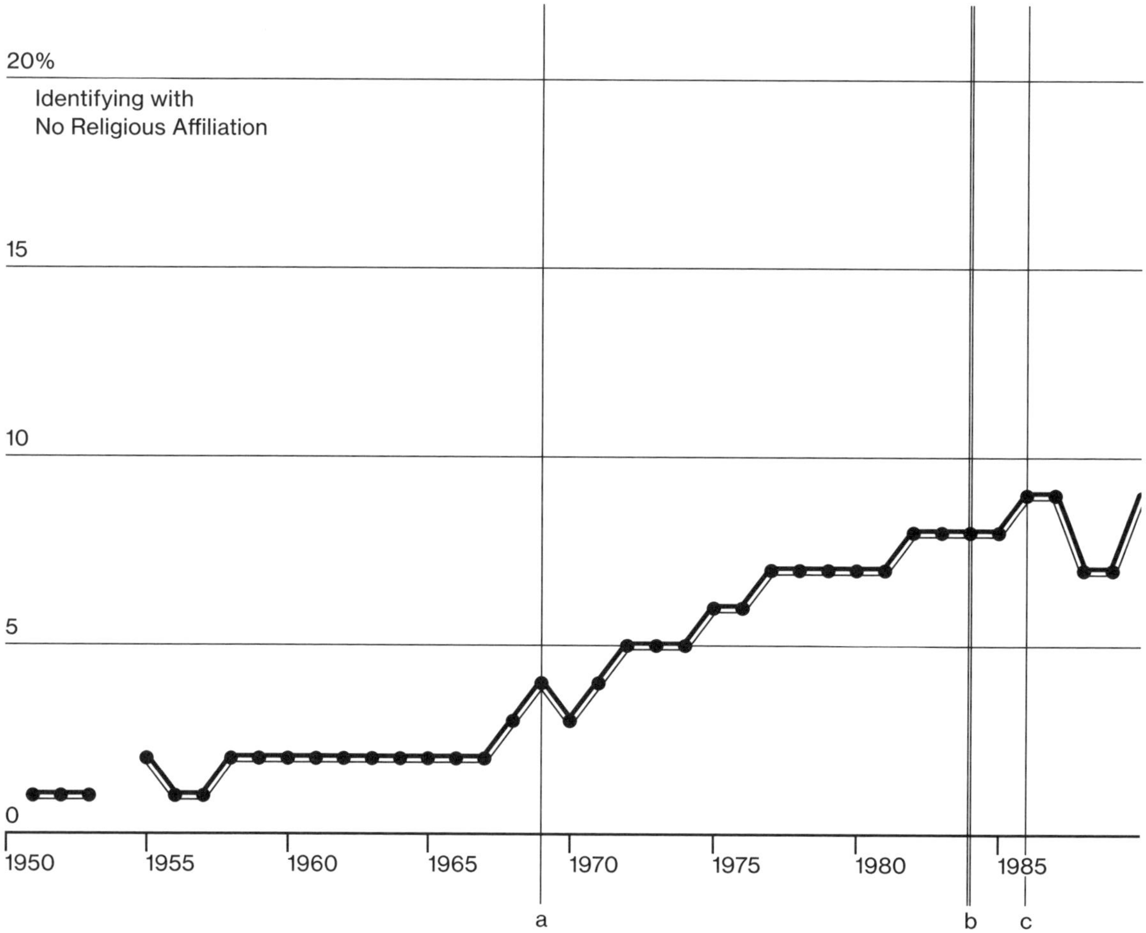

- a Club Paradiso
- b Church Court; The Limelight Nightclub
- c Eremitani Civic Museum
- d Art in the Chapels (L'art dans les chapelles)
- e Church Brew Works
- f Piazza Alicia
- g Montante Cultural Center
- h Library and Lecture Hall
- i Catalysis Corporation; Cultural Center of the Piarists in Lavapiés; Le Chic Resto Pop
- j Barcelona Supercomputing; Kruisherenhotel
- k Selexyz Dominicanen Bookstore
- l Our Lady of the Conception Gallery
- m Constable's Palace; Vertige Escalade
- n House in a Church
- o San Telmo Museum; The Sanctuary Museum (Museum of Divine Statues)
- p Convento das Bernardas
- q Waanders in de Broeren; Culture House DC

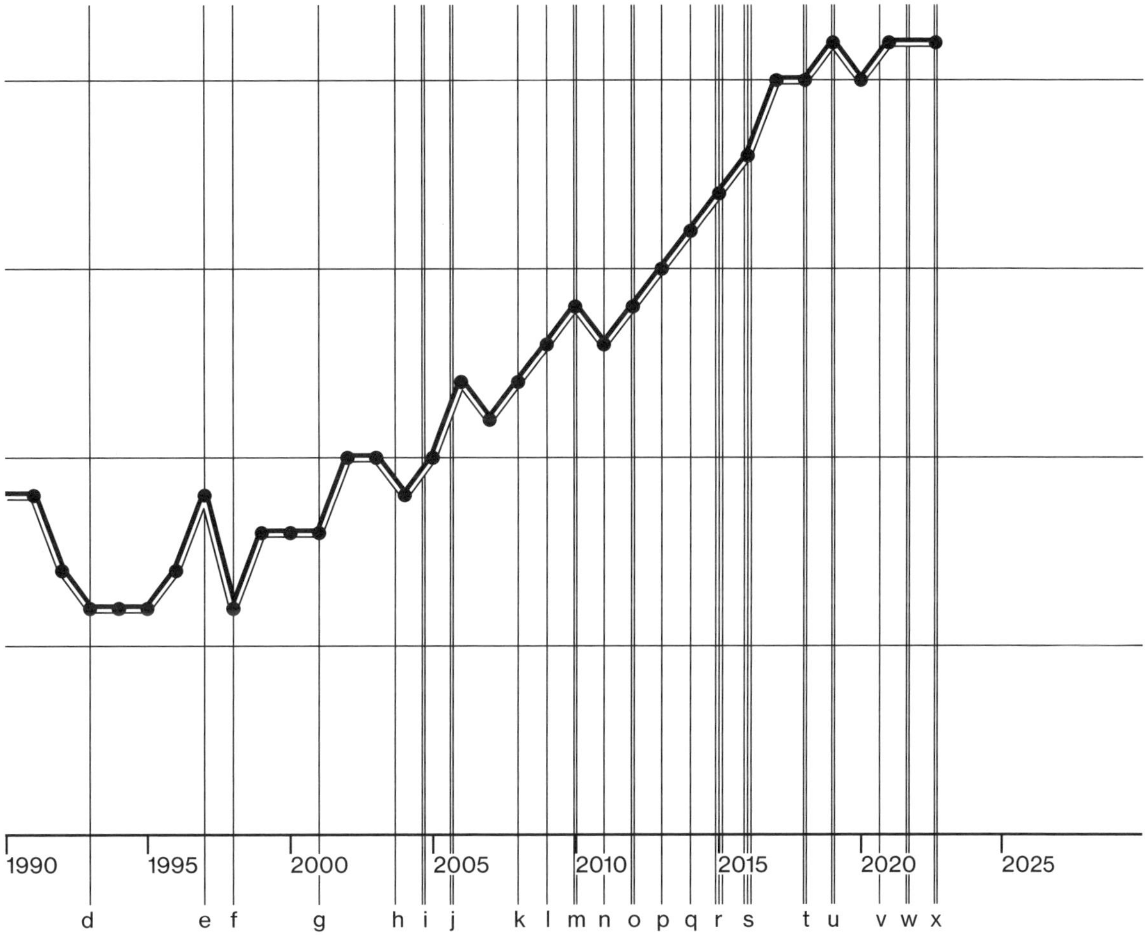

r Grey Nuns Reading Room; Royal Abbey of Fontevraud; The Limelight David Barton Gym; Théâtre Paradoxe

s Children's Day School; Kaos Temple; König Galerie; Masjid Isa Ibn Maryam (Jesus, Son of Mary Mosque); Quarry Theater at St. Lukes; Tafts Ale House

t Nyamata Genocide Memorial Centre; Santa María de Vilanova de la Barca

u Lucas Condominiums; The Line Hotel

v Sinan Books Poetry Store

w Espai Santa Eulàlia; Tap Holding Headquarters

x Monastero Arx Vivendi Hotel; San Juan de Ruesta Hermitage

* Source: Gallup Poll

In 1844, when the Church of the Holy Communion opened, its architect Richard Upjohn could not have imagined that, 139 years later, Andy Warhol would host the opening party of its conversion into the infamous Limelight Nightclub, "the epicenter for rave culture in New York."[1] Built at the height of Anglican Catholicism, the Gothic Revival Evangelical church served the spiritual needs of some of the wealthiest citizens of New York City. In 1966, the church was designated a landmark by the New York City Landmarks Preservation Commission. Despite this architectural honor, it was decommissioned shortly thereafter due to post-Second World War urban flight and the trend toward secularization. From 1976 on, the church served various functions: artist and scholar collective, drug and alcohol rehabilitation center, marketplace and, since 2014, the David Barton Gym. From religion to sex, drugs and body shaping, the trials of this Gothic Revival church exemplify the trials and tribulations of many Christian churches in the West at the end of the 20th century.

IMG 1 — James Brown performing at Club Paradiso, located in a former Amsterdam church.
IMG 2 — A religious celebration at a megachurch.

Hundreds of vacant churches and religious properties are for sale in 2022 across Europe, the United States and Australia, some of which hold heritage designation. They are the physical manifestation of secularization trends in the Western world. A *Wall Street Journal* study in 2015 found that the Church of England closed 20 churches annually, Germany's Roman Catholic Church closed 515 in a decade, Denmark has deemed approximately 200 of its churches underused, and the Netherlands estimates that 700 Protestant churches will close within four years and two-thirds of its 1,600 Roman Catholic churches will be decommissioned in ten years.[2] In the US in 2019, 3,000 Protestant churches opened but 4,500 closed.[3] In the Catholic Church, however, there are conflicting developments, with decades of church closures in the northeast but a demand for new churches in the south and west.[4] In addition, megachurches are thriving in parts of the US, Asia, Africa and Australia. These, at times contradictory, trends are the result of decades of shifting beliefs, many of which are the product of changing cultural and social norms from the 1970s. The impact of these trends is tangible as numerous unused or decommissioned churches in the 20th century have since become adaptive reuse projects in their afterlife.

American church membership throughout the mid-1970s was at approximately 70%.[5] A Gallup poll survey on religious preferences from the 1970s indicates that 96% identified with a religion, 3% with none and less than 0.5% did not answer, whereas in 2021, 76% identified with a religion (Protestant, Christian, Catholic, Jewish, Mormon or other), 21% with none and 3% did not answer.[6] A 2021 Pew Research survey found that "three-in-ten U.S. adults (29%) are religious 'nones' – people who describe themselves as atheists, agnostics or 'nothing in particular' when asked about religious identity."[7] Of these "nones," 20% were not atheists but were those who identified with "nothing in particular."[8] Religious "nones" also saw an increase in 19 European countries.[9] This shift of the "nones," with their lack of religious beliefs, is one of the main factors leading to secularization. The shift peaked most dramatically from 2005 when it increased steadily by 10% in 16 years.[10] As the "nones" increased, church membership decreased. This direct relationship is borne out by the numbers of notable reused church projects that steadily increased in the 21st century. This is especially so with churches in Europe, where "the level of religious observance is considerably lower ... than in the United States" and "the process of secularization is extremely advanced throughout the continent."[11] The town of Maratea in Italy, dating to the 15th century, boasts 44 churches as part of its history of strong religious traditions. Today, these churches have been incorporated into the town's touristic activities.

The shift away from religious affiliation was one of many factors contributing to the increase of decommissioned churches. Other factors, developed as a result of changes that began in the 1970s, included a growing awareness of diversity. At a time when population growth slowed, "more immigrants from different countries arrived ... than at any previous time in American history." "Nearly five million immigrants arrived in the United States during the 1970s, the greatest influx of people to America since the 1920s. Of these five million, the vast bulk came from countries in Asia, the Caribbean, and Central America; more immigrants came from Mexico during the 1970s than from any other country."[12] [13] A recognition of ethnicity developed by way of advocacy for these different ethnic groups and their rights. The Chicano Movement of the 1960s rallied against discrimination toward people of Mexican heritage. The movement was advanced in the 1970s with strikes by the farm workers, mostly migrants from Mexico, that led to California's 1975 Agricultural Labor Relations Act. The Act established the right to collective bargaining with the objective to "ensure peace in the agricultural fields by guaranteeing justice for all agricultural workers and stability in labor relations."[14] In New York's Chinatown, Asian Americans protested for equal employment rights in 1974. "The meticulously organized protest, similar to those that have been taking place at sites in black and Puerto Rican areas for 11 years in the city, is something new to Chinatown. While residents have often complained of discrimination and short changing on city services, public protest has been rare."[15] The American Indian Movement (AIM), an American Indian civil rights organization founded in the late 1960s, advanced the rights of American Indians and their right to Indian lands. In 1972, they marched on Washington, DC and, in 1973, together with members of the Oglala Lakota tribe, occupied the land at Wounded Knee, South Dakota, to demand reparations for past unmet treaties made by the US Government. This increasing diversity in the US populace triggered demands for a national recognition of their rights. In 1975, legislation recognizing these various ethnic groups came about through an amendment to the Voting Rights Act of 1965. An achievement of the civil rights movement, the 1965 Act declared that all discrimination based on race was illegal, with the then objective to protect the rights of Blacks. However, by the 1970s, Congress found extensive evidence of voting discrimination against "citizens of language minorities."[16] This led to an Amendment in 1975 that defined these citizens as "persons who are American Indian, Asian American, Alaskan Native, or of Spanish heritage."[17]

This formal acknowledgment, together with growing diversity in the American populace, would lead to a changed religious landscape over half a century. In 2021, a Pew Research Study found that in North America, "Muslims and followers of 'other religions' are the fastest-growing religious groups. Christians are projected to decline from 78% of the US population in 2010 to 66% in 2050, while the unaffiliated are expected to rise from 16% to 26%."[18] And, by 2035, Muslim births will outpace Christian births while all other religions combined are predicted to decrease slightly by 2060.[19] In contrast, between 2010 and 2015, Christian deaths in Europe outpaced births in 24 of 42 countries.[20] In total, "Europe's Christian population is expected to shrink by about 100 million people in the coming decades."[21] In addition, Christians (66 million people) are predicted to switch out of the religion, including the net departure of twice as many men (44 million) as women (22 million).[22] These trends and predictions corroborate declining membership in Western Christian churches, especially in Europe, confirming what is noted in the built environment.

The issue of religious affiliation and the belief in the importance of a religious community were not directly part of the counterculture of the 1960s and the 1970s. But two separate movements from that time impacted religion and, by association, both religious affiliation and church membership: the women's rights movement and the gay rights movement. The end of the 1960s was marked by the November 1969 Congress to Unite Women Meeting in New York City, organized by the National Organization for Women (NOW), with the aim to find common ground between the moderate and radical parts of the women's rights movement. In the early years of the 1970s, gains for women were made on different levels from the church to the stadium. In 1970, the Lutheran Church approved women's ordination and 11 female deacons were ordained as the first female Episcopal priests four years later. In 1972, the US Congress passed Title IX of the Higher Education Amendments that prohibited discrimination on the basis of sex in federally funded educational programs. This legislation paved the way for women's participation in athletics. The same year, the Equal Rights Amendment prohibiting discrimination based on sex was approved, 49 years after it was first drafted. (Although it was approved by the Congress in 1972, to date it has not received enough states for its ratification.) The critical achievement in women's rights, though, was the 1973 Supreme Court decision on *Roe v. Wade* that protects a woman's right to an abortion. (In 2022, 49 years after this decision, a different Supreme Court overturned this ruling.)

At the same time, there was also positive development in the fight for gay rights. In 1969, the Stonewall Inn, a gay club in Greenwich Village in New York City, was raided by the police. This raid sparked a six-day riot that was the catalyst for the gay rights movement. To commemorate

IMG 3 — The Chapel Torre Girona reused as the MareNostrum Supercomputing Center, Barcelona.
IMG 4 — The wine bar cafe occupying the altar and apse of the Selexyz Dominicanen Bookstore.

the raid, the Christopher Street Liberation Day, the first gay pride parade, was held in New York City in 1970. It inspired similar protests in Europe: the first meeting in 1970 of the London Gay Liberation Front (GLF) held at the London School of Economics, the 1971 founding of the FHAR (Front homosexuel d'action révolutionnaire) in France, the HAW (Homosexuelle Aktion Westberlin) in West Germany,[23] and the 1978 transnational founding of the National Lesbian and Gay Association in Coventry, UK. In the US there were small victories for the societal perception of gay people as they became more visible on different fronts. In 1973, the Board of Trustees of the American Psychiatric Association "approved a change in its official manual of psychiatric disorders. 'Homosexuality per se,' the trustees voted, should no longer be considered a 'psychiatric disorder.'"[24] In 1977, the New York Supreme Court ruled to allow a transgender woman to play in the U.S. Open tennis tournament as a woman. And in 1978, Harvey Milk became the first openly gay man to be elected to office in San Francisco, California. These were the first steps on the long road to the 2015 U.S. Supreme Court case *Obergefell v. Hodges* that ruled all bans on same-sex marriage unconstitutional. This led to marriage equality in the United States.

These developments within the women's rights movement and the gay rights movement took place alongside the rise of conservative politics and the emergence of the New Religious Right. The Christian Right comprised political action groups that included the voices of religious organizations such as the Moral Majority (founded in 1979), the Religious Roundtable and the Christian Voice (founded in 1978). The legalization of abortion and same-sex marriage, viewed as moral decline, "gave certain general themes of the Right's moral traditionalism concrete political application and thus helped stimulate a new wave of conservative political activism and the rise of the New Religious Right."[25] The Christian Right consisted of different religions, including Catholicism, Protestantism and Mormonism, with a majority within the Protestant Church. These evangelical Christians within the Protestant Church cleaved the Protestant Christians into Mainline Protestants and Evangelical Protestants. In the United States, of 70.6% Christians, 25.4% are Evangelical Protestants while 14.7% are Mainline Protestants.[26] In 2020, "the evangelical branch of Protestantism has 660 million adherents worldwide and is growing dramatically. In the early 20th century, 94% of South Americans were Catholic and only 1% Protestant. Currently, the number of Protestants there has grown to 20%, while that of Catholics has fallen to 69%."[27] Evangelical Christians practice in different church spaces, often to accommodate the size of their congregations. With up to 2,000 congregants at mass at a given time, these spaces of worship have earned the name of "megachurch." The emergence of the Religious Right has had the dual effect of siphoning membership from existing churches, thereby contributing to the loss of congregations, as well as through the creation of new megachurches.

The Catholic Church itself contributed to the issue of declining membership in the 1990s when news came to light of the sexual abuse of minors by the clergy. The church abuse scandal, as it became known, was not new. Investigations from the 1990s by *The Boston Globe* culminated in a 2002 Pulitzer Prize-winning report that exposed the scandal. The investigations revealed global instances of such abuse stemming from the 1950s in the

United States, but also in many other countries, including Ireland, Australia, France, Scotland and Austria. A case from the early 1970s of a Roman Catholic cardinal and archbishop of Washington, DC – the highest ranked priest to be removed from the church – is one of hundreds of cases of accused priests around the world.[28] In a 2019 Gallup poll, "Thirty-seven percent of U.S. Catholics, up from 22% in 2002, say news of the abuse has led them to question whether they would remain in the church."[29] The editor of *Catholic World News* wrote, "I think probably, for a lot of people, it was sort of a reason to leave the church, but they were going to leave anyway."[30] In addition to contributing further to a membership decline, the scandal was followed by lawsuits that required cash for both legal fees and settlements. "Within a year of *The Boston Globe* report, the Boston archdiocese paid out $85 million in settlements. By 2007, that number was $615 million."[31] Many Catholic Church properties were closed and sold.

These factors – secularization, multiculturalism, conservatism, scandal – all contributed to the declining membership of Christian churches and ultimately, over time, their closure. The adaptive reuse of the many closed or decommissioned churches follows this trajectory. Reflecting the timeframe between the event and its implications on the built environment, the timeline of notable church conversions includes a few projects in the 1980s and 1990s, but shows a steep rise from the turn of the 21st century. In 2022, breaking news of sexual abuse in evangelical churches will most likely cause further decline in religious structures. The reuse of the megachurch may well become a new category of religious reuse.

Churches have been reused in many different ways: retail, hospitality, housing, entertainment, exercise, recreation, culture, performance, education and even storage. Despite this variety of new programs, the church as a host structure differentiates itself from other host structures in that some programs of reuse have the potential to inflict damage on the authenticity of the host. The Christian church as a vast, empty shell for assembly invites the consideration of many different new functions. Volumetrically, it has the potential to accommodate enormous programs of use, from nightclubs to condominiums. The characteristically high nave, similar to the voluminous interiors of airports or power plants, offers the possibility of vertical subdivision and the accommodation of dense programmatic requirements. This is achieved, especially in the conversion to housing, with the insertion of new floors and walls within the void. Such lucrative considerations provide a financial incentive for reuse development. Unlike airports and power plants, however, the church is uniquely imbued with an architecture of ritual, in which holy rites performed over millennia are imprinted on its elements, from the floorplan to the detail. They are part of its aura and inseparable from the physical material. While subdividing the church is feasible, doing so renders irreparable damage to its integrity. Of the many church conversion projects, the ones that are most successful are those that retain this aura in assembly, be it as a new skateboard park, bookstore or concert venue. Conversely, the subdivision of the church into additional levels and rooms destroys what is salient. In the case of the church as a host structure, afterlife is indeed only attained by capturing the spirit of the place.

IMG 5 — Jesus, Son of Mary Mosque located in the former Holy Trinity Church in Syracuse, NY.
IMG 6 — The church of Santa Barbara Asturias transformed into a skateboard park.

- Art in the Chapels (L'art dans les chapelles) — Brittany, France, 1992
- Barcelona Supercomputing — Barcelona, Spain, 2005
- Catalysis Corporation — Seattle, WA, USA, 2004
- Children's Day School — San Francisco, CA, USA, 2015
- Church Brew Works — Pittsburgh, PA, USA, 1996
- Church Court — Boston, MA, USA, 1983
- Club Paradiso — Amsterdam, the Netherlands, 1968
- Constable's Palace — Pamplona, Spain, 2009
- Convento das Bernardas — Tavira, Portugal, 2012
- Convento do Beato Complex — Lisbon, Portugal, 2022
- Cultural Center of the Piarists in Lavapiés — Madrid, Spain, 2004
- Culture House DC — Washington, DC, USA, 2013
- Eremitani Civic Museum — Padua, Italy, 1985
- Espai Santa Eulàlia — Gironella, Spain, 2020
- Grey Nuns Reading Room — Montreal, Canada, 2014
- House in a Church — Rotterdam, the Netherlands, 2010
- Jesus, Son of Mary Mosque — Syracuse, NY, USA, 2015
- Kaos Temple — Llanera, Asturias, Spain, 2015
- König Galerie — Berlin, Germany, 2015
- Kruisherenhotel — Maastricht, the Netherlands, 2005
- Le Chic Resto Pop — Montreal, Canada, 2004
- Library and Lecture Hall — Madrid, Spain, 2003
- Lucas Condominiums — Boston, MA, USA, 2017
- Monastero Arx Vivendi Hotel — Arco, Italy, 2021
- Monastery of San Juan — Burgos, Spain, 2015
- Montante Cultural Center — Buffalo, NY, USA, 2000
- Nyamata Genocide Memorial Centre — Kigali, Rwanda, 2016
- Our Lady of the Conception Gallery — Lisbon, Portugal, 2008
- Piazza Alicia — Salemi, Italy, 1997
- Quarry Theatre at St. Lukes — Bedford, UK, 2015
- Royal Abbey of Fontevraud — Fontevraud, France, 2014
- San Juan de Ruesta Hermitage — Ruesta, Spain, 2022
- San Telmo Museum — San Sebastián, Spain, 2011
- Santa María de Vilanova de la Barca — Lleida, Spain, 2016
- Selexyz Dominicanen Bookstore — Maastricht, the Netherlands, 2007
- Sinan Books Poetry Store — Shanghai, China, 2019
- Tafts Ale House — Cincinnati, OH, USA, 2015
- Tap Holding Headquarters — Paderborn, Germany, 2020
- The Limelight David Barton Gym — New York, NY, USA, 2014
- The Limelight Nightclub — New York, NY, USA, 1983

• The Line Hotel	Washington, DC, USA, 2017
• The Sanctuary Museum (Museum of Divine Statues)	Lakewood, OH, USA, 2011
• Théâtre Paradoxe	Montreal, Canada, 2014
• Vertige Escalade	Sherbrooke, Canada, 2009
• Waanders in de Broeren	Zwolle, the Netherlands, 2013

1 Priya Krishna, "From House of Worship to House of Sin: The History of Chelsea's Limelight Building," *Curbed*, 30 November 2016.

2 Naftali Bendavid, "Europe's Empty Churches Go on Sale," *The Wall Street Journal*, 2 January 2015.

3 Aaron Earls, "Protestant Church Closures Outpace Openings in the U.S.," Lifeway Research, 25 May 2021. https://www.christianitytoday.com/news/2021/may/lifeway-church-close-open-2019-planting-revitalization.html, accessed 16 March 2021.

4 Robert David Sullivan, "Two U.S. Churches: One is Closing Down Parishes, the Other is Standing-room Only," *America*, 19 April 2019. https://www.americamagazine.org/faith/2019/04/19/two-us-churches-one-closing-down-parishes-other-standing-room-only, accessed 16 March 2022.

5 Jeffrey M. Jones, "U.S. Church Membership Down Sharply in Past Two Decades," Gallup, 18 April 2019. https://news.gallup.com/poll/248837/church-membership-down-sharply-past-two-decades.aspx, accessed 16 March 2022.

6 "What is Your Religious Preference – Are You Protestant, Roman Catholic, Mormon, Jewish, Muslim, Another Religion or No Religion?" Gallup. https://news.gallup.com/poll/1690/religion.aspx, accessed 17 March 2022.

7 Gregory A. Smith, "About Three-in-Ten U.S. Adults Are Now Religiously Unaffiliated," Pew Research Center, 14 December 2021.

8 Ibid.

9 "The Changing Global Religious Landscape," Pew Research Center, 5 April 2017. https://www.pewforum.org/2017/04/05/the-changing-global-religious-landscape/, accessed 21 March 2022.

10 Smith,"About Three-in-Ten U.S. Adults," op. cit.

11 Danièle Hervieu-Léger, "The Role of Religion in Establishing Social Cohesion," *Religion in the New Europe* [online]. Budapest: Central European University Press, 2006. http://books.openedition.org/ceup/1275, accessed 21 March 2022.

12 John Robert Greene, "Gerald Ford: The American Franchise," Miller Center, University of Virginia. https://millercenter.org/president/ford/the-american-franchise, accessed 21 March 2022.

13 Ibid.

14 "What is the Agricultural Labor Relations Act?" Agricultural Labor Relations Board – State of California. https://www.alrb.ca.gov, accessed 23 March 2022.

15 Paul L. Montgomery, "Asians Picket Building Site, Charging Bias," *The New York Times*, 1 June 1974.

16 "An Act to Amend the Voting Rights Act of 1965," Public Law 94–73. H.R.6219 – 94th Congress (1975–1976). 6 August 1975.

17 Ibid.

18 "The Future of World Religions: Population Growth Predictions, 2010–2050," Pew Research Center, 2 April 2015, p. 17. https://assets.pewresearch.org/wp-content/uploads/sites/11/2015/03/PF_15.04.02_ProjectionsFullReport.pdf, accessed 21 March 2022.

19 Ibid.

20 "The Changing Global Religious Landscape," op. cit.

21 Ibid., p. 17.

22 "The Future of World Religions," op. cit.

23 Régis Schlagdenhauffen, "Gay Rights and LGBTQI Movements in Europe," Encyclopédie d'histoire numérique de l'Europe [online], ISSN 2677-6588, 6 February 2022. https://ehne.fr/en/node/12402, accessed 17 March 2022.

24 "The Issue is Subtle, The Debate Still On," *The New York Times*, 23 December 1973.

25 Jerome L. Himmelstein, *To the Right: The Transformation of American Conservatism*. Berkeley: University of California Press, 1990, p. 99.

26 "America's Changing Religious Landscape," Pew Research Center, 12 May 2015, p. 3.

27 Akram Belkaïd and Lamia Oualalou, "The Rise of Evangelical Christianity," *Le Monde diplomatique*, September 2020. https://mondediplo.com/2020/09/06evangelicals, accessed 22 March 2022.

28 "U.S. Ex-cardinal Theodore McCarrick Defrocked over Abuse Claim," BBC, 16 February 2019. https://www.bbc.com/news/world-us-canada-47264130, accessed 22 March 2022.

29 Jones, "U.S. Church Membership," op. cit.

30 Karen Hensel, "Priest Sex Abuse Scandal Accelerated Declining Catholic Church Attendance in Boston," NBC Universal Media, 20 December 2017. https://www.nbcboston.com/news/local/priest-sex-abuse-scandal-accelerated-declining-catholic-church-attendance-in-boston/35128/, accessed 24 March 2022.

31 Ibid.

		Project		Architect
R-1		Piazza Alicia Salemi, IT	1997	Álvaro Siza and Roberto Collovà
R-2		Convento das Bernardas Tavira, PT	2012	Eduardo Souto de Moura
R-3	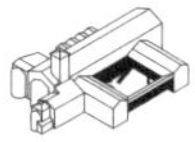	Eremitani Civic Museum Padua, IT	1985	Studio Albini
R-4	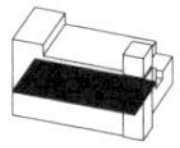	König Galerie Berlin, DE	2015	Arnold Brandlhuber
R-5		Monastery of San Juan Burgos, ES	2015	BSA
R-6		San Juan de Ruesta Hermitage Ruesta, ES	2022–	Sebastián Arquitectos
R-7		Selexyz Dominicanen Bookstore Maastricht, NL	2007	Merkz + Girod

Religion

New Program

	Cultural	Education	Hospitality	Infrastructure	Office	Residential	Retail	Recreational	Memorial
								●	
			●			●			
	●								
	●								
	●								
	●		●						
							●		

R-1 Piazza Alicia

In 1968, the earthquake of Belice in southwestern Sicily killed more than 200 people and left 100,000 homeless. Salemi, a nearby town, was one of the many affected. With a population of approximately 10,000, Salemi was built on the slopes of a hill where the streets wound upward toward the Chiesa Madre, the main church at the top. Built in the 17th century, the church was badly damaged by the earthquake. Parts of the dome and a few columns of the nave were the only parts that remained standing amidst the wreckage. The project of reconstruction and conservation comprised several distinct parts: the stabilization of the remaining church structure, the stabilization of the adjacent alley and rectory, and the transformation of the remains. Compromised structures both in the church and the adjacent areas were stabilized through the addition of exposed new elements in accordance with the Venice Charter. Once cleared, the church was transformed to an urban square through the addition of a new horizontal plinth, using customized materials and means replicating those from the 17th century. The new square, Piazza Alicia, is now a communal outdoor space where kids kick a soccer ball in what was the nave and couples vie for the nooks within the remains of the altar. What was once the heart of the town as a church still is today as an urban plaza. In the transformation of the mother church to an urban piazza, the civic and the sacred merge.

Location:	Salemi, Italy	
Year of Conversion:	1997	
Architects:	Álvaro Siza and Roberto Collovà	
Original Use:	Church	[religion]
New Use:	Urban plaza	[recreation]

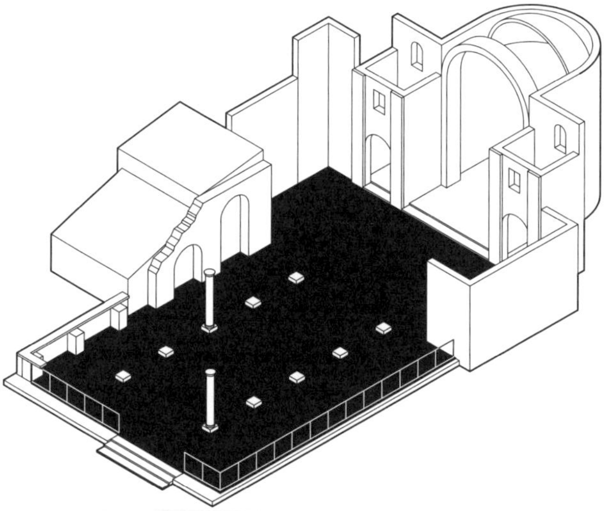

R-2 Convento das Bernardas

For more than 500 years, the Bernardas Convent, founded in 1509, housed the members of the Cistercian Order of southern Portugal. The extinction of the order in 1834 left the convent abandoned and eventually it was acquired in a public auction. In 1890, it was converted into the Steam Mill and Pasta Factory, which closed in the 1960s. Subsequent character-altering transformations took place over the next decades until it fell out of use. In 2006, when Eduardo Souto de Moura received the commission, it was a ruin but one with cultural patrimony that includes a Manueline portal. Tavira, a city of 25,000 inhabitants, is relatively undeveloped and now adjusting to tourism. This dovetailed with the program of a residential resort complex with 78 units of different sizes. The architectural tasks were to, first, recover and restore the existing structure and, second, to develop the new construction within it. The units – single-family townhouse, triplex – are spread out amongst the different wings, each displaying a different typology to best fit into the varying conditions of the restored complex from convent to church and tower. This 'Tetris' approach to spatial manipulations exemplifies the work of adaptive reuse in heritage structures.

Location:	Tavira, Portugal	
Year of Conversion:	2012	
Architects:	Eduardo Souto de Moura	
Original Use:	Convent	[religion/heritage]
New Use:	Residential complex	[residence/hospitality]

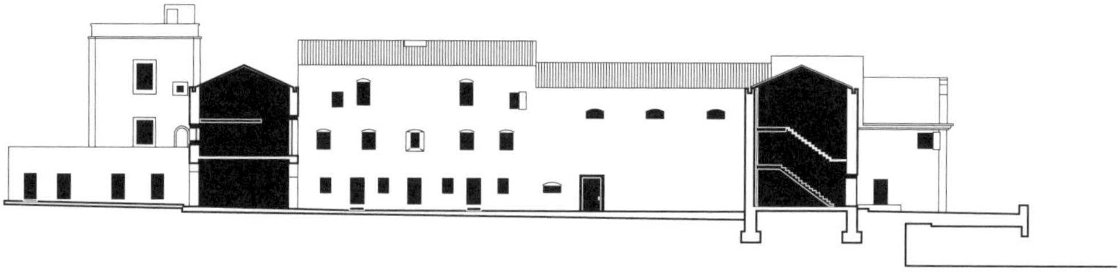

R-3 Eremitani Civic Museum

The Eremitani convent of the 13th-century basilica in Padua is today the Eremitani Civic Museum. It is part of a complex that includes the Scrovegni Chapel with its treasured Giotto frescoes. The double-cloistered convent was severely damaged in WWII and, by the mid-1960s, was selected to host Padua's civic art and archaeological collection. Studio Albini's proposals included a restoration of the relatively undamaged major cloister, revitalization of the destroyed minor cloister, an addition to the entry and a new block of galleries. The additions never materialized. The renovated galleries and especially the interventions in the minor cloister, however, demonstrate the recommendation by the Venice Charter of 1964 for 'a contemporary stamp' when restoring historic structures. The use of exposed steel in different applications, from the long-span I-beams supporting a second-floor loggia to column supports at the ground level, floating stairs and the vertical exhibition stands, introduces a spare and weathered tectonic against the existing brick and stucco of the cloister. A pair of stairs under a thin segmented roof plate leading to the second floor floats effortlessly in front of the existing cathedral wall. The corner column at the cloister is missing – a silent gesture to the new layer in time.

Location:	Padua, Italy	
Year of Conversion:	1985	
Architects:	Studio Albini	
Original Use:	Monastery	[religion/heritage]
New Use:	Museum	[culture]

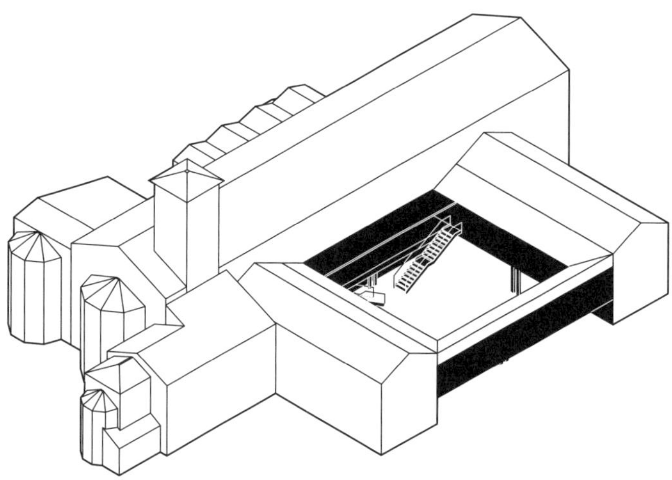

R-4 König Galerie

The König Galerie occupies what was Saint Agnes Church in Berlin. A Catholic parish, Saint Agnes was founded in the Kreuzberg neighborhood in 1925 in a converted riding stable. The entire area was razed in 1945. Reconstruction of this part of the city began in the late 1950s and Saint Agnes was completed in 1967 in the Brutalist style by German architect Werner Düttmann, who served as Berlin's Director of Urban Development from 1960–1966. Religious services ceased after a sharp decrease in church membership that led to parishes being merged, deconsecrated and leased. Without funding for maintenance, the church fell into disuse and advocates fearing its demolition termed it an endangered structure. The church is listed for heritage protection due to such advocacy. Composed of monolithic concrete volumes, the complex includes a sacristy, a rectory, a courtyard, a community center and a 20-m-high tower. The church, the centerpiece of the complex, is without decoration. Its stark concrete walls are lit by slits behind the altar and skylights. Berlin gallery owner Johann König acquired the church in 2012 with a focus on redeveloping the church as an exhibition space. In its new form, the complex has largely been preserved with its original architecture. It is valued for both its religious heritage and its new architectural heritage through its Brutalist design.

Location:	Berlin, Germany	
Year of Conversion:	2015	
Architects:	Brandlhuber + Emde, Burlon / Riegler Riewe Architects	
Original Use:	Church	[religion / heritage]
New Use:	Gallery	[culture]

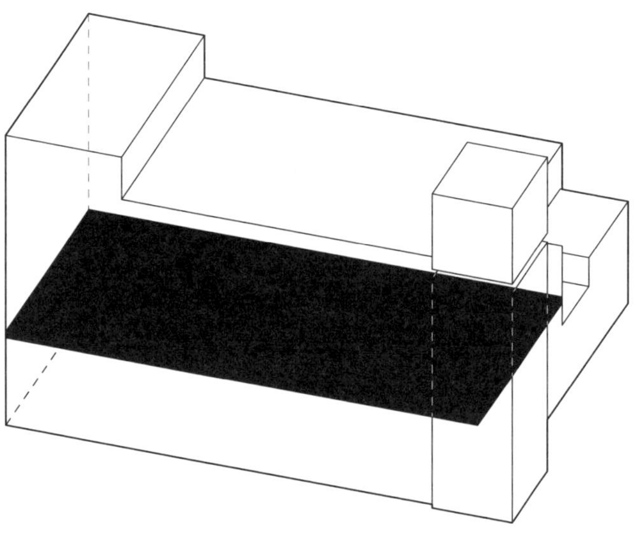

R-5 Monastery of San Juan

The Monastery of San Juan in Burgos is a stop on the Camino de Santiago (Way of St. James), one of the three major pilgrimages of Christianity and a declared cultural route of the Council of Europe. Built in the 11th century, the monastery suffered damage through the years from successive fires in the 15th and 16th centuries to a conflict in the 18th century. Today, the remaining structure – a set of exterior walls – is a heritage ruin that is reasonably preserved due to conservation efforts in the latter half of the 20th century. The addition of a roof that hovers over these ruins protects the remaining walls and provides a new covered event space for the Marceliano Santamaría Museum residing in an adjacent accessory building. The new horizontal roof plane floats above the remains at different levels, recalling the placement of past naves. Extending just beyond the walls, it is independently supported by center columns that leave the original walls untouched. A perfect application of the Venice Charter in differentiating between old and new, the intervention at the Monastery of San Juan is simultaneously an act of preservation and one of transformation. It is an intervention that maintains the authenticity of the ruins while giving them new life.

Location:	Burgos, Spain	
Year of Conversion:	2015	
Architects:	BSA Barrio & Sainz de Aja	
Original Use:	Monastery	[religion/heritage/ruin]
New Use:	Event/Museum (Marceliano Santamaría)	[culture]

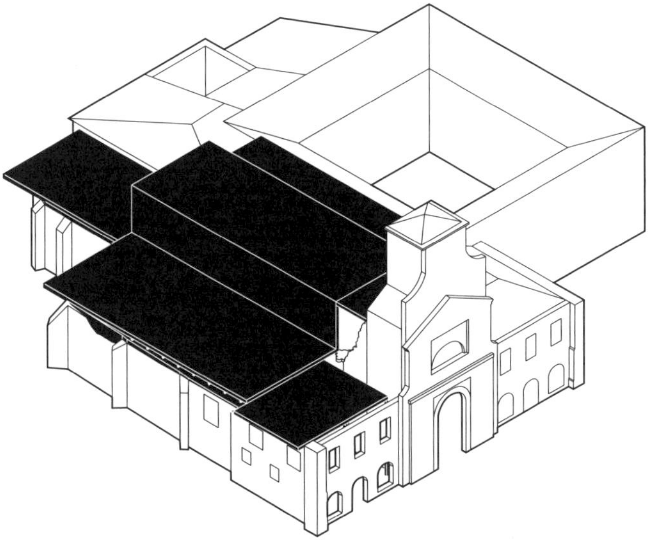

R-6 San Juan de Ruesta Hermitage

Pilgrims have traversed the Camino de Compostela (Way of St. James) since the Middle Ages. This phenomenon, which had declined from the 18th century, reappeared in the 20th century, especially with the inscription of the Way of St. James on the UNESCO World Heritage List in 1993. The hermitage of San Juan de Ruesta is part of an important and ambitious project by Sebastián Arquitectos to recover and revitalize the wealth of heritage in the abandoned town of Ruesta and its surrounds, once an important stop along the pilgrimage route. The master plan for Ruesta proposes simple acts of cleaning, consolidating and reinforcing the ruined structures to maintain their integrity. Once completed, they will be used for a new nomadic tourism as a means to give life to this restored heritage site. In addition to the town, the project includes the restoration of several hermitages related to adjacent monasteries. The Hermitage of San Juan de Ruesta was in ruins by the 21st century, stripped of its precious objects and paintings. Intervention required the recovery of the destroyed volume. Working within the remains of the masonry foundation and base and in a conjecture of what might have been, the new volume arises with its own abstract architectural vocabulary in a dialogue with the old.

Location:	Ruesta, Spain	
Year of Conversion:	2022–	
Architects:	Sebastián Arquitectos	
Original Use:	Houses, hermitage	[residence/religion/ruin]
New Use:	Heritage, “camp” site, hospitality	[heritage/culture/recreation]

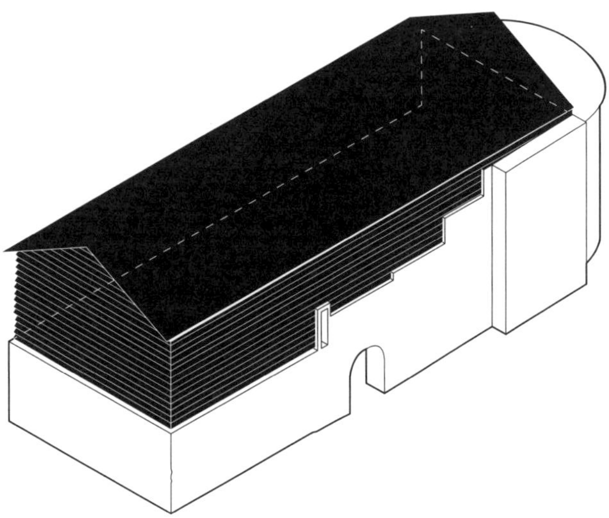

R-7 Selexyz Dominicanen Bookstore

The Dominicanenkerk (Dominican church) in Maastricht is a Gothic church built in the 13th century and consecrated in 1294 as part of the Order of the Dominicans. In 1794, Maastricht was taken by the French and, in 1796, the church was expropriated by French troops as part of the dissolution of spiritual institutions subsequent to the French Revolution. While it served as a parish church for a few years, from the early 19th century the building was used for many different purposes: city warehouse, a printing press, a school, a place for art exhibitions, concert hall, city archives, library reserve depot, post office, party venue and bicycle shed. Its newest use is as a bookstore for Selexyz, a Dutch distribution center for books with bookstores in venues of architectural interest. The program for the books required more than twice the surface available in the church. The accommodation of this requirement, together with respect for the Gothic church, was achieved using monolithic "furniture." Bookshelves, cantilevered floors and stairs are all incorporated into an autonomous, lightweight and abstract steel insertion in the nave that never touches the church itself. Browsing books on the upper-story shelves also permits close examination of the Gothic architecture. A wine bar/cafe occupies the altar in a cruciform-shaped table. One of many afterlives of the Dominican church, the Selexyz bookstore is an exemplary reversible intervention within a historic host structure.

Location:	Maastricht, the Netherlands	
Year of Conversion:	2007	
Architects:	Merkx + Girod	
Original Use:	Church	[religion/heritage]
New Use:	Bookstore and café/bar	[retail]

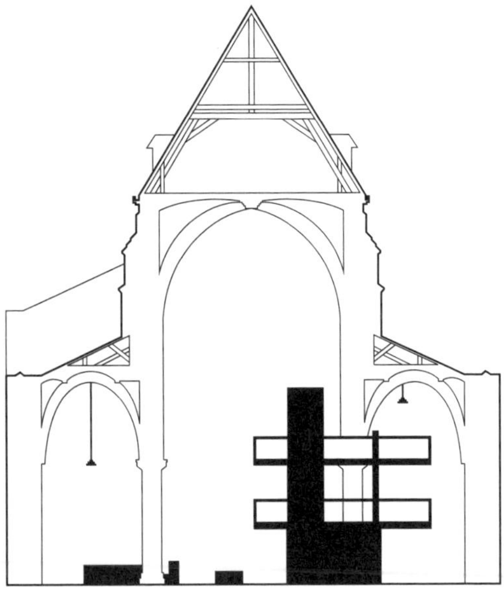

New Heritage

Reuse of Structures of Negative Heritage
+ Deaths from Terrorism 1970–2019*

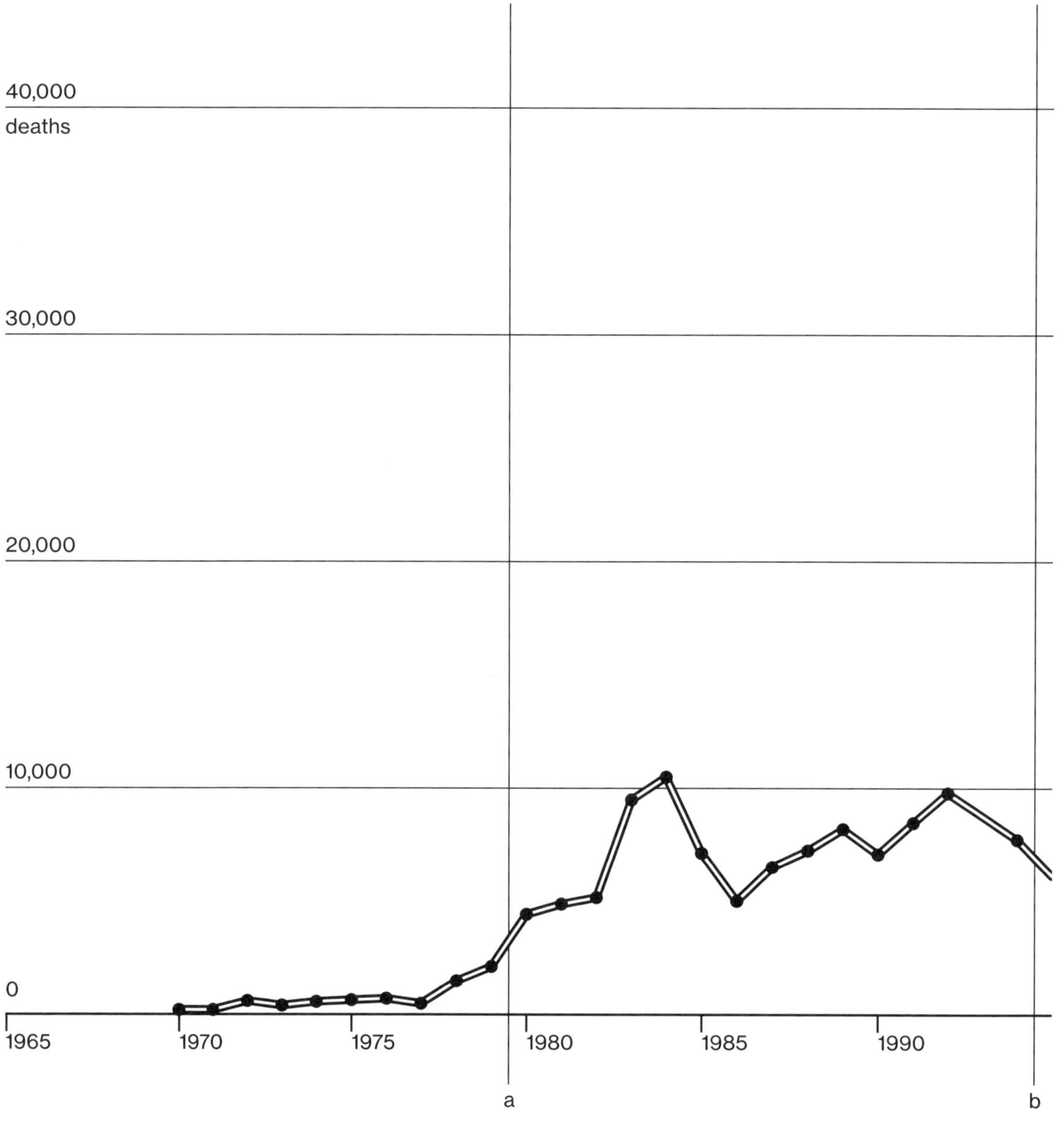

a S.21 Tuol Sleng Genocide Museum

b Documentation Centre Nazi Party Rally Grounds

c Hiroshima Peace Memorial

d New German Parliament

e Malcolm X & Dr. Betty Shabazz Memorial and Educational Center

f Park Street Armory

g Moritzburg Museum

h Neues Museum

i Bunker 599; Waterhouse at South Bund

j	9/11 Memorial & Museum; Blockhaus – La Fabrique; Dresden Military History Museum Extension
k	Memorial to the Abolition of Slavery
l	Castillo de la Luz; Castle of Garcimuñoz; Conde Duque Barracks
m	Archaeological Space; Klan KOSOVA TV Station; Pombal Castle Visitor Centre
n	The Kommandant's House; Naval Museum
o	Nyamata Genocide Memorial Centre
p	Design Academy Saaleck

* Sources: Global Terrorism Database from OurWorldinData

The National Historic Preservation Act of 1966 (NHPA) was passed in the United States after almost a century of attempts at codifying policy for built heritage. The impetus for passing this legislation in the 1960s came about as a result of a specific incident related to a post-Second World War decline in rail use. This trend and its financial implications led to a reevaluation of rail service and, eventually, the pertinence of the railroad stations themselves. At Pennsylvania Station (Penn Station) in New York City, a Beaux-Arts railroad station designed by McKim, Mead & White, this assessment led to the sale of the air rights above the rails. Constructed in 1910, the aboveground head house was demolished despite the advocacy of many groups to save it. The loss of this architectural masterpiece caused an outrage that served as a catalyst in the demand for a national preservation policy. The passage of the NHPA defined a clear process of historic preservation in the US, decades and even centuries after such regulations were enacted in other Western countries. The NHPA was enacted by the US Senate and

IMG 1 — Mount Vernon, a house museum on the U.S. National Register of Historic Places.
IMG 2 — The Waterhouse at South Bund is a boutique hotel in Shanghai built into an existing Japanese Army headquarters – a site of negative heritage recalling the WWII Japanese occupation.

House of Representatives through Public Law that defined the term "historic preservation" as follows: "To include the protection, rehabilitation, restoration, and reconstruction of districts, sites, buildings, structures, and objects significant in American history, architecture, archeology, or culture."[1] The Act enabled the US Government to become part of the evolving conversation about buildings and landscapes that are part of the nation's heritage. The early days of the NHPA led to the preservation of buildings from American history, architecture and culture by freezing them in time as historic sites. Mount Vernon, the home of George Washington, the first US president, is an example of the many houses turned museums that were placed on the US National Register of Historic Places and declared US National Historic

Landmarks. The turbulence of the 1960s and the decades that followed would lead to changed perceptions of American history. Such changed perceptions would, in turn, challenge what constituted significance in history and culture and the type of heritage associated with it.

An expansion of the concepts of heritage evolved unofficially, outside of American preservation, as a repercussion of a postwar phenomenon taking place in urban environments, namely the desire "to clear out the slums, get rid of 'obsolete' buildings, make space for an exploding population, and accommodate the burgeoning car culture."[2] In the name of urban renewal, not only buildings but entire neighborhoods and city blocks were demolished. While Jane Jacobs' seminal 1961 *The Death and Life of Great American Cities* voiced opposition to urban renewal, which often affected the most disadvantaged, it was not until the early 1970s that this disaffection became action. In particular, the US Department of Housing and Urban Development (HUD) enacted the Community Development Block Grant in 1974 that allocated funds for the rehabilitation of housing and commercial buildings. In the wake of this, one of HUD's longest running programs, large cities such as New York pursued various initiatives including one to "Reuse Vacant Space in Existing Buildings." Among the pioneers of adaptive reuse practice as we know it today is art entrepreneur Alanna Heiss, who rehabilitated "derelict warehouses and unused city-owned property in an environment reeling from blight and decay, creating nonprofit art spaces that blurred the lines between studio, gallery, theater, and community center."[3] These initial instances included the reuse in 1971 of the abandoned First Ward School or Queens Public School No.1 (PS1) in Long Island City and the 1972 founding of an artists' gallery in the clock tower of a 19th-century McKim Mead & White building in Lower Manhattan. PS1 was reused as the Institute for Art and Urban Resources, Inc, an organization devoted to organizing exhibitions in underutilized and abandoned spaces across New York City. In 2001, it would become MoMA PS1, a branch of the Museum of Modern Art.

Taking place just prior to the first noted use of the term "adaptive reuse," Heiss' projects put into practice Article 1 of the Venice Charter of 1964, which broadened the designation of heritage projects to include "not only great works of art but also to more modest works of the past which have acquired cultural significance with the passing of time."[4] The reuse of commonplace structures such as schools or clocktowers expanded the concept of cultural significance beyond the narrow confines of American historic preservation.

A different post-war phenomenon taking place outside of the US would expand the concept of heritage in an international setting. The United Nations Educational, Scientific and Cultural Organization (UNESCO) was founded in 1945, just after the end of the Second World War, with representatives of 44 countries who "decided to create an organization that would embody a genuine culture of peace. In their eyes, the new organization would establish the 'intellectual and moral solidarity of mankind' and thereby prevent the outbreak of another world war."[5] In looking to build peace through dialogue and mutual understanding, the organization embraced different values that were reflected in their many programs from education to sustainable development methods and the alleviation of poverty. Among those values, UNESCO advocated "the equal dignity of all cultures,"[6] which they looked to protect through the promotion of cultural heritage. In 1972, the UNESCO General Conference was held in Paris where the session focused on the threat to cultural and natural heritage by decay, but also by changing social and economic conditions. It concluded with the adoption of the World Heritage Convention and its proposed system of collective protection of cultural and natural heritage. The Convention defined cultural heritage to include monuments, groups of buildings and sites.[7] Monuments included architectural works but also monumental sculpture and paintings, elements or structures of an archaeological nature. Monuments and groups of buildings were defined as heritage of "outstanding value from the point of view of history, art or science."[8] In 1975, the World Heritage Convention was formally ratified and both the List of World Heritage in Danger and the World Heritage Fund were established. A process was put in place for proposing projects for inclusion in the World Heritage Site List. Over the next decades, many projects were protected as UNESCO heritage sites. In addition, the World Heritage Convention led to the introduction of new categories of world heritage: Cultural Landscapes, 1992, Underwater Cultural Heritage, 2002, Intangible Heritage, 2003. Singlehandedly, this achievement of the 1970s would lead to a broadened definition of heritage. And through the implication of the Venice Charter, which recommends the occupancy of heritage structures, this broadening led to an expansion of reuse projects. Over the next half-century, the scope of adaptive reuse projects in both the US and Europe extended farther and farther in both scale and heritage types.

Today, projects of reuse often comprise more than a single abandoned or decommissioned heritage host structure. Host structures extended to groups of buildings (Le Fresnoy), neighborhoods and even a pilgrimage route through more than one country (Ruesta). An increase of site size was not the only consideration. The opposite offered creative opportunities as well, as in projects in which single rooms within a city, adapted through a creative and unifying intervention (Pixel Hotel), or rooms in an unfinished construction, adapted through the act of squatting (Torre de David), furthered the limits of cultural significance. These different projects of reuse provided the blank canvases on which to probe various issues from the nuances of authenticity (Rosa Parks House Project) to translocation

(Yin Yu Tang House). Expanded concepts of heritage reflecting cultural and societal changes prompted new approaches to intervening in existing built heritage and even spurred new types of heritage for adaptation. Structures deemed historically significant by today's values include negative heritage, Black heritage and architectural heritage.

Negative Heritage: War and Conflict Sites

One type of heritage structure emerged from the mindset and culture influenced by the anti-war and civil rights movements. While the protests of the 1960s emerged from the abundance and optimism of the post-war boom, the 1970s inherited these movements in a dramatically different context. Developments at home and abroad, from the Vietnam War to the Yom Kippur War, the first airplane hijacking and the banning of literacy requirements for US voter registration provided a testing ground for those ideals, with real-time constraints. Together, the spirit of the 1960s and the adjusted expectations of the 1970s offered new ways of perceiving history as the anti-war and civil rights movements came of age.

Provoked by US involvement in the Vietnam War, the anti-war protests of the 1960s were one of the most significant displays of opposition to government policy.[9] Events such as the 1967 March on the Pentagon attracted more than 100,000 protesters and inspired others. Anti-war protest rallies and demonstrations continued, especially in reaction to the US invasion of Cambodia in 1970. At a multi-day protest against the expansion of the Vietnam War into Cambodia at Kent State University in Ohio, four students were killed and nine wounded by the Ohio National Guard in what would become known as the Kent State Massacre. The tragic outcome of this event on 4 May 1970 shocked and outraged Americans as the deadly violence changed the tenor of the previous protests. Some believe that it was a turning point in the protest movement. The following year, *The New York Times* published the first Pentagon Papers, revelations of deceptive governmental conduct related to the war. The May Day Protest of 1971 put "increasing pressure on the [Nixon] administration to try and find some way to get out of the war."[10] Robert D. Schulzinger, historian and expert on the Vietnam War said: "The anti-war movement did not end the war in Vietnam, but it did alter almost irrevocably, the perceptions of ordinary citizens of their society and their government; it also altered the perceptions of leaders toward the public."[11] Enabled in great part by the protest mindset of the previous decade, these altered perceptions of war policies evolved into a more general skepticism of government policy, even in democratic contexts. The erosion of citizens' trust for government policies grew, melding into mainstream culture. In literature and media, Kurt Vonnegut's bestseller,

Slaughterhouse Five, is said to have “few if any equals in creating the kind of distance that can offer insight into the mass insanity of modern warfare”[12] and television’s *M*A*S*H*, a 14-time Emmy award-winning dark comedy about a mobile army surgical hospital, aired in 1972 with its cynical depiction of the horrors of war.

IMG 3 — Students fleeing during the shooting at Kent State University, May 4, 1970.
IMG 4 — The cast of TV show *M*A*S*H*.

Such portrayals of government and war were translated into the built environment as new ways of engaging with war-related structures. Disenchantment with war was by no means new, as anti-war sentiments existed throughout history. Historically, the reuse of war-related structures was driven by economics. War waged through hand combat – such as with the many conquests of the Roman Empire – resulted in damaged structures. Such damage allowed for the structures’ reuse as adapted buildings or as construction material. The evolution of modern-day weaponry, however, led to a destruction that left little remaining for reuse or adaptation. Even in 1918, the Belgian city of Ypres was completely destroyed with the weaponry of the early 20th century. Today’s city of Ypres is instead the product of new construction. This was all the more so in the Second World War, with the introduction of large-scale bombing and nuclear weapons, both of which wreaked destruction in dimensions not seen before. The remains of some Second World War structures that were adapted were not reused as salvage. Rather, with the immensity of the destruction and the hope that such devastation would not reoccur, they were adapted as witnesses to atrocities humans inflicted upon each other. The Genbaku Dome in Hiroshima, Japan, was the only building left standing after the first atomic bomb. Its use as the Hiroshima Peace Memorial is to memorialize through bearing witness. Concentration and extermination camps such as Auschwitz-Birkenau were preserved as they were and today fulfill the functions of both a memorial and a museum: “There is no way to understand postwar Europe and the world without an in-depth confrontation between our idea of mankind and the remains of Auschwitz."[13] These two projects of war heritage served as reminders that such destruction and inhumanity should not happen again. Unfortunately, that would not be the case and, in fact, it would be the contrary with the rise of post-Second World War conflicts. S.21 (security prison 21) is a byproduct of conflict in the 1970s. A school in Cambodia turned security prison and torture site by the Khmer Rouge in 1975 is now the Tuol Sleng Genocide Museum. It came under the protection of the UNESCO Memory of the World Register and was adapted as a museum in 1979. Like Auschwitz-Birkenau, it serves to educate and memorialize these tragic events. This type of war and conflict-related reuse would come to be called negative heritage, "a conflictual site that becomes the repository of negative memory in the collective imaginary."[14]

Beyond their roles in education and memorialization, adapted war-related structures have at times been employed to express anti-war sentiments. Such adapted host structures serve different purposes, varying from documentation to redemption and even the administration of justice. Damaged host structures of war attest to the horrors of war through the very nature of their destruction and serve these purposes well. Walls pockmarked by bullets serve as evidence of the destruction. In the rebuilding of August Stüler's war-damaged Neues Museum in Berlin, David Chipperfield elected to let the horrors of war speak for themselves through the meticulous decades-long mapping and preservation of the scars of combat. In contrast, Günther Domenig's Dokumentationszentrum Reichsparteitagsgelände (Documentation Center Nazi Party Rally Grounds) in Nuremberg, a transformation of a wing of the Nazi Party Rally Grounds complex, consists of the addition of a glass and steel passageway that pierces the Congress Hall. In plan and in section, the new glass shaft penetrates the classical plan envisioned by Albert Speer, Hitler's architect, "as a way of reappraising history" and "a confrontation with Nazi architecture."[15] At the Westerbork concentration camp in the Netherlands, Oving Architekten's encasement in glass of the house of a Nazi commandant pushes the envelope of architectural interventions with its imprisonment of the structure. Here, architecture is a means of dispensing justice with the house as the personification of its occupant's crimes. These different expressions through architecture expand the scope of projects for adapting war-related structures. Architect Daniel Libeskind speaks of his transformation of the neoclassical arsenal into the Dresden Military History Museum as representational. The addition of the enormous geometric metal shard that pierces the existing stone facade "represents the severity of the authoritarian past, while the former reflects the transparency of the military in a democratic society."[16] The 21st-century reuse of war and war-related structures has evolved in the last half-century with the shifting sentiment for war that has its roots in the last quarter of the

20th century. From serving as memorials and witnesses to atrocities, the existing host structures of war in recent adaptive reuse projects are canvases for anti-war protests and redemption.

Different associations of war-related projects lead to different responses for reuse. The proposed conversion of the home of German architect Paul Schultze-Naumburg, a member of a Nazi art propaganda unit, into a design academy for promoting diversity is a less-charged repurposing of an "uncomfortable" monument. Decommissioned defense structures such as fortresses and castles that have long performed the role of defense without specific incriminations of violence served not as war-related sites but as heritage tourism. Their adaptation through additions to often partially complete ruins serves to enhance visitor experience. At the Pombal Castle in Portugal and the 15th-century Moritzburg Castle in Germany, elegant and minimal additions transform the castle ruins. Following the recommendations of the Venice Charter of 1964 that mandates a distinct contemporary stamp for additions to the host structure, these adaptive reuse interventions demonstrate a respect for the military host architecture as a part of history.

Negative Heritage: Structures of Trauma

A different type of heritage emerged in the wake of the civil unrest stemming from the anti-war protests and race riots of the 1970s. The tragic outcome of the anti-war protest at Kent State was followed by numerous public shootings. The Jackson State killings, the Marin County Civic Center attacks, the Sterling Hall bombings at the University of Madison-Wisconsin, the Boston busing desegregation crisis, the Symbionese Liberation Army shootout and the Greensboro massacre all resulted from civil unrest related to anti-war and racial tensions. The decade was also plagued by some of the most notorious serial killings, including the Manson murders, the Son of Sam killing spree, and Ted Bundy and the Chi Omega killings. The violence in the US in the 1970s was matched by spates of global violence. On 6 September 1970, four planes were hijacked by Palestinian guerillas and a month-long hostage negotiation ensued in an international arena. On 5 September 1972, athletes from the Israeli Olympic Team were taken hostage at the XX Olympics in Munich, Germany, by Palestinian militants from the Black September group. A one-day long standoff included an attempted rescue that ultimately resulted in the death of 11 Israelis, one Munich policeman and five Palestinian terrorists. "Between 1970 and 1979 nationalist and ethnic terrorists, religious zealots, and anti-war militants frequently attacked American targets."[17] Acts of terror – bombs, shootings, hijackings – were prevalent, with violent incidents in Europe peaking in the 1970s.[18] While terrorism has existed for centuries – the term was coined during the French Revolution[19] – the decade of the 1970s became known as one "when terrorism came of age." "A time of rapidly evolving threats at home and abroad as radical elements exploited a new age of mass international air travel and television to advance political agendas by targeting civilians."[20]

"During times of national crises, television galvanized the country by preempting regular programming to provide essential coverage of significant events."[21] By the 1970s, 95% of households owned at least one television set.[22] The rescue attempt at the Munich Olympics and its ultimate failure were "broadcast live to nearly 1 billion people around the world and to the many televisions throughout the Olympic Village."[23] This type of news coverage "brought increasingly disturbing reports as the decade progressed"[24] and exposed viewers to violence in their own living rooms. This ever-expanding violence, together with the accessibility of media coverage, placed such events squarely in the public consciousness. Since the start of the 21st century, violent incidents have become random occurrences not only in the US but globally and in places of everyday life: schools, synagogues, Christmas markets, nightclubs and soccer stadiums.

These tragic events in the 1970s were the start of a culture of pervasive violence in the US that has steadily increased in the last 50 years. A US Congressional study carried out in 2015 found that "For 44 years (1970–2013), the prevalence of mass public shootings has increased: 1.1 incidents per year on average in the 1970s, 2.7 in the 1980s, 4.0 in the 1990s, 4.1 in the 2000s, and 4.5 in the first four years of the 2010s."[25] By May 2022, the US had already experienced 214 mass shootings.[26] An omnipresent

IMG 5 — The Genbaku Dome, the only structure left standing after the dropping of the atomic bomb on August 6, 1945, is now the Hiromshima Peace Memorial.
IMG 6 — Terrorist from Black September at the Munich Olympic Massacre, 1972.

media enables these horrific acts to permeate the lives of everyone in all age groups and walks of life. In addition, the ubiquitous use of smartphones with cameras has enabled the capture of such events on video that are disseminated in seconds through social media. The current war in Ukraine is an example of intense media coverage that brings real-time war tragedy

24/7 to viewers both on television and social media. "Traditional and social media now broadcast collective traumas across the country – and globally – in record time."[27]

These collective traumas engender collective remembrance. In the built environment, these random horrific acts outside of war and military conflict gave rise to a new type of negative heritage. In contrast to the Auschwitz-Birkenau concentration and extermination camps, where the memorial and the site of tragedy are the same, early memorials of unexpected violence did not necessarily relate to the site of the tragedy or the victims. Memorials for the victims of such acts were typically in the form of statuary or sculpture. For example, the May 4 Memorial at Kent State, dedicated in 1986, is a sculpture in a wooded park, distanced from the site of the shooting, where stone structures commemorate the lost lives. The Munich Olympic Massacre, at first memorialized by a statue and a plaque, is now the focus of a memorial pavilion in Munich's Olympic Park erected in 2017, 45 years after the event. With the increase over decades of both violent acts and their unceasing coverage in the media, there is demand for assuaging collective grief through memorials, especially those incorporating physical material evidence related to the event. At the 9/11 Memorial in New York City, the physical void left by the bombing of the World Trade Center is at the heart of remembering the victims. In contrast, the victims of the 2011 Norway attacks, in which a lone gunman opened fire on a Workers' Youth League summer camp on Utøya Island, are memorialized through several types of memorials. One such memorial repurposes the café building in which 13 of the 69 victims died. A new learning center is built around the café and preserves the physical evidence of trauma in an act of enclosure. In Kosovo, an abandoned factory converted into a television station memorializes the ethnic Albanians driven out by the Serbian forces in the Kosovo conflict of 1998–1999 by reusing the materials of the 200,000 burnt residences.[28] At

IMG 7 — Protest on Boston Common against the Kent State Massacre.
IMG 8 — The glass corridor of Gunther Domenig's Documentation Center addition pierces the Nazi Rally Center in Nuremburg.
IMG 9 — The TV section of a popular department store in the 1970s.

the Nyamata Church in Nyamata, Rwanda, where members of the Tutsi minority ethnic group were killed in the 1994 Rwandan genocide, the clothes of the 10,000 victims are conserved in the church interior.[29] The many colors and patterns of the preserved clothing serve as a reminder of each person who perished in what is now the Nyamata Genocide Memorial Centre. The increase of violence in society today, the ensuing collective grief and the need for remembrance have engendered a type of negative heritage in sites and physical evidence of trauma.

Black Heritage

The civil rights protests were part of the civil rights movement that came to prominence from the mid-1950s. This turbulent time in the 1960s was defined by leaders such as Martin Luther King, Jr. and Malcolm X. The Black Power movement that began at that time continued on through the 1970s. This civil rights era closed with the passing of the Fair Housing Act (Civil Rights Act) of 1968 that prohibited discrimination based on race, sex, religion and national origin. The decade of the 1970s marked the beginning of the post-civil rights era and a time for testing and implementing the provisions of the Civil Rights Act. A critical gain came in the form of the extension in 1970 and 1975 of the Voting Rights Act of 1965. Other gains include the 1971 Supreme Court decision to uphold busing of students for integration, the 1972 nomination of Shirley Chisholm for the Democratic presidential nomination, the 1976 publication of Alex Haley's bestselling book *Roots: The Saga of an American Family*, which raised enormous interest in African American genealogy, and the 1977 appointment of Andrew Young to serve as the American ambassador to the United Nations. Some strides were made in this decade but certainly not enough given the rise of the Black Lives Matter Movement 40-some years later in 2013, to protest the continued racism and discrimination against Black people. Although not enough, especially in the wake of the conservative government in the 1980s, those achievements were not insignificant for that time in placing emphasis on Black history and the inclusion of Black people in positions of importance.

Evidence of Black lives in the built environment is scant. Often their achievements are remembered through memorials in the form of statuary (Martin Luther King, Jr., Malcolm X, Medgar Evers, Harriet Tubman, Adam Clayton Powell, Joe Louis). A few homes of prominent members of the Black community – Frederick Douglass, Martin Luther King, Jr. – are house museums and preserved as national heritage sites. Some humble slave dwellings on southern plantations have been preserved as touristic heritage sites. Until the 21st century, examples of the adaptive reuse of

Black sites were almost non-existent because there were so few surviving sites of such heritage. In the 21st century, some sites of negative memories for the Black community have become memorials. In 2005, the Audubon Ballroom in New York City, where activist Malcolm X was assassinated, was converted into the Malcolm X & Dr. Betty Shabazz Memorial and Educational Center. In Nantes, France, the Quai de la Fosse was transformed into the Mémorial de l'Abolition de l'Esclavage, a memorial to the Abolition of Slavery. A quay in the port city of Nantes, from which many slave ships sailed in the 18th century to Africa for the bustling slave trade, the underside of the quay structure was adapted as an exhibition of slave commerce and the city's role in it. The infrastructural host site is implicated by its location and purpose. Its material neutrality allows for this confrontation with history to condemn slavery as a crime against humanity. In both of these projects, adaptive reuse of negative heritage serves the purpose of redemption, albeit much delayed.

Attempts at adapting sites of Black heritage have met with varying results in great part because first of all, these sites have not been recognized and, second, they are in extreme disrepair. The Rosa Parks House Project is an example of a host structure site imbued with such difficult issues. The small house on S. Deacon Street in Detroit, Michigan, was the home of activist Rosa Parks' brother and 13 children. It served as her place of refuge from 1957 to 1959 when she migrated to the north after receiving death threats for her act of resistance in Montgomery, Alabama. In 2015, the house had been abandoned due to deterioration and rot. Placed on Detroit's demolition list, it was purchased for US$ 500 by Parks' niece Rhea McCauley and given to Ryan Mendoza, an American artist living and working in Germany and Italy, to salvage. Mendoza deconstructed what was left of the house, moved it to Berlin and rebuilt it in his garden. The translocated house gained the recognition in Europe that it had not in Detroit, where its significance as a two-year refuge was questioned. It subsequently travelled back to the US in 2017 where it met with obstacles, was auctioned without success and returned across the Atlantic Ocean where it was most recently displayed in "Almost Home," a solo exhibition at the Royal Palace in Naples, Italy, in 2021. The Rosa Parks House Project epitomizes the charged nature of sites related to civil rights: their fragile states, their limited recognition as heritage and the funding required to support their preservation. Architecturally, it also raised interesting issues: the relationship between translocation and authenticity, the significance of reconstruction in eroded structures, the boundary of art and monument, the concept of adaptive reuse as art. The controversy surrounding this small house, a brief home to a civil rights icon, in being recognized as an American monument perhaps reflects the work begun in the civil rights movement that is still required today. As Mendoza said of the Rosa Parks House Project's aborted return to US soil: "Rhea McCauley and I invite the American consciousness to remember a house it didn't know it had forgotten."[30]

The case of the preservation/reuse of the childhood home of musician and activist Nina Simone, just a year later, is a more hopeful and less charged recent example of the plight of Black heritage. In disrepair and threatened by demolition, as was Rosa Parks' two-year refuge in Detroit, the 660sf (61m²) clapboard house was purchased by a group of African

IMG 10 – The 9/11 Memorial uses the void of the destroyed World Trade Center building as remembrance.
IMG 11 – Shirley Chisholm, candidate for President 1972.

American visual artists in 2017. In 2018, in the context of the heated national discussion about monuments celebrating Confederate heritage of the American Civil War, the National Trust for Historic Preservation, a non-profit organization to save America's historic sites, advocated for the representation of African American history. In the same year, the African American Cultural Heritage Action Fund came into being. It was through this fund – the National Trust for Historic Preservation's African American Cultural Heritage Action Fund – and in partnership with World Monuments Fund (WMF) and Preservation North Carolina – that protection was secured for the childhood home of Nina Simone in Tryon, North Carolina. Proposed plans for its preservation would maintain its integrity as a modest cottage without plumbing, running water, heat or air conditioning. Original materials would be maintained or, where deteriorated, reconstructed. But other options are under discussion with the community for its reuse for performances or community programs, where this authenticity would be augmented by modern systems.

Since its beginning in 2013, the Black Lives Matter movement has had an increasing impact on the American mindset in the fight against racism and racial inequality. In June 2020, the Pew Research Center found that "Two-thirds of U.S. adults say they support the movement, with 38% saying they strongly support it."[31] Such advocacy in the fight against racism may bolster support for the preservation and adaptive reuse of Black heritage. The founding of efforts such as the African American Cultural Heritage Action Fund is crucial in this endeavor. Hopefully, it is just the beginning for this new type of heritage and its reuse. The George Floyd Square in Minneapolis is the site memorializing the brutal murder of George Floyd by a police officer in 2020. There is no formal memorial as yet. Would Cup Foods, the convenience store where Floyd bought the cigarettes that eventually led to his murder directly outside, be considered a site of trauma?

Architectural Heritage

A specific type of heritage emerged in the last decades of the 20th century with the aging of iconic buildings designed by revered contemporary architects. Some of these projects, sacred to the architectural community, but viewed as aging and outdated structures otherwise, were demolished. Others were saved from this fate through monument designation. In 1965, Le Corbusier's Villa Savoye in Poissy, France, completed in 1929 and slated for demolition, received France's Monument Historique designation while the architect was still living – a rare occurrence. Such designations are the exception, however. In Karachi, for instance, Richard Neutra's 1961 US Embassy, later downgraded to US Consulate, faced demolition or a new use as a shopping mall. After a two-year-long battle, it finally received Sindh cultural heritage designation in 2012. It has since been sold and is now the property of a private developer. It is to be hoped that a landmark status

IMG 12 — The Audubon Ballroom where Malcolm X was shot is now the Malcolm X & Betty Shabazz Memorial.

will help to protect its architectural significance even in its new use, whatever that may be. Robin Hood Gardens in London, the famed 1972 Brutalist housing project of Alison and Peter Smithson, could not be rescued through heritage designation despite the efforts of many in the architectural community and was demolished in 2017.

The work of DOCOMOMO (Documentation and Conservation of buildings, sites and neighborhoods of the Modern Movement), a non-profit organization that was founded in 1988, exemplifies the desire to preserve architectural masterpieces of the Modern Movement. If saved as architectural landmarks, these works remain as they were and a testament to their importance in the history of architecture. The fervor of the architectural community to save these works, however, is not necessarily always shared by the owners of the structures, who are required to bear the cost of maintaining the monuments.

These works can also be saved through repurposing. Adaptations of revered and canonical works of architecture pose a unique design dilemma for the commissioned architect or designer: How does one alter or transform an architectural masterpiece? The reuse of the 1976 Montreal Olympic Tower was conducted through interventions, mostly interior, that left the iconic form intact. The current renovation and addition to Aldo van Eyck's 1994 Tripolis office building in Amsterdam, granted Municipal Status in 2019, is inspired by the desire to protect the architectural heritage by guarding and sheltering it with an addition. Similarly, the Centraal Beheer Building in Apeldoorn, the Netherlands, by Herman Hertzberger will be preserved and yet transformed at the same time by becoming the focus of a new project – a sustainable green neighborhood that "echoes the design of the existing building."[32] This project will be undertaken in consultation with Hertzberger's office. Such collaboration highlights the insular nature of such adaptive reuse projects, embedded within the thorny context of the architectural community and their reverence for the architectural work and its creator. This category of architectural heritage illustrates the salient "difference between architecture and other artistic disciplines. It is not admitted, in principle, that a pictorial, sculptural, musical, cinematic, or literary work of art could be modified by another author, but it has always been assumed that buildings can change or be extended and transformed by other architects."[33]

Broadening the Field

In 2009, Dutch architect Rem Koolhaas gave the Paul S. Byard Memorial Lecture at Columbia University's Graduate School of Architecture, Planning & Preservation. Titled "Preservation is Overtaking Us," he pointed out, among other things, the increasing number and decreasing age of the structures/objects we preserve – an example being the 2002 Monument Historique registration of his own project, Maison à Bordeaux, completed in 1998.[34]

The objectives of the nascent National Historic Preservation Act, as those of other countries' codification of heritage protection, were intended to safeguard the objects significant to a nation's history. As a nation's history evolved, what constituted that history also evolved. This is reflected in the history of the French Commission for Historic Monuments (Commission des monuments historiques), one of the first efforts at safeguarding a nation's architectural heritage. It was established in the mid-19th century as a reaction to the buildings damaged in the French Revolution. The Commission's first statute, passed in 1887, was intended to safeguard only the property of the state.[35] But by 1913, with a different set of political and societal circumstances, a new statute passed in which "the term 'historic monument' refers, not only to buildings, but to all works whose preservation has a public interest from an artistic or historic point of view."[36] In 2022, a historic monument is instead defined as "a building (built or not built: park, garden, cave, etc.) or a movable object (furniture or building by destination) receiving a special legal status intended to protect it for its historical interest, artistic, architectural but also technical or scientific so that it is preserved, restored and enhanced."[37] The accretion of items defined as historic monuments in the development of the Commission des monuments historiques over 125 years, demonstrates that preservation is far from a static endeavor. The adoption of the UNESCO World Heritage Convention in 1972 and the creation of the World Heritage List were catalysts in broadening heritage not as national assets but global ones. Today, there are 1,154 UNESCO World Heritage Sites – natural and cultural sites to be protected and preserved. This includes many different types of heritage. War heritage such as Auschwitz-Birkenau was added to the list in 1979 and the Hiroshima Peace Memorial (Genbaku Dome) was added much later, in 1996, at the same time as the Dutch Water Defence Line in the Netherlands. Industrial heritage includes the Zollverein Coal Mine Industrial Complex in Essen, added in 2001, and the major mining sites of Wallonia in Belgium, added in 2012. Sites related to transportation include the naval port of Karlskrona, added in 1998, and the Rhaetian Railway in 2008. And architectural heritage includes the Rietveld Schröder House, added in 2000, the Luis Barragán House and Studio in 2004, Walter Gropius' Fagus Factory in 2011, 17 works by Le Corbusier in 2016 and 8 projects by Frank Lloyd Wright in 2019. The emergence of UNESCO World Heritage expanded the conservation standards set by previously accepted definitions of heritage. It gave credence to the growth of new types of heritage and influenced the establishment of various organizations for protecting heritage as well as the broadening of scope of existing preservation societies and organizations.

Within the built environment, the concepts of the 1970s inspired a reevaluation of built heritage through different and critical eyes, yielding new types of heritage. In turn, these new types with their unique contexts are hosts for groundbreaking reuse interventions, launching a sea change for the practice of adaptive reuse in the 21st century.

IMG 13 — A map of UNESCO World Heritage Sites, 2019.

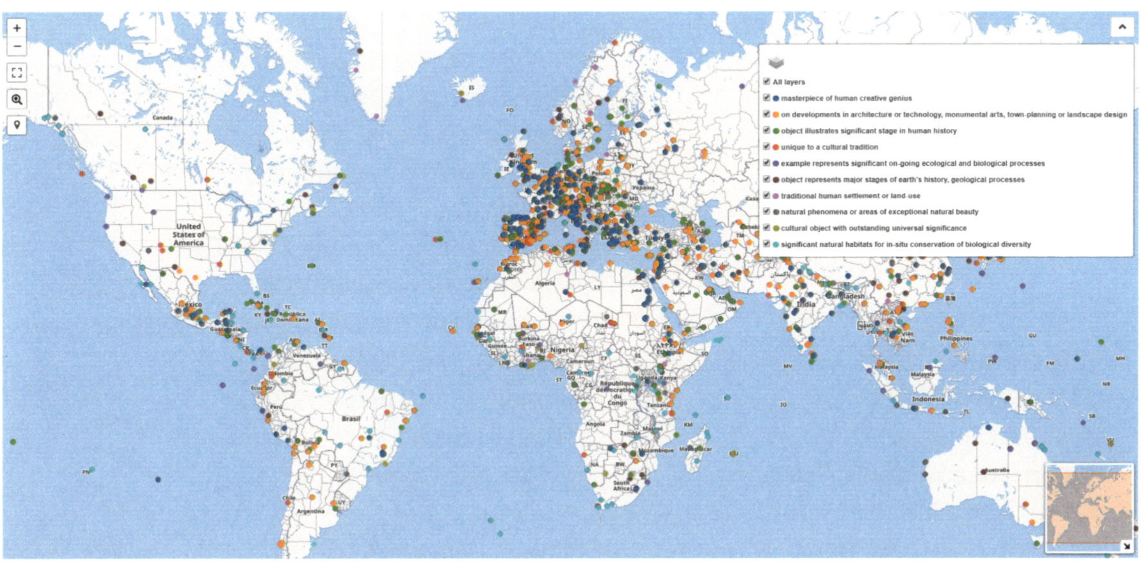

• 9/11 Memorial & Museum,	New York, NY, USA, 2011
• Archaeological Space	Daroca, Spain, 2014
• Auschwitz-Birkenau Museum	Oświęcim, Poland, 1947
• Blockhaus – La Fabrique	Nantes, France, 2011
• Bunker 599	Gelderland, the Netherlands, 2010
• Castelvecchio	Verona, Italy, 1958–1974
• Castillo de la Luz	Las Palmas, Spain, 2013
• Castle of Garcimuñoz	Cuenca, Spain, 2013
• Conde Duque Barracks	Madrid, Spain, 2013
• Design Academy Saaleck	Naumburg, Germany, 2021–
• Documentation Centre Nazi Party Rally Grounds	Nuremburg, Germany, 1994
• Dresden Military History Museum Extension	Dresden, Germany, 2011
• Hiroshima Peace Memorial	Hiroshima, Japan, 1996
• Klan KOSOVA TV Station	Pristina, Kosovo, 2014
• The Kommandant's House	Westerbork, the Netherlands, 2015
• Le Fresnoy Art Center	Tourcoing, France 1997
• Malcolm X & Dr. Betty Shabazz Memorial and Educational Center	New York, NY, USA, 2005
• Memorial to the Abolition of Slavery	Nantes, France, 2012
• Montreal Olympic Stadium Building	Montreal, Canada, 2018
• Moritzburg Museum	Halle, Germany, 2008
• Naval Museum	Cartagena, Spain, 2015
• Neues Museum	Berlin, Germany, 2009
• New German Parliament	Berlin, Germany, 1999
• Nina Simone House	Tryon, NC, USA, 2018–
• Nyamata Genocide Memorial Centre	Kigali, Rwanda, 2016
• Park Street Armory	New York, NY, USA, 2007–
• Pixel Hotel	Linz, Austria, 2006
• Pombal Castle Visitor Centre	Pombal, Portugal, 2014
• Rosa Parks House Project	Berlin, Germany/Detroit, MI, USA/ Naples, Italy, 2015–
• S.21 Tuol Sleng Genocide Museum	Phnom Penh, Cambodia, 1979
• Torre de David	Caracas, Venezuela, 2007
• Tripolis Park	Amsterdam, the Netherlands, 2022–
• TWA Hotel	Queens, NY, USA, 2019
• *USS Arizona* Memorial	Honolulu, HI, USA, 1962
• Village of Ruesta	Ruesta, Spain, 2022–
• Waterhouse at South Bund	Shanghai, China, 2010
• Yin Yu Tang House at the Peabody Essex Museum	Salem, MA, USA, 2003

Notes and Sources

1 Public Law 89-665, An Act of the Senate and House of Representatives of the United States of America in Congress, 15 October 1966 [S.3035], p. 916.

2 "National Historic Preservation Act," National Park Service – US Department of the Interior. https://www.nps.gov/subjects/historic preservation/national-historic-preservation-act.htm, accessed 30 May 2022.

3 "Introduction – The Artist in Place: The First 10 Years of MoMA PS1," Museum of Modern Art. https://www.moma.org/interactives/exhibitions/2012/artistinplace/, accessed 30 June 2022.

4 The International Charter for the Conservation and Restoration of Monuments and Sites (The Venice Charter 1964).

5 "UNESCO's History," UNESCO. https://www.unesco.org/en/brief, accessed 30 July 2022.

6 "Our Vision," UNESCO. https://www.unesco.org/en/brief, accessed 30 July 2022.

7 "Convention Concerning the Protection of the World Cultural and Natural Heritage," UNESCO, 16 November 1972, p. 2.

8 Ibid.

9 "Anti-war Protests of the 1960s–70s," The White House Historical Association. https://www.whitehousehistory.org/anti-war-protests-of-the-1960s-70s, accessed 25 February 2022.

10 Ibid.

11 Robert D. Schulzinger, *A Time for War: The United States and Vietnam, 1941–1975*, Oxford: Oxford University Press, 1997 p. 245.

12 Kevin Powers, "The Moral Clarity of 'Slaughterhouse-Five' at 50," *The New York Times*, 6 March 2019.

13 "Education," from the website for Auschwitz-Birkenau. https://www.auschwitz.org/en/education/, accessed 27 February 2022.

14 Lynn Meskell, "Negative Heritage and Past Mastering in Archaeology," *Anthropological Quarterly*, Vol. 75, No. 3, The George Washington University Institute for Ethnographic Research, 2002, pp. 557–574. http://www.jstor.org/stable/3318204, accessed 10 March 2022.

15 "Architecture," The Documentation Centre Museum Website. https://museums.nuernberg.de/documentation-center/architecture, accessed 28 February 2022.

16 "Military History Museum," Studio Libeskind website. https://libeskind.com/work/military-history-museum/, accessed 28 February 2022.

17 Peter Bergen, "The Golden Age of Terrorism," CNN, 21 August 2015. https://www.cnn.com/2015/07/28/opinions/bergen-1970s-terrorism/index.html, accessed 11 March 2022.

18 Anthony H. Cordesman, "Trends in European Terrorism: 1970–2016," CSIS Center for Strategic & International Studies, 18 August, p. 10. https://www.csis.org/analysis/trends-european-terrorism-1970-2016, accessed 11 March 2022.

19 Noah Webster of the *Merriam-Webster Dictionary* first entered this term in 1840 as a term translated from the French during the Reign of Terror.

20 Stephen Collinson, "Nixon's Own 9/11: When Terrorism Came of Age," CNN, 29 July 2015. https://www.cnn.com/2015/07/27/politics/terrorism-1970s-richard-nixon/index.html, accessed 10 March 2022.

21 Robert J. Thompson and Steve Allen, "Television in the United States," Encyclopedia Britannica, 1 July 2019. https://www.britannica.com/art/television-in-the-United-States, accessed 1 March 2022.

22 "Media Utilization – Telephone and Telegraph Systems," Statistical Abstract of the United States 1982–1983, 103rd Edition, US Department of Commerce, p. 555.

23 The Editors of the Encyclopedia Britannica, "Munich Massacre," Encyclopedia Britannica, 29 August 2021. https://www.britannica.com/event/Munich-Massacre, accessed 1 March 2022.

24 Thompson and Allen, "Television in the United States," op. cit.

25 William J. Krouse, and Daniel J. Richardson, "Mass Murder with Firearms: Incidents and Victims: 1999–2013," Congressional Research Service Report, 30 July 2015, p. 2.

26 Shayenne Gai and Madison Hall, "The U.S. Has Had 214 Mass Shootings So Far in 2022," *Insider*, 26 May 2022.

27 Roxane Cohen Silver, E. Alison Holman and Dana Rose Garfin, "Coping with Cascading Collective Traumas in the United States," *Nature Human Behavior*, Vol. 5, January 2021, p. 4. https://www.nature.com/articles/s41562-020-00981-x.pdf, accessed 12 March 2022.

28 Astrit Nixha, "Klan Kosova – Resisting New Order," *Int|AR Journal of Interventions and Adaptive Reuse*, Volume 09, 2018, p. 46.

29 JoAnn Greco, "Protecting 'Negative Heritage' in Rwanda," *The Pennsylvania Gazette*, January/February 2017, p. 29.

30 Ryan Mendoza, Taped Presentation at "Everybody's House – The Rosa Parks House Project Symposium," Rhode Island School of Design and WaterFire, Providence, RI, 18 May 2018.

31 K. Parker, J. Menasce Horowitz and M. Anderson, "Amid Protests, Majorities Across Racial and Ethnic Groups Express Support for the Black Lives Matter Movement," Pew Research Center, 12 June 2020. https://www.pewresearch.org/social-trends/2020/06/12/amid-protests-majorities-across-racial-and-ethnic-groups-express-support-for-the-black-lives-matter-movement/, accessed 3 March 2022.

32 MVRDV to Transform Herman Hertzberger's Centraal Beheer Building – an Icon of Structuralism – into a New Residential District," MVRDV, 16 June 2022.

33 Luis Sacristán Murga, "Between Memory and Intervention, *Int|AR Journal of Adaptive Reuse*, Vol. 6, 2016.

34 "Maison Lemoine," Ministère de la culture. https://www-pop-culture-gouv-fr.translate.goog/notice/merimee/PA33000068?_x_tr_sl=fr&_x_tr_tl=en&_x_tr_hl=en&_x_tr_pto=sc, accessed 14 August 2022.

35 Mathilde Roellinger, "Centenary of the French Law on Historic Monuments," *Art, Antiquity and Law*, Vol. XIX, Issue 4, December 2014, p. 328.

36 Ibid.

37 "The Historical Monument," Ministère de la Culture. https://www.culture.gouv.fr/en/Thematiques/Monuments-Sites/Monuments-historiques-sites-patrimoniaux/Les-monuments-historiques, accessed 27 July 2022.

		Project		Architect
NH-1 (military)		Bunker 599 Gelderland, NL	2010	Atelier Lyon, RAAAF
NH-2 (military)	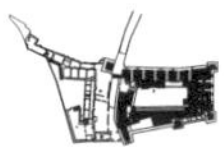	Castelvecchio Verona, IT	1958–1974	Carlo Scarpa
NH-3 (conflict/trauma)		The Kommandant's House Westerbork, NL	2015	Oving Architecten
NH-4 (trauma/Black heritage)	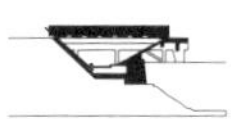	Memorial to the Abolition of Slavery Nantes, FR	2012	Wodiczko + Bonder
NH-5 (military)	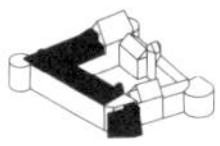	Moritzburg Museum Halle, DE	2008	Nieto Sobejano Arquitectos
NH-6 (war/conflict)	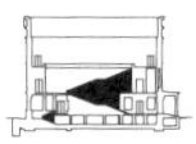	Neues Museum Berlin, DE	2009	David Chipperfield Architects
NH-7 (trauma)		Nyamata Genocide Memorial Centre Kigali, RW	2016–	PennPraxis & expert teams
NH-8 (military)	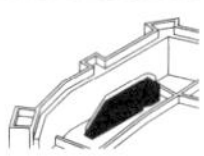	Pombal Castle Visitor Centre Pombal, PT	2014	COMOCO Architects
NH-9 (conflict/Black heritage)		Rosa Parks House Project Berlin, DE/Providence, US/Naples, IT	2015/2018/2021	Ryan Mendoza
NH-10 (conflict/trauma)	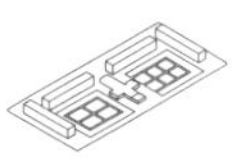	S.21 Tuol Sleng Genocide Museum Phnom Penh, KH	1979	–
NH-11 (scale)		Le Fresnoy Art Center Tourcoing, FR	1997	Bernard Tschumi
NH-12 (scale)	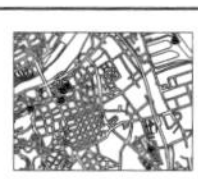	Pixel Hotel Linz, AT	2006	Funk, Grugl, Haller, Steger, Weidinger
NH-13 (unfinished structure)	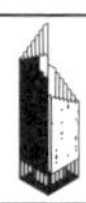	Torre de David Caracas, VE	2007	–
NH-14 (architectural heritage)	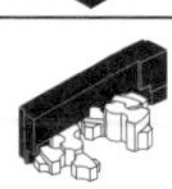	Tripolis Park Amsterdam, NL	2022–	MVRDV
NH-15 (architectural heritage)		TWA Hotel New York, US	2019	Beyer Blinder Belle
NH-16 (translocation)	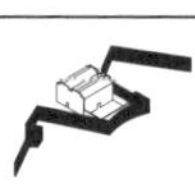	Yin Yu Tang House at the Peabody Essex Museum Salem, US	2003	John G. Waites Associates

New Heritage

New Program

Cultural	Education	Hospitality	Infrastructure	Office	Residential	Retail	Recreational	Memorial
	●							●
●								
	●							●
●	●							●
●								
●								
								●
●	●							
●								
●								●
●	●							
		●						
					●			
				●				
		●						
●								

NH-1 Bunker 599

Bunker 599 is a concrete bunker built along the New Dutch Waterline, a water-based military defense route from Muiden to Biesbosch. From 1815 to 1940, this waterline was used to protect the Netherlands from invaders through the use of intentional flooding. Today, without such dangers, the waterline has become a recreational area and, in 2021, was placed on UNESCO's list of World Heritage Sites. Built in 1940 with the capacity to shelter a dozen soldiers in case of bombing, Bunker 599 was transformed through the physical removal of a slot through the monolithic concrete block, a sawing process that required 40 days. The remaining opening accommodates the insertion of a walkway through it, leading to the floodplains below. Visitors can enter through the narrow slot that reveals the history of the waterline and descend to a long boardwalk at the water's edge. This subtractive intervention has transformed a structure of defense into a revelatory exhibition of a long military secret. One of 700 other concrete bunkers along the waterline, this act of adaptive reuse has transformed a structure of municipal significance into a project of national heritage. In a reversal of custom where heritage sites are transformed for new use through adaptive reuse, the adaptive reuse of Bunker 599 has elevated a common structure to a monument.

Location:	Diefdijk 5 – Highway A2, the Netherlands	
Year of Conversion:	2010	
Architects:	Atelier Lyon, RAAAF	
Original Use:	Military bunker	[war / military]
New Use:	Installation	[culture]

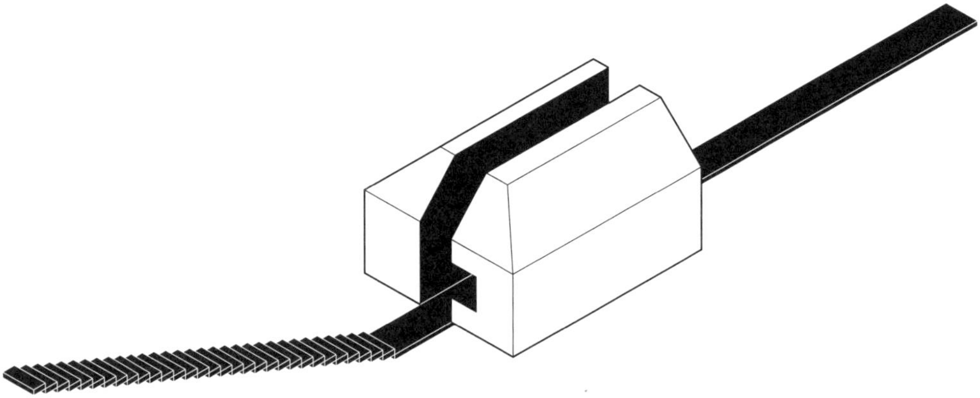

NH-2 Castelvecchio

The Museo Civico di Castelvecchio is sited in a castle that has had many different lives: the 14th-century fortress of the La Scala ruling family, a munitions depot and military academy, barracks under 18th-century French rule that continued with the 19th-century annexation of Verona to the Kingdom of Italy. Under fascist rule, the castle was transferred to the city with plans to restore and convert it into a museum. In the early 1920s, it was restored to the ideal of a medieval castle it never was. From 1958–1974, it was renovated by Carlo Scarpa and remains one of his best-known projects and an oeuvre on every level. As an adaptive reuse of a complex site with multi-layered lives, Scarpa's intervention is most notable for its distinct creation of a layer of its own time. Additions – from stairs to windows, doors and marble exhibit platforms – and artwork (statues, painting, sculptures, archaeological finds) hover and levitate above and from the floors and walls of the existing host structure through seemingly effortless and minimal detail. This poetic distance is most poignant at a rectangular sash placed on the interior, directly in front of the Gothic windows created in the fascist renovation. The Castelvecchio remains an unsurpassed example of adaptive reuse.

Location:	Verona, Italy	
Year of Conversion:	1958–1974	
Architects:	Carlo Scarpa	
Original Use:	Fortress / munitions / barracks	[war / military / heritage]
New Use:	Museum	[culture]

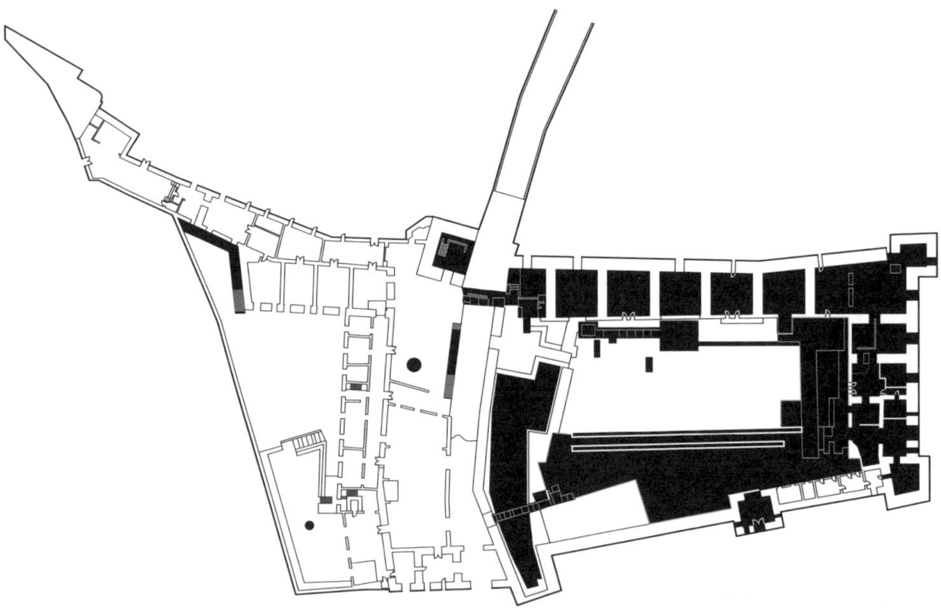

NH-3 The Kommandant's House

The project, the Kommandant's House at Kamp Westerbork, breaks new ground in the treatment of war and trauma heritage. Originally a Dutch detention center to receive Jewish refugees, Kamp Westerbork was seized by the Germans in 1940 and transformed into a transit hub for deporting Jews to extermination camps. By 1945, almost 100,000 refugees had been deported from Westerbork, including Anne Frank. The green clapboard house, the residence of the SS camp commander Albert Konrad Gemmeker, was the last remaining structure of this tragic site and was declared a national monument in 1994. Concentration camps such as Auschwitz have been preserved in situ as heritage, with the purpose of bearing witness to atrocities and to educate. The new project encases the house in a gigantic vitrine with the dual purpose of first, providing an additional conservation skin to the structure and, second, to create a place for educational activities directly with the artefact. Through this intervention of adaptive reuse, the house and its former occupant are now perpetually imprisoned in a skin of glass in an act of judgment facilitated through architecture.

Location:	Westerbork, the Netherlands	
Year of Conversion:	2015	
Architects:	Oving Architecten	
Original Use:	House for commandant of concentration camp	[residence/war/military/heritage]
New Use:	Exhibition/memorial	[culture/education/memorial]

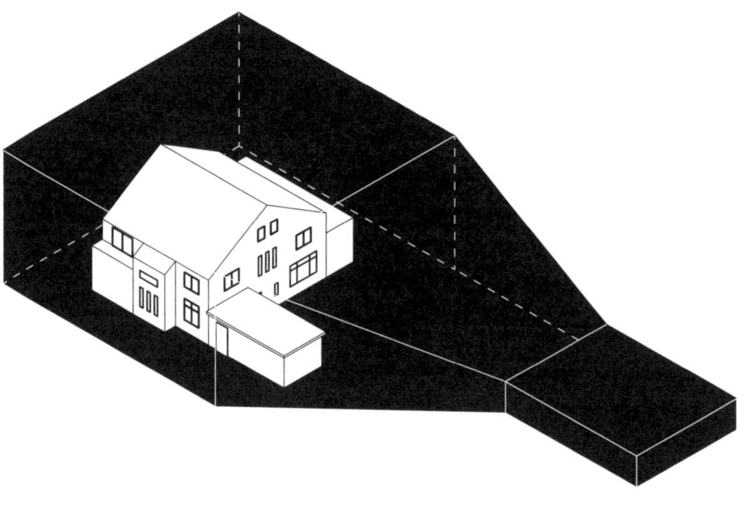

NH-4 Memorial to the Abolition of Slavery

The Memorial to the Abolition of Slavery is located on the Quai de la Fosse, the wharf from which ships sailed to Africa as part of the slave trade. In the 18th century, the city of Nantes derived much of its income and wealth as the busiest French slave port, responsible for "43% of the French slave trade shipments and [the deportation of] 450,000 black captives to the American colonies."[1] With slavery nowadays recognized as a crime against humanity, the siting of the Memorial at the place of that crime is a powerful new program of use for the wharf. An open-air staircase leads from the esplanade to an underground exhibition space created in the underbelly of the wharf structure. Hemmed in on one side by continuous inclined glass plate exhibits of text and water on the other, the cramped atmosphere evokes that of the slave ship. Commemorating past and present acts of resistance to slavery, the reuse of the wharf understructure as a memorial is an example of negative heritage. The power of the placement of memorials such as this one in the actual place of crimes and acts of violence emphasizes the unique role of context in projects of adaptive reuse.

Location:	Nantes, France	
Year of Conversion:	2012	
Architects:	Wodiczko + Bonder	
Original Use:	Wharf	[transportation]
New Use:	Museum and memorial	[culture/memorial]

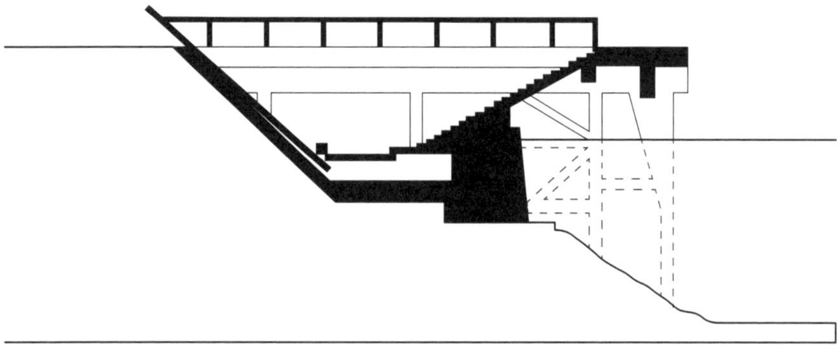

1 The Memorial of the Abolition of Slavery Nantes Press Kit.

Freiheit
Liberte
Vryheid
Kimpwanza

NH-5 Moritzburg Museum

The Moritzburg Museum resides in the Moritzburg, a fortified castle built in the late 15th century. Built as the archbishop's residence, the castle has played a role in the city's defense over different periods in history. In a siege during the Thirty Years' War, fire destroyed various parts of the castle that were never rebuilt. Plans from 1829 for its restoration as a university by K. F. Schinkel did not materialize due to a lack of funding. The intact portions of the castle were established as a museum in 1904, holding one of the best collections of Expressionist art. Finally, in 2004, a reconstruction was approved to expand the museum. A ruin as a host structure requires an intervention to make it whole. The addition of a particular roofscape solved many issues simultaneously. As a large, rigid aluminum platform that rises and falls, the new roof provided much-needed building closure, structural support for hanging two new, column-free exhibition spaces, and indirect lighting through its well-placed skylights. This single intervention juxtaposes existing and new, protecting the ruins while creating new spatial opportunities. The aluminum roof is a departure from the existing red-tiled roof; when asked, the architects indicated that the silver-gray aluminum melded into the cloudy Germanic sky, at times disappearing altogether – leaving only the ruin.

Location:	Halle, Germany	
Year of Conversion:	2008	
Architects:	Nieto Sobejano Arquitectos	
Original Use:	Castle	[war/military/heritage]
New Use:	Museum	[culture]

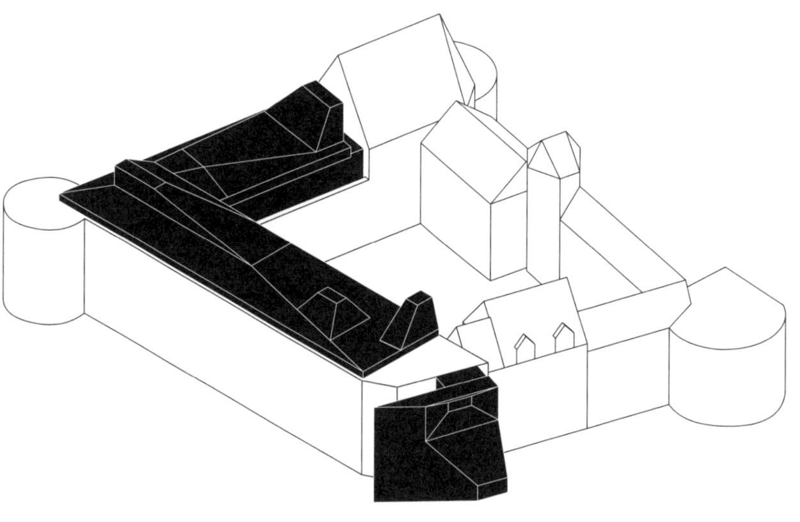

NH-6 Neues Museum

The Neues Museum on Berlin's Museum Island was designed by Friedrich August Stüler and opened in 1859. World War II left it in ruins, damaged and missing entire sections of the building. It remained a ruin for more than half a century until David Chipperfield Architects won the commission to restore the structure. Their work exemplifies the recovery of ruins as laid out in the principles of the Venice Charter of 1964. One aspect of this work was archaeological restoration in which a decades-long mapping process was undertaken to record the damage; including that from bullet holes and machine gun fire. Some of this damage remains today as part of the history of the structure. Where reparations of this damage were made, they were completed according to the Venice Charter with a new material to differentiate between old and new. This can be seen in missing portions of walls and ceilings where an abstract concrete has been applied. A demonstration of this process performed on a large scale pertained to the loss of the original grand staircase. Replaced in the exact location as before the war, the monumental stairs are rendered in abstract modern materials. The process by which the ruins of the Neues Museum were resurrected serves as a classic precedent for the treatment of not only war-damaged ruins but heritage structures of all types.

Location:	Berlin, Germany	
Year of Conversion:	2009	
Architects:	David Chipperfield Architects in collaboration with Julian Harrap	
Original Use:	Ruin of museum	[war/military/heritage]
New Use:	Museum	[culture/heritage]

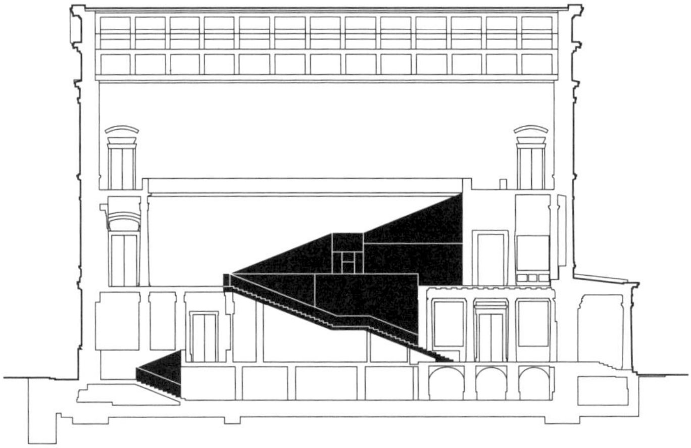

NH-7 Nyamata Genocide Memorial Centre

The Rwandan Civil War was a result of decades of struggles between the Tutsi and Hutu tribes. In 1959, many Tutsis were forced to relocate to the Nyamata Refugee Camp in Bugesera District and, in the 1980s, the Nyamata Church was built for their worship. Decades of ethnic persecution culminated in genocide from April to July of 1994 when killings of the Tutsis began after the assassination of President Habyarimana on April 6th. Between April 14th and 16th, Tutsis sheltered in the Nyamata Church, a religious place regarded as sacred and therefore safe. Thousands were slaughtered in the church where more than 45,000 victims are laid to rest today. The church was desacralized in 1997 with the remains of the victims left in situ. In 2016, the Commission Nationale de Lutte contre le Génocide (CNLG) began work on a conservation plan for Nyamata with PennPraxis, a research and practice arm of the University of Pennsylvania's Weitzman School of Design. The conservation of the site included different experts in the field including preservationists and textile conservators. The desacralized church is pockmarked by bullet holes and its walls stained with blood. The clothing of the many victims – approximately 35 m^3 – is conserved and remains in piles draped on the pews, a testament to the number of those who perished. One of six genocide memorials in Rwanda, the Nyamata Church is a registered UNESCO site. Its tragic existence is an example of today's negative heritage.

Location:	Kigali, Rwanda	
Year of Conversion:	2016–	
Architects:	Teams assembled by PennPraxis	
Original Use:	Church	[war/military/religion]
New Use:	Memorial	[memorial]

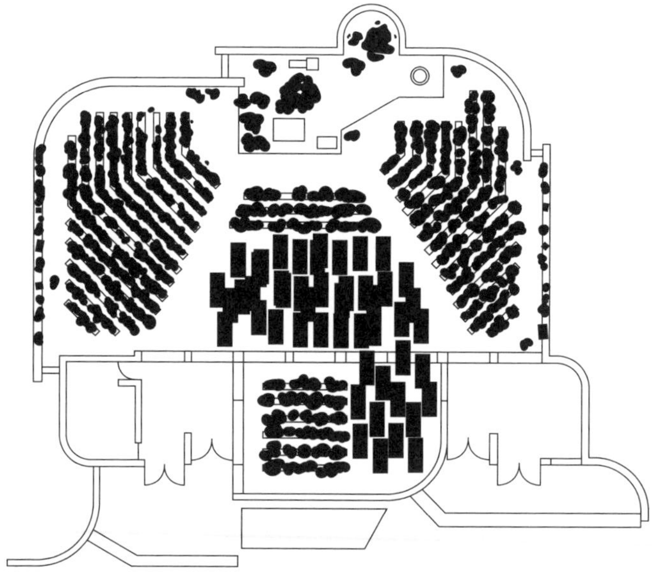

NH-8 Pombal Castle Visitor Centre

On the top of a hill overlooking the Arunca river, Pombal Castle is today a former fortification dating back to Roman occupation. It continued in its vital role of defense throughout the 19th century until the loss of its military significance during the Napoleonic Wars. The castle fell into disrepair despite various attempts at restoration. In the 21st century, the castle was reassessed by the Portuguese Institute for Architectural Patrimony and converted into a museum in 2005. The commission for a visitor center follows an earlier 2011 commission to reorganize Pombal Castle's hill by creating connections between the urban center at the base of the hill to the castle. Strong but simple volumes were introduced – in wood and concrete – that led the visitor up the hill. The design of a visitor center is a continuation of this vocabulary with the addition of a limestone structure housing a reception area, a screening room and storage. This simple rectangular volume with an open staircase on one side is simultaneously ambiguous and conspicuous. Its monolithic quality allows it to integrate with the existing elements of the fortification ruins and establish its own voice in this touristic phase of the military structure's long history.

Location:	Pombal, Portugal	
Year of Conversion:	2014	
Architects:	COMOCO Architects	
Original Use:	Castle	[war/military/heritage/ruin]
New Use:	Tourist accommodation	[culture]

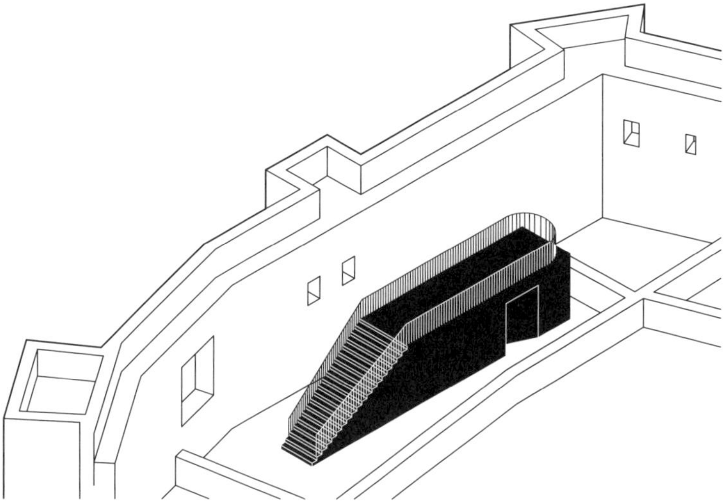

NH-9 Rosa Parks House Project

The Rosa Parks House Project is the result of a series of interactions that began in Detroit, Michigan, in 2014 when a decaying house on South Deacon Street was placed on a list for demolition. The home of American civil rights activist Rosa Parks from 1957–1959, it was saved from demolition when her niece, Rhea McCauley, purchased it from the City of Detroit and gave it to the artist Ryan Mendoza. The building catapulted out of obscurity due to the intervention of Mendoza, who moved the structure, or what was left of it, across the Atlantic Ocean to Berlin. There it gained a new identity and notoriety through reconstruction on German soil. Transformed through translocation, the structure would recross the ocean in the spring of 2018, with hopes of a repatriation in Providence, Rhode Island, through the sponsorship of Brown University. Due to complex issues, this did not take place. The house was auctioned but did not sell. It crossed the Atlantic Ocean once more to Naples, Italy, where it was the focus of an exhibition at the Palazzo Reale titled "Coming Home." Once a humble wood home in Detroit, the Rosa Parks House Project became an "art object" when placed out of context and repatriated. With claims to being an American civil rights monument, the Rosa Parks House Project is an example of Black heritage and its plight in and outside of the United States. The controversy surrounding it embodies the troubled American dialogue on race and equity.

Location:	Detroit, MI, USA/Berlin, Germany/Providence, RI, USA/Naples, Italy	
Year of Conversion:	2015/2018/2021	
Architects:	Ryan Mendoza	
Original Use:	Home	[residence]
New Use:	Monument/installation	[heritage/culture]

NH-10 S.21 Tuol Sleng Genocide Museum

The Preah Ponhea Yat High School (later renamed Tuol Svay Prey), built in 1962, comprised four buildings arranged around a courtyard. The buildings were converted in 1976 by the Khmer Rouge as a detention center and the school was renamed Security Office 21 or S.21. The design of the high school incorporated many of Le Corbusier's principles, especially those of shading and air circulation. In its transformation into a detention and torture center, the well-proportioned classrooms were subdivided into tiny prison and torture chambers. The windows and outdoor covered hallways were enclosed with iron bars and electrified barbed wire. Between 1975–1979, it is estimated that between 15,000–20,000 people were imprisoned at S.21. The site became the Tuol Sleng Genocide Museum in 1979, after the liberation of the city by the Kampuchea United Front of National Salvation and Vietnamese troops. It was one of three such crime sites that are now safeguarded as memorial sites for remembering the victims and for preserving the evidence for history. The Museum is under UNESCO protection and its archives are part of the UNESCO Memory of the World Register. S.21 is a precedent for negative heritage and its conversion into memorials.

Location:	Phnom Penh, Cambodia	
Year of Conversion:	1979	
Architects:	–	
Original Use:	School / Torture center	[education / war / military]
New Use:	Memorial / museum	[memorial / cultural]

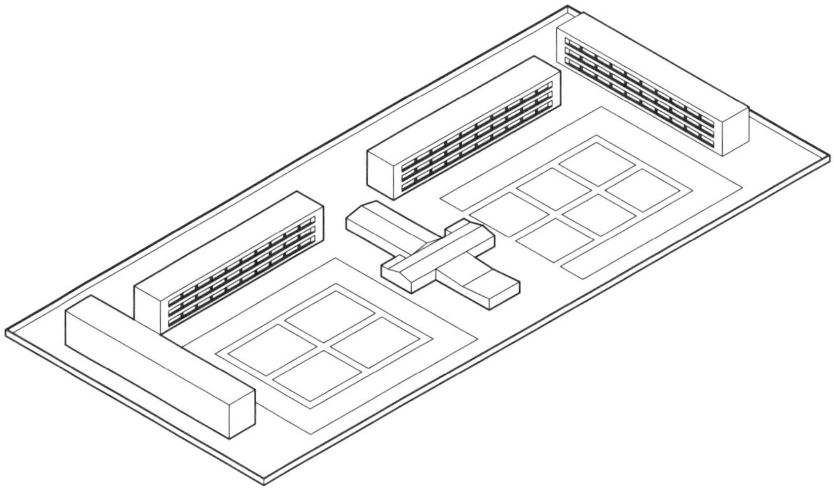

NH-11 Le Fresnoy Art Center

Le Fresnoy is an art and audiovisual research center in northern France created from a leisure and entertainment complex built in the 1920s. The host structure is unique in this project as it comprises a group of dilapidated assembly buildings that includes a cinema, a ballroom, skating and horseback riding rinks. The transformation of many volumes of different scales, without their demolition, into a single-use space was achieved through the addition of one large volume over the existing complex. A contemporary facade topped by a vast roof provided enclosure for the group of buildings – a box over a series of unrelated smaller boxes. The steel and polycarbonate roof is a single unifying intervention as an assembly containing glazed openings for light, ductwork for ventilation and cooling, structure for suspending circulation stairs and walkways. Support spaces for the new program including exhibition areas, sound studios, production facilities, a library, administrative offices, and apartments for faculty and students are inserted in the upgraded existing structures or between and above them. Completed shortly before the turn of the 20th century, Le Fresnoy Art Center sets a precedent for reuse both in its sheer scale of adapting multiple structures and its groundbreaking perspective toward preservation and reuse of structures.

Location:	Tourcoing, France	
Year of Conversion:	1997	
Architects:	Bernard Tschumi	
Original Use:	Neighborhood	[recreation]
New Use:	Art center	[culture/education]

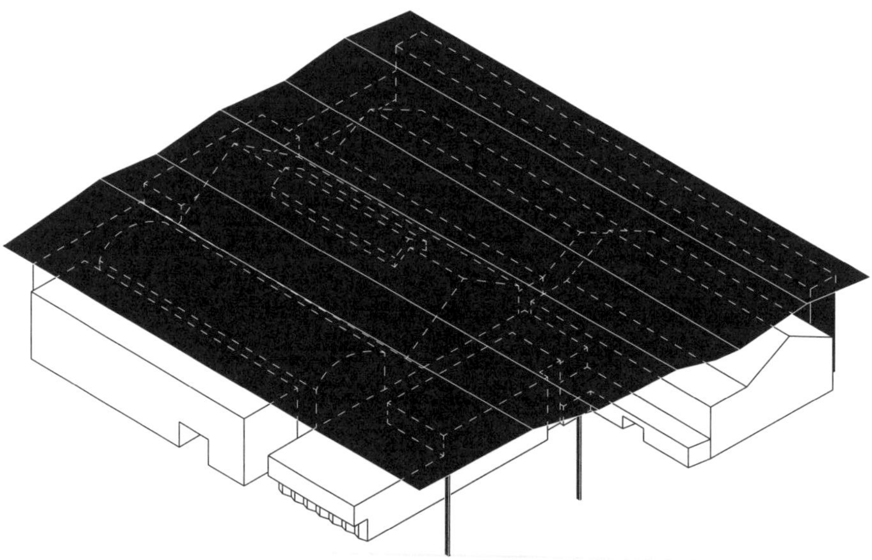

NH-12 Pixel Hotel

Designed for Linz's year as 2009 European Capital of Culture, the Pixel Hotel merges urban heritage and hospitality in a new type of hotel. Hotel rooms are re-envisioned not as private bedrooms within a single building but rather as rooms spread across the city in a unique form of tourism. Located across the historic city, these rooms, or pixels, offer varied experiences that are outside the realm of the typical traveler. In Pixel in der Galerie, one inhabits modern sculpture within an art gallery. In Pixel am Wasser, a room is found on a restored 1958 tug boat, MV Traisen, anchored in the Linz harbor. Pixel mit Garten is an experience in the social history of Linz with a room in the working-class neighborhood of Franckviertel – part of a low-cost housing project, begun in 1919, where a communal garden was provided for the tenants to grow their own vegetables. Pixel in der Volksküche takes the traveler to the Altstadt Ost, the eastern part of the old town, to sleep in what was once a coal warehouse from the late 19th century, transformed into a soup kitchen for the needy that was fully operational until 1968. These unconventional pixels give new life to old spaces, reinventing a tradition of travel through real life experiences.

Location:	Linz, Austria	
Year of Conversion:	2006	
Architects:	Sabine Funk, Michael Grugl, Jürgen Haller, Richard Steger, Christoph Weidinger	
Original Use:	Spaces in the city	[culture/industry/residence/heritage]
New Use:	Hotel	[hospitality]

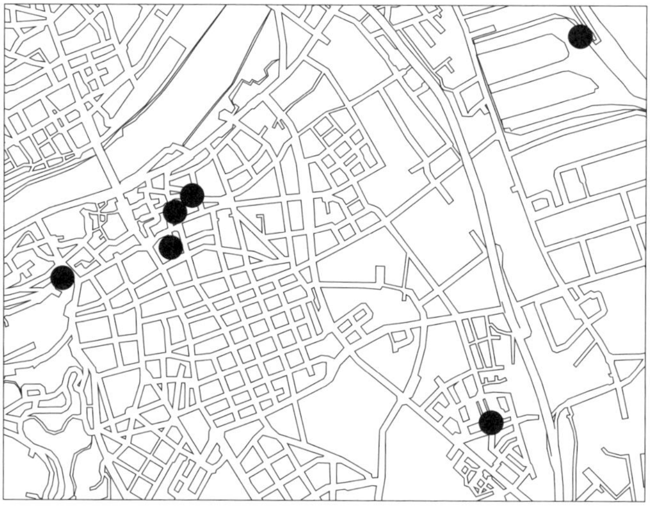

E

NH-13 Torre de David

The Torre de David or Centro Financiero Confinanzas in Venezuela's capital city is an abandoned 45-story skyscraper whose construction began in 1990. Named for its main investor, who subsequently died in 1993, the construction was halted due to the Venezuelan banking crisis that took place in the same year. The government took control of the unfinished building that lacked many basic elements including vertical systems, windows, water, electricity and even walls. An auction was held in 2001 but did not result in any offers. In October 2007, squatters from Caracas' "informal communities" occupied the unfinished tower, eventually improving basic services in the unfinished high-rise up to the 22nd floor. Through what they had at hand, these residents – estimated at 700 families at the peak – transformed the structure to accommodate not only homes but bodegas, beauty salons and barbershops. In 2011, the housing shortage for the poorest communities was a critical issue for the reelection of President Hugo Chávez, especially in the wake of torrential rains that destroyed many hillside slums. The transformational project to alleviate the plight of these families was documented and won a Golden Lion at the 2012 Venice Architecture Biennale. Many of the families have been relocated since. The tower remains after suffering significant damage in an earthquake in 2018. Torre de David exemplifies reuse by way of appropriation through informal means.

Location:	Caracas, Venezuela	
Year of Conversion:	2007	
Architects:	–	
Original Use:	Unfinished office tower	[ruin]
New Use:	Housing	[residence]

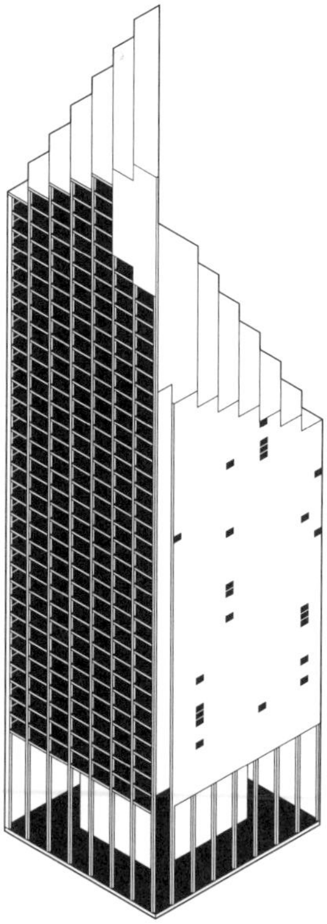

NH-14 Tripolis Park

It is said that Dutch architect Aldo van Eyck's "effect on the Dutch architecture scene can hardly be overestimated,"[1] from his contribution to the development of Dutch structuralism to his participation in Team 10. Van Eyck's Tripolis Park office complex, completed in 1994, is not one of his masterpieces and has not proven commercially successful with low occupancy. But it is sited in close proximity to the Amsterdam Orphanage, a project that gained him international recognition in 1960. Tripolis Park was designated a municipal monument in 2019, conferring a status of hallowed ground to the area containing both projects. MVRDV's project is an update achieved through the addition of an 11-story office building, one that serves to protect the van Eyck project from the noise and bustle of the adjacent highway. The new block is linear and austere on the south – the side of the highway – with a glazed facade that offers glimpses of van Eyck's buildings. On the north – the side of van Eyck's buildings – the new structure devolves into van Eyck's geometry in homage. The gap between old and new structures contains the circulation of the new project. A meandering path that unifies the two parts, its form is a testament to the respect for the work and the man behind it. This iteration of Tripolis Park exemplifies a new type of heritage, a status conferred upon modern works held sacred by the architectural community.

Location:	Amsterdam, the Netherlands	
Year of Conversion:	2022–	
Architects:	MVRDV	
Original Use:	Office	[heritage]
New Use:	Office	[office/heritage]

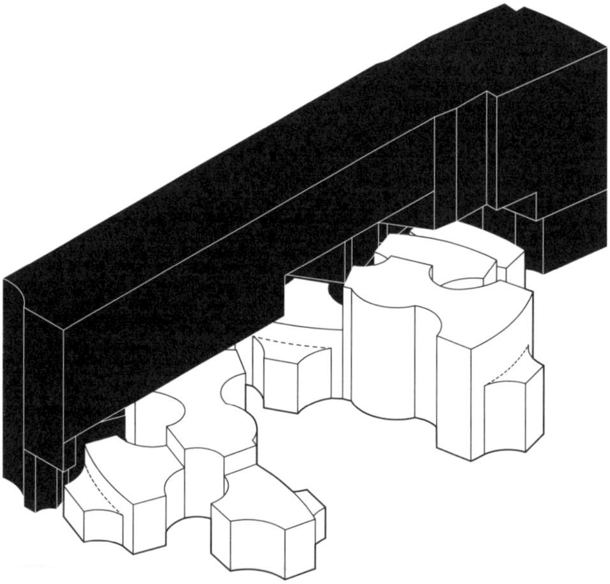

1 "Aldo van Eyck (1918–1999," http://www.team10online.org/team10/eyck/index.html#top Accessed July 13, 2022.

NH-15 TWA Hotel

The Trans World Airlines Flight Center designed by Eero Saarinen and Associates operated as a terminal building of the John F. Kennedy International Airport from 1962 to 2001. Its wing-shaped roof of four curving segments is a pioneer in thin-shell construction. Built when commercial flight became commonplace post-WWII, its iconic form and fluid spaces capture that sense of flight, claiming a place in the history of architecture. Designed for the flight requirements of the late 1950s, the terminal was not able to accommodate the needs of larger and more complex jet airliners that followed. Operating as an air terminal until 2001, it was closed in the same year. It had been declared a New York City landmark in 1994 and was added to the National Register of Historic Places in 2005. The terminal remained vacant for more than 15 years until it was adapted as a hotel, restaurant and conference center. The reuse maintains the legacy of the Saarinen structure where the landmark Flight Center serves as the lobby for the different functions. Two wings, one on each side of the Flight Center, have been added that house more than 500 hotel rooms. The development of the TWA Flight Center into the TWA Hotel demonstrates the relationship between technology and obsolescence in transportation structures. Its preservation serves as an example of the new heritage found in iconic architectural works of the 20th century.

Location:	New York, NY, USA	
Year of Conversion:	2019	
Architects:	Beyer Blinder Belle	
Original Use:	Airport terminal	[transportation]
New Use:	Hotel	[hospitality/heritage]

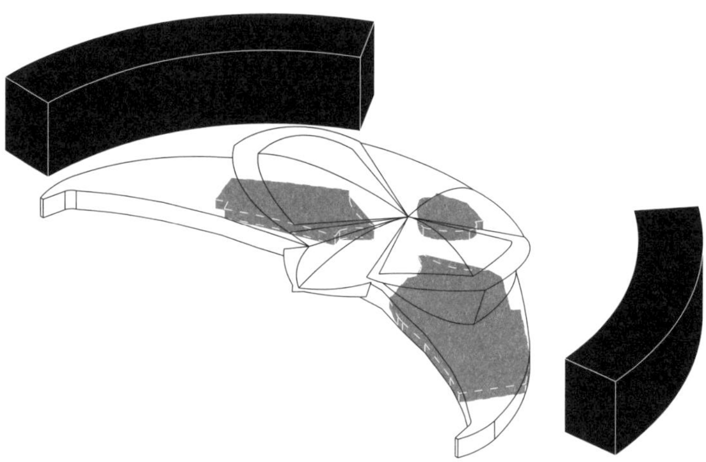

NH-16 Yin Yu Tang House at the Peabody Essex Museum

In the ancestral villages of the Huizhou District of southeastern China are thousands of folk houses, the ancestral homes of merchants who dominated the trade community during the Ming and Qing dynasties. These lavish ancestral halls were the product of their accumulated wealth. But by the 20th century, their descendants had fled the villages for the city. Outstanding examples were protected as heritage but many of the homes were abandoned. The Yin Yu Tang was the 16-bedroom house of the Huang family, descended from a Qing Dynasty merchant. The last Huang descendant left in 1982 and, due to a chance meeting with American Nancy Berliner who purchased the house, the home was relocated to the United States. Meticulously deconstructed, joint by joint, to 2,735 wooden pieces, the house was reconstructed, piece by piece, as a permanent exhibit at the Peabody Essex Museum in Salem, Massachusetts. Replete with objects of domestic life, the Yin Yu Tang House offers visitors a glimpse into daily life from centuries past through the exhibit of this architectural heritage. Translocation as an intervention preserves unprotected heritage by removing their physical context. At the Yin Yu Tang House, this removal of context transformed the house into a museum object. Typically a last resort, translocation offers new and fertile ground for adaptive reuse practice.

Location:	Salem, MA, USA	
Year of Conversion:	2003	
Architects:	John G. Waites Associates	
Original Use:	Home	[residence]
New Use:	Object	[culture]

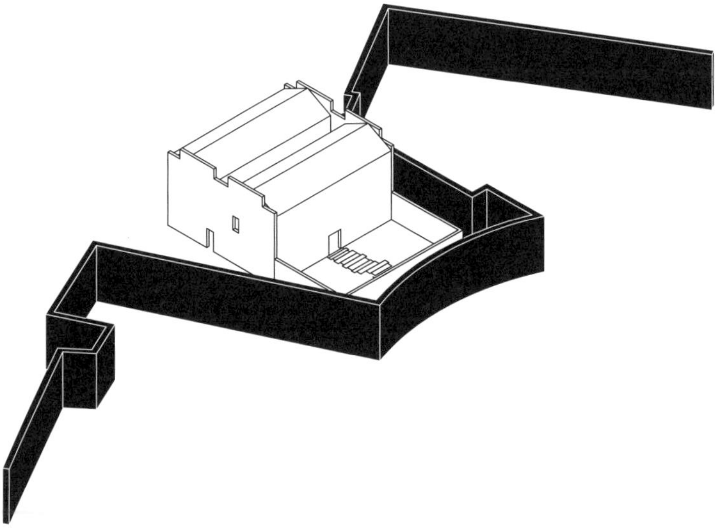

Looking Ahead

Critical Moments in Current Phase of Adaptive Reuse
+ Average Annual OPEC Crude Oil Price from 1960–2022*

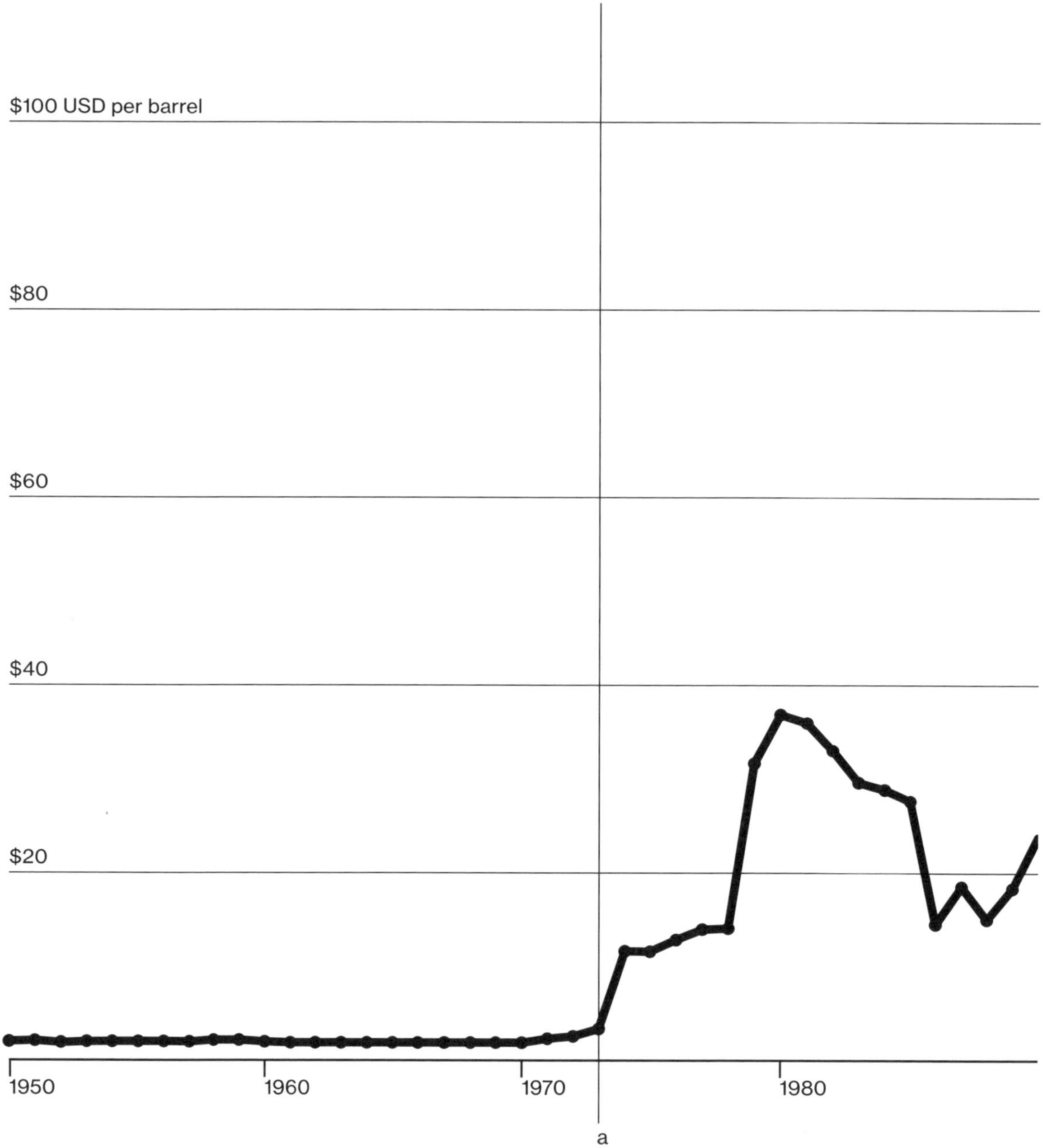

a First use of the term “adaptive reuse” in the *Merriam-Webster Dictionary* in 1973

b Founding of the initiative Architecture 2030, establishing the importance of the existing building stock (2002)

c “The Greenest Building Is One That Is Already Built” (2007)

d *The Greenest Building: Quantifying the Environmental Value of Building Reuse* (2011)

* Source: OPEC en2X @statista 2022

On Monday, 23 May 2022, the last public pay phone was removed from New York City, whereas, in the year 2000, there were 30,000 such booths from which one could make a phone call.[1] This final removal concludes a chapter in the history of communications that began in 1973 with the introduction of the first battery-operated DynaTAC phone. There is symmetry to this closure as the final event in a 50-year shift to wireless device use, where many born in the 21st century have no knowledge of wall telephones. Transitions over time are at the heart of the previous chapters that offer the reader hypotheses on shifts in six aspects of modern life that were rooted in ideas from the 1970s. Over decades, these ideas developed and evolved, culminating in the built environment as decommissioned/abandoned and subsequently reused structures. These six types of buildings – energy production, manufacturing, agricultural, transportation, religious and heritage – were examined as standalone explorations within a modern context leading to their respective abandonment or decommissioning. Individually, each exploration revealed connections to events in the 1970s that served as catalysts for the eventual abandonment/decommissioning of that type. As a group, these six types were connected by the fact that many of the abandoned/decommissioned buildings were reused in the early 21st century instead of demolished. These two common factors, one of the 1970s and the other of the early 21st century, are bookends of a half century of change spanning two eras. They provide the background to understanding a parallel phenomenon that begin in 1973 when the term "adaptive reuse" was officially defined. This formal gesture signaled a new period in the long, long history of reuse practice, one fueled by the needs of a different time.

As Climate Action

"Adaptive reuse" was defined during the first oil crisis, when the terms "green" and "sustainability," as related to the environment, did not yet exist. Awareness of the environment was in its infancy. By the end of the 1980s, however, environmentalism was becoming a global concern; there was ever-increasing recognition of the threats to our planet's viability and the action needed to claim a livable future. Within this context, the role of the built environment in global warming was acknowledged in various ways. In 2002, Architecture 2030, a non-profit organization, was created with the objective to "achieve a dramatic reduction in the energy consumption and CO_2 emissions of the built environment by 2030." With buildings being "the largest source of the world's carbon emissions globally," the organization has alerted attention to the fact that "in 2040, two thirds of the global building stock will be buildings that exist today,"[2] thereby uniquely acknowledging the importance of the role of existing structures and their reuse in climate change action. Building reuse would be a crucial part of Architecture 2030's mission "to rapidly transform the built environment from the major contributor of greenhouse gas emissions to a central solution to the climate crisis."[3] Despite this recognition, most contributions toward the decarbonization of buildings and cities, the most effective as stringent criteria of high-performance building energy codes, have addressed new construction. However,

IMG 1 — Phone booths, once a common object in New York City, have now all been removed.
IMG 2 — Lacaton & Vassal's trademark transformations of social housing.

"even if every new building designed from today forward meets the zero-carbon operations standard, buildings and cities will continue emitting more carbon pollution than industry, agriculture, or transportation."[4] In 2007, future American Institute of Architects (AIA) President Carl Elefante wrote in the *Forum Journal* that "the greenest building is one that is already built."[5] Four years later, in 2011, the Preservation Green Lab, a research arm of the National Trust for Historic Preservation, completed a report titled, *The Greenest Building: Quantifying the Environmental Value of Building Reuse*. It found that "it takes 10 to 80 years for a new building that is 30 percent more efficient than an average-performing existing building to overcome, through efficient operations, the negative climate change impacts related to the construction process."[6] It is said that "there is no pathway to a zero-emissions building sector without zeroing out emissions from America's 325 billion square feet of existing buildings."[7] Through science, these findings directly connect adaptive reuse and sustainability. They render the reuse of existing structures the viable option for the future of net-zero energy building in the time of climate change action. These findings shed light on the connection between the many abandoned buildings of six different use groups that, in the 21st century, were reused instead of demolished. They also shed light on why projects of reuse have become the highlight of the architectural profession. Lecturing at the Harvard Graduate School of Design in March 2022, Anne Lacaton of Lacaton & Vassal admonished: "Never demolish. Never subtract, remove, or replace. Always add, transform, and utilize."[8] In many ways, her words expand upon those in the Athens Charter and Venice Charter regarding heritage-designated structures and apply them to all buildings. These findings offer us the *raison d'être* for the spate of reuse projects that mark the beginning decades of the 21st century. Formally named adaptive reuse, these works of a half-century constitute the most recent chapter in the long history of reuse practice. The viability of our planet's future can now be added to the other factors – economy, power transitions, conservation of heritage, war recovery – that have triggered reuse practice over time. This relationship between adaptive reuse and the future of humanity is to date the most urgent reason for this practice. It is apt that it finally received a formal name at this time after existing for years without one. The first known use of the term in 1973 marks an epoch in this practice, signaling a new chapter in the history of reuse.

As climate change action, the implementation of reuse has extended in many directions beyond the transformation of a single or even several structures. At a minimum, adaptive reuse is now part of urban planning strategies. In France, the Réinventer Paris initiative that began in 2014 is a large-scale urban development project for Paris to reuse 23 different sites in the city. They include heritage buildings such as the 17th-century Hotel de Coulanges, but also the Voltaire, a former electric substation, and Masséna, a disused railway station. But less glamorous projects of upgrades and refurbishment are now embraced and given their due in the architecture and design world. The Moreland Mixité, a repair and reuse project along the Seine, a commission won by David Chipperfield Architects, exemplifies the first steps of this new regenerative spirit. Such a regenerative spirit, however, is not all pervasive in the construction and development process. In the United Kingdom, a VAT of 20% is charged on all refurbishment and renovation.[9] This is an incentive to build or rebuild rather than to reuse and renovate. Reform of the VAT rate is one of the aims of the RetroFirstcampaign in 2019.[10]

The practice of reuse as it exists today is a retroactive one that is dependent on the decommissioning or abandonment of buildings that have already served one lifespan. A new trend to amend the reuse of underused or abandoned sites as 'after-the-fact' action is emerging. Making a pre-construction plan for considering the reuse of a building is now a nascent practice. For a few new projects, there are now requirements within the design process to include proposals for its future reuse. This type of requirement operates within the assumption that a building's function will at some time become obsolete and embraces the concept of reuse as the viable future of new construction. While planning for distant futures is not easy, applying the concept of architectural fit – as in the reuse of the pagan Baths of Diocletian as the Christian Santa Maria degli Angeli e dei Martiri – in planning reuse ahead of time is a fascinating idea. In this scenario, infrastructure and systems, at the very least, could be planned in advance to serve a second, distant life. While this concept may take some time to implement for the design of all new buildings, its application is ideal and feasible for the design of structures for one-off events, including expositions and sports events such as the Olympics or the World Cup. With the recognition of the role that building reuse plays in our climate future, plans for a second life that accompany the designs for the first is a critical step toward making regenerative design a principle of architecture.

The Shape of Change

In hindsight, the examination of a half-century makes it possible to perceive connecting threads within a bracketed period of time. In the case of this book, the brackets were determined by the first use of the formalized name for the practice of reusing structures. Our wireless phone culture today is such an example of a 50-year transition, from the introduction of the battery-operated phone to the removal of the last phone booth. The six subjects explored in this book demonstrate transitions that left physical evidence in the built environment as quantities of abandoned, decommissioned or underused structures of similar types. Many new ideas introduced in society, however, did not necessarily follow such a path. These changes instead culminated in hybrid scenarios in which new functions did not lead to the demise of a building type. Instead, the structures were adapted to fit those new functions. For example, many predicted the demise of books with the advent of the e-book in the 1990s, and with it the demise of the library. This did not happen. Digital media has dramatically changed the operations

IMG 3 — Today, the public library includes many activities outside of lending books.
IMG 4 — Mass at the New Roads Community resembles a concert.

of a library, but the library has remained. As a type, it has evolved beyond that of a container of texts. Today, public libraries serve as living rooms for communities and include services from secondary education to health clinics and childcare. The evolution of the library from a place for physical books is a success in adaptation. Other building types that are in flux include, for example, post offices, rendered less necessary by the advent of email; office supply stores, rendered less in demand due to the reliance on digital practices; and toy stores, rendered less in demand with the advent of the iPad and phone apps. Between changing societal practices, they may initiate their own adaptive strategies.

Adaptation strategies are also pertinent for building types that struggle to remain relevant. A church project for an American Catholic community offers an example of such adaptation. In the church crisis of the late 1990s, Catholic parishes were combined for financial reasons. Two parishes in Massachusetts joined to become New Roads Community. While both parish churches exist, the newly combined parishes chose to celebrate mass in the church's community center, albeit transformed. Today, masses are delivered in a black box theater environment, devoid of most Christian

IMG 5 — Co-locating energy and agriculture
IMG 6 — Careful deconstruction of sites yields materials for reuse.

iconography. Instead of an altar there is a large flat screen wall lit in neon lights that spotlight the rock band belting out new wave Christian hymns. At a time when abandoned and decommissioned churches have been transformed for different uses, from hospitality to entertainment and retail, a church community chose a nightclub setting for its religious celebrations as an adaptation strategy in a changed world.

A different approach to the adaptation of a building type struggling for relevance lies in the introduction of a new type of use while maintaining the original use. This strategy of co-location provides its own type of transition that has the potential to bypass the decommissioning or abandonment of a structure. Agrivoltaics, which refers to the simultaneous use of land for both energy and food production, is one example of such a strategy for ailing farms. On farms engaging in this practice, rows of plants alternate with rows of solar panels, yielding a combined harvest of food and energy.

The introduction of new ideas does not always come through the luxury of a long transition period. The effects of unforeseen and violent circumstances, such as war, on the built environment have contributed to the development of reuse practice in staccato fashion; the Athens and Venice Charters can be described as critical policy gains arising from the effects of war. The recent and unforeseen circumstances of the Covid-19 pandemic provided a new insight on sudden changes of functions in the built environment. Many buildings were made redundant, with the most impact on office towers, retail and hospitality. In addition, there were new and urgent functions to accommodate, but little time to construct new structures. The temporary repurposing of redundant structures to support the new functions resulted in a type of reuse dictated by economy and efficiency. Hotels close to hospitals were used as temporary housing for medical staff, while hotels near universities served as dormitories to provide socially distanced housing. Parking lots were used as drive-in testing sites, stadiums as vaccination sites, and ice rinks as morgues. In many ways, the reuse related to the Covid-19 pandemic recalls the reuse of the Arles amphitheater during the Saracen invasion as a reuse of necessity.

As this half-century since 1973 draws to a close, recent developments in the second half of 2022 will most likely cause dramatic changes in different aspects of life that will reverberate in the built environment. The six aspects already discussed will certainly be affected again by events taking place in the world today. The Russian war on Ukraine has created many issues that affect these aspects. The dire repercussions that the weaponizing of oil will have on the supply and consumption of energy in the European Union and other countries may reopen discussions about decommissioned coal plants. The EU's potential switch to liquified natural gas and the need for its transport and storage may transform certain ports and harbors. In addition, the storage and transportation of Ukraine's grain could immediately impact both structures of agriculture and transportation. In Ukraine, parts of Mariupol and Bucha are sites of trauma waiting for memorialization.

The recent passage of a climate change bill in the United States will lead to the fabrication of parts related to green energy – this time, probably in the US. Will this reverse the trend of outsourcing and, if so, what will it portend for sites of manufacturing? The rise of "fake" or vegan meat in the US may diminish the demand for cattle, with consequences for the

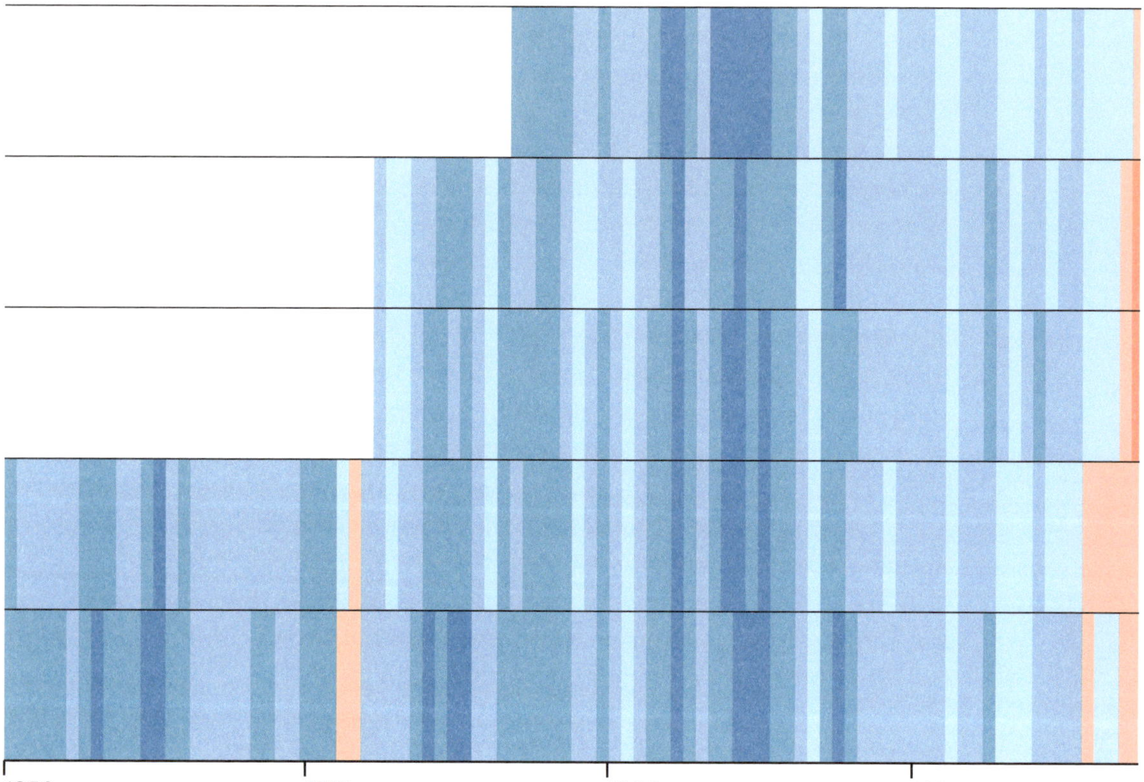

a Geothermal Steam Act; *Future Shock*, Alvin Toffler; Clean Air Act; Agricultural Act; Introduction of the Boeing 747; Establishment of international shipping container service; Clean Air Act; First Gay Pride parade, NY; US invasion of Cambodia; Kent State Massacre; Dawson's Field hijackings

b Publication of the Pentagon Papers 1971; Introduction of the Intel 4004 chip 1971; US Ping-pong team invited to China 1971; Founding of FHAR (Front homosexuel d'action révolutionnaire 1971; US Supreme Court upholds busing 1971

c U.N. Conference on Human Environment 1972; Rural Development Act 1972; UN Conference on Human Environment 1972; UN adoption of the World Heritage Convention 1972; Title IX of the Higher Education 1972; Nomination of Shirley Chisholm for Democratic presidential candidate 1972; Premiere of *M*A*S*H** 1972; Munich Olympics Massacre 1972

d Introduction of Dynatac phone 1973; Yom Kippur War 1973; Energy crisis 1973; EU energy summit in Copenhagen 1973; Karl Böer creates Solar One 1973; *The Coming of Post-Industrial Society*, Daniel Bell 1973; Consumer Protection Act 1973; Consumer Protection Act 1973; US Supreme Court decision *Roe v. Wade* 1973

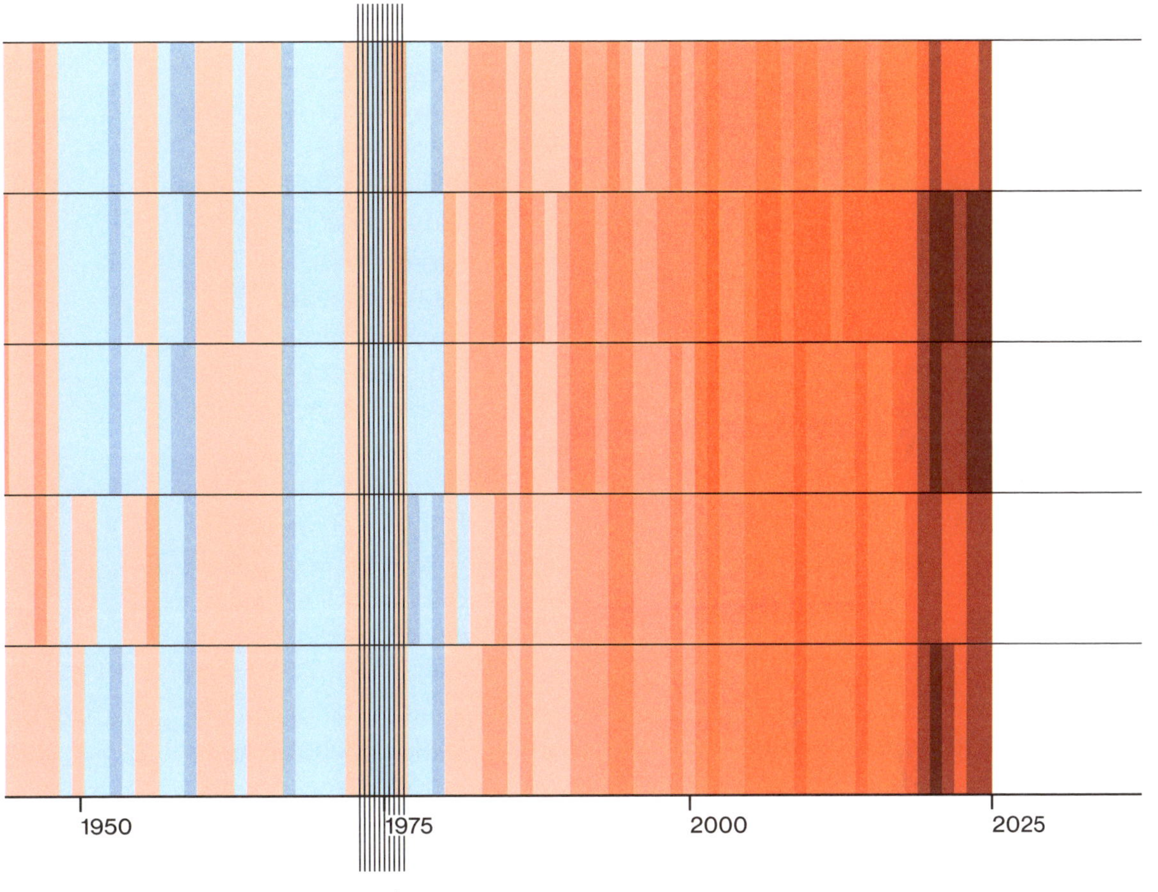

e	Community Development Block Grant 1974; Energy Reorganization Act 1974
f	Agricultural Labor Relation Act 1975; Amendment to the Voting Rights Act of 1965, 1975; Ratification of UNESCO World Heritage Convention 1975; Establishment of the UNESCO List of World Heritage in Danger 1975; Establishment of the UNESCO World Heritage Fund 1975
g	Railroad revitalization and Regulatory Reform Act 1976; Publication of *Roots* by Alex Haley 1976
h	Food and Agricultural Act 1977; Solar Research Institute 1977;
i	Humane Methods of Slaughter Act 1978; Airline Deregulation Act 1978; Founding of the National Lesbian and Gay Association 1978; Founding of Christian Voice 1978
j	2nd Energy Crisis 1979; Founding of the Moral Majority 1979

* Source: RCraig09 comparing 5 datasets: NASA; GISS; HadCrut; NOAA; Japan BerkeleyE

agricultural landscape. Revelations of abuse in Southern Baptist churches, one of the few Christian congregations that continued to grow in the midst of secularization trends, may curtail or even reduce the rise of the convention/megachurch. The increased gun violence in the US has already left many sites of trauma.

Recent developments will also engender new types of reuse. With the US Supreme Court's reversal of women's right to have an abortion, what will happen to the more than 1,500 facilities that provide abortions?[11] What of the country of Ukraine, where entire cities have been destroyed? And the ongoing and increasing impact of climate change itself? It is predicted that migration due to "heat, rising seas and drought [will] render swaths of the planet uninhabitable, millions, if not billions of people may eventually have to relocate."[12] What of the structures they abandon?

Despite the many initiatives for reusing structures today, many of them will not be reused. Rather, they will be demolished. A 2020 study by the UK's Department for the Environment, Food and Rural Affairs (Defra) indicated that in 2016, "the UK generated 66.2 million tonnes of non-hazardous construction and demolition waste," which is representative of 62% of the total waste generated in that year.[13] This type of recognition has led to a new approach to construction waste and a general embrace of such debris to create a circular materials economy. The Danish firm Lendager has completed several projects that are designed around the use of discarded construction materials from a demolished building or buildings. Upcycle Studios, completed in 2018, repurposes waste concrete, wood and old windows and, in doing so, "demonstrates how 3,000m² row houses can save 45% CO_2 and turn 1000 tonnes of waste into building materials."[14] Their project Resource Rows in Copenhagen, a brick housing complex of 92 flats and row houses, demonstrates the principle of materials upcycling. The facade is constructed from brick panels from the demolished Carlsberg Brewery. They claim that such reuse saves "as much as 29% CO_2 by upcycling only 10% of all building materials."[15] The project Karstadt Re-Parked in Berlin, to be completed in 2025, is an office and retail building created directly within the host structure, the historical Karstadt building and parking lot. "The architecture of Re-Parked grows from what is already present on-site in terms of materials, spatial constraints."[16] The new design is one that not only embraces but maintains the existing structure as a point of departure. Material that is demolished is reintegrated into the new design as a "reconfiguration of existing materials that demonstrates the possibilities of re-use – possibly creating the most sustainable retail and office building in the world."[17] While such an approach is tailored to a specific site and building, the recent development of databases for reuse will make the process more accessible. Madaster is an online global registry of materials and products in the built environment. This system posits a structure as a "reservoir of materials" that is organized and managed throughout the life of the building, facilitating a reuse of materials at a later date.[18] Registered buildings are given a materials passport that provides "insight into the material, circular and financial (salvage) value of those buildings."[19] Some countries offer a tax incentive for buildings that hold such a materials passport. This strategy as the future of reuse would, in some ways, harken back to the Roman concept of *spolia* but as a point of departure instead of an afterthought.

What will the terrain of adaptive reuse resemble a century from the time of the term's formal definition? Recent developments in the reuse of coalmines for renewable energy production, factories for manufacturing food, and churches as mosques hint at what might be new and fascinating cycles of change. In 1970, the book *Future Shock* was released and instantly became an international bestseller. Penned just a few years before Daniel Bell's *The Coming of Post-Industrial Society*, American writer and futurist Alvin Toffler speculated on the speed of post-industrial life. He introduced the term "information overload," referring to the exponential rate of change and our ability to process it. Like Bell, Toffler's predictions have long arrived a half-century later. Despite the vast reaches of technology, however, there is no easy way to predict the future. Projects such as FutureMap utilize applied data science "to identify salient factors across the political, economic, social, environmental and technological domains."[20] The joint expertise of globalization and international relations experts, data scientists and research analysts utilizes geography to advise clients in a "hyper-connected world of opportunity and risk."[21] This knowledge, intended for investors, developers and municipal authorities, would also serve adaptive reuse well in predicting trends. The investigations in this book are made in hindsight. With the secure knowledge that adaptive reuse has served different purposes over thousands of years, foresight that includes reuse is the way forward. With the urgency of climate change action and the connection of such action to the reuse of existing structures, adaptive reuse holds an important role in the future of our planet.

N.B.: On the eve of printing, newspaper headlines announced changes to the world even since the final words to this book were penned. These included: "Boeing says farewell to the 'Queen of the Skies,'" CNN News, January 31, 2023, on the delivery of the last 747 Boeing to be manufactured; "U.S. downs Chinese spy balloon, resulting in a tense exchange between the two nations," NBC News, February 5, 2023, on the shooting of a Chinese spy balloon over the US Atlantic coast; "Why Chinese Companies Are Investing Billions in Mexico," New York Times, February 2, 2023, on the term 'nearshoring' to describe a trend of "international companies moving production closer to customers to limit their vulnerability to shipping problems and geopolitical situations" and "'Future World of Fusion Energy' one step closer after Oxford reactor breaks record," BBC, February 9, 2023. These events are closing brackets on some of the trends discussed in the chapters on Transportation, Manufacturing and Energy: closure to a half-century of flight on the jumbo jet, new twists on the global trade market since ping-pong diplomacy and the introduction of the term outsourcing, and the potential of a new source of energy. These news items allude to the ever-changing events in a global context that wield a ripple effect in the built environment, effects that will determine the future path of adaptive reuse.

IMG 7 — Built from recycled concrete, repurposed double-glazed windows and discarded flooring boards, Upcycle Studios demonstrates how 3,000 m² row houses can save 45% CO_2 and turn 1,000 tonnes of waste into building materials.
IMG 8 — Resource Rows, where the facade comprises materials cut from the facades of defunct buildings.

Notes and Sources

1 Ann Chen and Aaron Reiss, "The Only Living Pay Phones in New York," *The New York Times*, 27 May 2022.

2 "Existing Building Actions," *architecture 2030*. https://architecture2030.org/existing-building-actions/, accessed 10 February 2022.

3 https://architecture2030.org, accessed 28 April 2022.

4 Carl Elefante, "Carbon Positive: Retrofitting Renewal and Transformation," *Architect*, 20 June 2022.

5 Carl Elefante, "The Greenest Building is One That is Already Built," *Forum Journal*, Vol. 21, No. 4, Summer 2007, pp. 26–38.

6 "The Greenest Building: Quantifying the Environmental Value of Building Reuse," The Preservation Green Lab, National Trust for Historic Preservation, 2011. https://forum.savingplaces.org/HigherLogic/System/DownloadDocumentFile.ashx?DocumentFileKey=b6b14c78-e108-1931-3f6d-9df1a153f9e1&forceDialog=0, accessed 5 February 2022.

7 Elefante, "Carbon Positive," op. cit.

8 Celine Nguyen, "'Never Demolish. Always Transform, With and For the Inhabitants': Anne Lacaton Delivers Inaugural Jaqueline Tyrwhitt Urban Design Lecture," Harvard Graduate School of Design, 13 April 2022.

9 "VAT for Builders," GOV.UK. https://www.gov.uk/vat-builders, accessed 11 August 2022.

10 "RetroFirst," *The Architects' Journal*. https://www.architectsjournal.co.uk/news/retrofirst, accessed 12 August 2022.

11 Jeff Diamant and Besheer Mohamed, "What the Data Says about Abortion in the U.S.," Pew Research Center, 24 June 2022.

12 Parag Khanna, "Migration Will Soon Be the Biggest Climate Challenge of Our Time," *Financial Times*, 3 October 2021.

13 "Construction and Demolition Sites – Do You Know What's in Your Waste?" Creating a better place blog. https://environmentagency.blog.gov.uk/2021/03/28/construction-and-demolition-sites-do-you-know-whats-in-your-waste/, accessed 11 August 2022.

14 "Upcycle Studios," Lendager website. https://lendager.com/project/upcycle-studios/, accessed 11 August 2022.

15 "Ressourceraekkern e sekvens," Lendager website. https://lendager.com/project/resource-rows/, accessed 11 August 2022.

16 "Karlstadt Re-Parked," Lendager website. https://lendager.com/project/resource-rows/, accessed 11 August 2022.

17 Ibid.

18 "Madaster – The Digital Library of Materials," The Madaster website. https://madaster.com, accessed 11 August 2022.

19 Ibid.

20 "FutureMap." https://futuremap.io, accessed 28 June 2022.

21 "What we do," FutureMap. https://futuremap.io, accessed 28 June 2022.

Appendix

Chapter: Looking Back

Bell, Daniel. *The Coming of Post-Industrial Society: A Venture in Social Forecasting.* New York: Basic Books, 1973.

Galazzo, Richard. "Timeline from 1G to 5G: A Brief History on Cell Phones." *CENGN*, 21 September 2020.

Smil, Vaclav. "Energy Transitions." *World Economic Forum,* 2013.

Wilkins, Ann Thomas. "Lex Bosman, *The Power of Tradition: Spolia in the Architecture of St. Peter's in the Vatican." CAA Reviews*, 12 June 2007.

https://www.culture.gouv.fr/en/Thematiques/Monuments-Sites/Monuments-historiques-sites-patrimoniaux/Un-peu-d-histoire

https://www.icomos.org/en/167-the-athens-charter-for-the-restoration-of-historic-monuments

https://www.icomos.org/en/participer/179-articles-en-francais/ressources/charters-and-standards/157-thevenice-charter

https://www.pewresearch.org/

Chapter: Energy

Bellini, Emiliano. "Converting Coal Mines into Gravity-based Renewable Energy Storage Facilities." *PV Magazine*, 26 October 2021.

Braun, Karen. "How the 19th Century Boosted America to the Top of the World Corn Market: A History of U.S. Grain Trade." *Thomson Reuters*, 12 June 2020.

Brommer, Marit. "Geothermal in the Future Energy Mix." *GeoExPro*, Vol. 15, No. 4, 2018.

Buck, Alice. "A History of the Energy Research and Development Administration." US Department of Energy, March 1982. https://www.energy.gov/management/downloads/history-energy-research-and-development-administration.

Butti, K. and Perlin, J. "Solar Water Heaters in California, 1891–1930." *The Coevolution Quarterly*, Fall 1977, pp. 4–13.

"Clarence Kemp." *National Inventors Hall of Fame.* https://www.invent.org/inductees/clarence-kemp.

Duc, Christine Mai. "The 1969 Santa Barbara Oil Spill That Changed Oil and Gas Exploration Forever." *Los Angeles Times*, 20 May 2015.

European Commission. "Why the EU Supports Wind Energy Research and Innovation." https://ec.europa.eu/info/research-and-innovation/research-area/energy-research-and-innovation/wind-energy.

Fornari, Harry D. "U.S. Grain Exports: A Bicentennial Overview." *Agricultural History*, Vol. 50, No. 1, January 1976, pp. 137–150.

"France to Delay Atomic Disposal." *The New York Times,* 13 October 1960.

"Glenn Responds to the 1970s Energy Crisis." *National Aeronautics and Space Administration (NASA)*, 10 April 2008.

"In Memoriam: Karl W. Böer." *UD Daily,* University of Delaware, 23 April 2018.

Jian, Yang. "Over Century-old Power Plant Gets a New Lease on Life." *Shine: Shanghai Daily*, 4 January 2022.

Lepage, Michael. "Climate Myths: They Predicted Global Cooling in the 1970s." *New Scientist*, 16 May 2007.

Maizland, Lindsay. "China's Fight Against Climate Change and Environmental Degradation." *Council on Foreign Relations*, 19 May 2021.

May, Tiffany. "Extreme Weather Hits China with Massive Floods and Scorching Heat." *The New York Times*, 23 June 2022.

Mohr, Charles. "Carter Asks Strict Fuel Saving; Urges 'Moral Equivalent of War' to Bar a 'National Catastrophe.'" *The New York Times*, 19 April 1977.

Sabas, Matthew. "History of Solar Power," *IER Institute for Energy Research*, 18 February 2016. https://www.instituteforenergyresearch.org/renewable/solar/history-of-solar-power/.

Stingelin, Peter. "Europe and the Oil Crisis." *Current History*, Vol. 68, No. 403, 1975, pp. 97–134.

US Department of Energy. "Wind Vision: A New Era for Wind Power in the United States." April 2015. https://www.energy.gov/eere/wind/wind-vision.

https://commission.europa.eu/index_en

https://www.earthday.org/history/

https://www.energy.gov/eere/office-energy-efficiency-renewable-energy

https://www.environmentandsociety.org

https://globalenergymonitor.org/projects/global-coal-plant-tracker/

https://memento.heritagemontreal.org/en/site/silo-no-5/

https://www.seia.org/solar-industry-research-data

https://www.un.org/en/

Chapter: Manufacturing

"Architect Turns Cement Factory into Castle." *Paintsquare*, 3 March 2017

Bell, Daniel. "The Coming of Post-Industrial Society." *The Educational Forum*, Vol. 40, No. 4, 1976, pp. 574–579.

Bhutada, Govind. "The Top 10 Semiconductor Companies by Market Share," *Visual Capitalist*, 14 December 2021.

Bonvillian, William. "US Manufacturing Decline and the Rise of New Production Innovation Paradigms." *OECD Organization for Economic Cooperation and Development*, 2017.

Da Silva, Wilson. "The Microchip That Changed the World Turns 50." *Medium*, 14 November 2021.

Donahue, Doug. "Subcontracting Manufacturing in China: The Risks and Alternative Options." *Forbes*, 18 June 2021.

Ghosh, Prince. "The Exodus of Chinese Manufacturing: Shutting Down 'The World's Factory.'" *Forbes*, 18 September 2020.

"Global Crude Steel Output Increases by 3.4% in 2019." *World Steel Association*, 27 January 2020.

"Intel Marks 50th Anniversary of the Intel 4004." *Intel*, 15 November 2021.

Jones, Elizabeth. "The Chip That Changed the World." *Intel*, 15 November 2021.

Rogers, Paul G. "EPA History: The Clean Air Act of 1970." EPA – US Environmental Protection Agency web archive. https://www.epa.gov/archive/epa/aboutepa/epa-history-clean-air-act-1970.html.

Shearer, Derrick. "Fifty Years After the Nixon-Mao China Opening, U.S.-Chinese Relations Are Getting Worse." *Washington Monthly,* 11 February 2022.

"'The Week that Changed the World': The 40th Anniversary of President Nixon's China Trip." *The Wilson Center*, 17 February 2012.

"Which Sector is the Main Employer in the EU Member States?" *Eurostat*, 24 October 2017.

"World Manufacturing Production in December 2020 Report." United Nations Industrial Development Organization (UNIDO), 16 March 2021.

https://www.bls.gov/emp/tables/employment-by-major-industry-sector.htm

https://www.dpeaflcio.org/factsheets/the-professional-and-technical-workforce-by-the-numbers

https://www.eea.europa.eu/environmental-time-line/1970s

https://www.epa.gov/archive/epa/aboutepa/epa-history-clean-air-act-1970.html

https://www.industryselect.com/blog/new-us-manufacturing-companies-for-april-2022

https://massmoca.org/about/history/

https://www.nam.org/state-manufacturing-data/2021-united-states-manufacturing-facts/

https://www.statista.com/statistics/270072/distribution-of-the-workforce-across-economic-sectors-in-the-united-states/

https://www.wilsoncenter.org

https://worldpopulationreview.com/country-rankings/car-production-by-country

https://worldsteel.org/media-centre/press-releases/2020/global-crude-steel-output-increases-by-3-4-in-2019/

Chapter: Agriculture

"41 CFR § 102-83.50 – What is the Rural Development Act of 1972?" https://www.govinfo.gov/app/details/CFR-2021-title41-vol3/CFR-2021-title41-vol3-sec102-83-50.

Abrams, R. and Harshbarger, E. "U.S. Agricultural Trade in the 1970s: Progress and Problems." *Economic Review*, May 1979, pp. 3–11.

"Agribusiness is Devastating to Family Farmers, Rural Communities, and the Environment." *ActionAid USA*. https://www.actionaidusa.org/work/agribusiness-family-farmers/.

Baird, Robert. "'Living Climate Change Now': How WA Farmers Are Trying to Turn the Tide." *The Guardian*, 24 May 2021.

Dimitri C., Effland, A. and Conklin, N. "The 20th Century Transformation of U.S. Agriculture and Farm Policy." United States Department of Agriculture, Economic Research Service. *Economic Information Bulletin* No. 3., June 2005. https://www.ers.usda.gov/publications/pub-details/?pubid=44198.

"H. R. 12144 (90th): An Act to clarify and otherwise amend the Meat Inspection Act, to provide for cooperation with appropriate State agencies with respect to State meat inspection programs, and for other purposes." *GovTrack*, 2018. https://www.govtrack.us/congress/bills/90/hr12144/studyguide.

Hagerty, Brady. "Indiana Farm Bureau Supports Hoosier Farmers Impacted by Grain Elevator Closure." *Indiana Farm Bureau*, 16 April 2020.

Hribar, Carrie. *Understanding Concentrated Animal Feeding Operations and Their Impact on Communities*. Bowling Green, OH: National Association of Local Boards of Health, 2010.

Johnson, Roger. "We Must Reject the 'Go Big or Go Home' Mentality of Modern Agriculture." *The Hill*, 8 October 2019.

Katz, Bruce and Noring, Luise. "The Copenhagen City and Port Development Corporation: A Model for Regenerating Cities." Centennial Scholar Initiative, The Brookings Institute, 1 June 2017. https://www.brookings.edu/research/copenhagen-port-development/.

Kennedy, Pete. "The Wholesome Meat Act of 1967: Disaster for Small Slaughterhouses from the Start." *Farm-To-Consumer Legal Defense Fund*, 10 September 2015.

McGreal, Chris. "How America's Food Giants Swallowed the Family Farms." *The Guardian*, 9 March 2019.

Maier, Dirk. "Grain Ops: Grain Elevator of the Future." *World-Grain*, 8 August 2019.

Neeley, Todd. "Grain Elevator Closures." *Institute for Agriculture & Trade Policy*, 14 May 2008.

Pfunder, Krista. "Closing of Grain Elevator Leave Farmers in a Lurch." *Bay Weekly*. https://bayweekly.com/closing-of-grain-elevator-leaves-farmers-in-a-lurch/.

Risser, J. and Anthan, G. "Why They Love Earl Butz." *The New York Times*, 13 June 1976.

Ritchie, Hannah. "Which Countries Eat the Most Meat?" *BBC News*, 4 February 2019.

Ritchie, Hannah and Roser, Max. "Meat and Dairy Production." *OurWorldInData*, 2017.

Roser, Max. "Employment in Agriculture." *OurWorldInData* 2013

Spitze, R. G. F. "The Food and Agriculture Act of 1977: Issues and Decisions." *American Journal of Agricultural Economics*, Vol. 60, No. 2, May 1978, pp. 225–235.

Stucker, T. and Boehm, W. "A Guide to Understanding the 1977 Food and Agricultural Legislation." US Department of Agriculture, *Agricultural Economic Report* No. 411, September 1978.

"Valued Added Agriculture." *Iowa Area Development Group*. https://www.iadg.com/iowa-advantages/value-added-agriculture/.

https://data.worldbank.org

https://www.ers.usda.gov

https://www.fsis.usda.gov/about-fsis/history

https://www.gsa.gov/reference/statutes/42-usc-3122

https://www.guidovanhelten.com/projects

https://worldpopulationreview.com

Chapter: Transportation

"Airline Deregulation: When Everything Changed." *Smithsonian National Air and Space Museum*, 17 December 2021.

Armstrong, Martin. "How the World Commutes." *Statista*, 29 June 2021.

Badger, Emily. "The Myth of the American Love Affair with Cars," *The Washington Post*, 27 January 2015.

Baskas, Harriet. "Defunct Airports Take Flight with Creative New Uses." *USA Today*, 30 November 2017.

Dowling, Stephen. "The Boeing 747: The Plane that Shrank the World." *BBC*, 19 June 2020.

"Dr. Beeching's Axe." *Network Rail*. https://www.networkrail.co.uk/who-we-are/our-history/making-the-connection/dr-beechings-axe/.

Sonnichsen, N. "Number of Petrol Stations in Selected European Countries at the End of 2020." *Statista*, 14 September 2021.

"The History of the Maritime Industry: How Container Shipping Changed the World." *Nordic IT*. https://nordic-it.com/the-history-of-the-maritime-industry-how-container-shipping-changed-the-world/#.

"The Story of Malcom McLean." *The Maritime Executive*, 28 December 2016.

Timmons, Matt. "Car Ownership Statistics in the U.S." *ValuePenguin*, 17 April 2022.

"Top 10 World's Largest Container Ships in 2022." *Marine Insight News Network*, 23 February 2022.

US EPA. "Emission Facts: Greenhouse Gas Emissions from a Typical Passenger Vehicle." February 2005.

"What is the Maritime Industry?" *Northeast Maritime Institute*, 24 March 2020.

https://www.aar.org/chronology-of-americas-freight-railroads/

https://www.api.org/oil-and-natural-gas/consumer-information/consumer-resources/service-station-faqs

https://www.networkrail.co.uk/who-we-are/our-history/making-the-connection/dr-beechings-axe/

Chapter: Religion

"America's Changing Religious Landscape." *Pew Research Center*, 12 May 2015.

"An Act to Amend the Voting Rights Act of 1965" Public Law 94-73. H.R.6219 – 94th Congress (1975–1976). 6 August 1975. https://www.congress.gov/bill/94th-congress/house-bill/6219.

Belkaïd, Akram and Oualalou, Lamia. "The Rise of Evangelical Christianity." *Le Monde Diplomatique*, 1 September 2020.

Bendavid, Naftali. "Europe's Empty Churches Go on Sale." *The Wall Street Journal*, 2 January 2015.

Earls, Aaron. "Protestant Church Closures Outpace Openings in the U.S." *Lifeway Research*, 25 May 2021.

Greene, John Robert. "Gerald Ford: The American Franchise." Miller Center University of Virginia. https://millercenter.org/president/ford/the-american-franchise.

Hensel, Karen. "Priest Sex Abuse Scandal Accelerated Declining Catholic Church Attendance in Boston." *NBC Universal Media*, 20 December 2017.

Hervieu-Léger, Danièle. "The Role of Religion in Establishing Social Cohesion." In: Krzysztof Michalski, *Religion in the New Europe*. Budapest: Central European University Press, 2006.

Himmelstein, Jerome L. *To the Right: The Transformation of American Conservatism*. Berkeley: University of California Press, 1990.

Jones, Jeffrey M. "U.S. Church Membership Down Sharply in Past Two Decades" *Gallup*, 18 April 2019.

Krishna, Priya. "From House of Worship to House of Sin: The History of Chelsea's Limelight Building." *Curbed*, 30 November 2016.

Montgomery, Paul L. "Asians Picket Building Site, Charging Bias." *The New York Times*, 1 June 1974.

Schlagdenhauffen, Régis. “Gay Rights and LGBTQI Movements in Europe.” *Encyclopédie d’Histoire Numérique de l’Europe*, 6 February 2022.

Smith, Gregory A. “About Three-in-Ten U.S. Adults Are Now Religiously Unaffiliated.” *Pew Research Center*, 14 December 2021.

Sullivan, Robert David. “Two U.S. Churches: One Is Closing Down Parishes, the Other Is Standing-room Only.” *America*, 19 April 2019.

“The Changing Global Religious Landscape.” *Pew Research Center*, 5 April 2017.

“The Future of World Religions: Population Growth Predictions, 2010–2050.” *Pew Research Center*, 2 April 2015.

“The Issue Is Subtle, The Debate Still On.” *The New York Times*, 23 December 1973.

“U.S. Ex-cardinal Theodore McCarrick Defrocked over Abuse Claims.” *BBC*, 16 February 2019.

https://www.alrb.ca.gov

https://millercenter.org/president/ford/the-american-franchise

https://news.gallup.com/poll/1690/religion.aspx

https://www.pewresearch.org/religion/2017/04/05/the-changing-global-religious-landscape/

Chapter: New Heritage

“Anti-war Protests of the 1960s–70s.” *The White House Historical Association*. https://www.whitehousehistory.org/anti-war-protests-of-the-1960s-70s.

Bergen, Peter. “The Golden Age of Terrorism.” *CNN*, 21 August 2015.

Britannica, The Editors of the Encyclopedia. “Munich Massacre,” *Encyclopedia Britannica*, 29 August 2021. https://www.britannica.com/event/Munich-Massacre.

Collinson, Stephen. “Nixon’s Own 9/11: When Terrorism Came of Age.” *CNN*, 29 July 2015.

“Convention Concerning the Protection of the World Cultural and Natural Heritage,” UNESCO, 16 November 1972.

Cordesman, Anthony H. “Trends in European Terrorism: 1970–2016.” *CSIS Center for Strategic & International Studies*, 18 August 2017.

Gai, Shayenne and Hall, Madison. “The U.S. Has Had 214 Mass Shootings So Far in 2022.” *Insider*, 26 May 2022.

Greco, JoAnn. “Protecting ‘Negative Heritage’ in Rwanda.” *The Pennsylvania Gazette*, 21 December 2016.

Krouse, William J. and Richardson, Daniel J. “Mass Murder with Firearms: Incidents and Victims: 1999–2013.” *Congressional Research Service Report*, 30 July 2015.

Mendoza, Ryan. Taped presentation at “Everybody’s House – The Rosa Parks House Project Symposium.” Rhode Island School of Design and WaterFire, Providence, RI, April 2018.

Meskell, Lynn. “Negative Heritage and Past Mastering in Archaeology.” *Anthropological Quarterly*, Vol. 75, No. 3, Summer 2002, pp. 557–574.

“MVRDV to Transform Herman Hertzberger’s Centraal Beheer Building – An Icon of Structuralism – into a New Residential District.” *MVRDV*, 16 June 2022.

Nixha, Astrit. “Klan Kosova – Resisting New Order.” *Int|AR Journal of Interventions and Adaptive Reuse*, Vol. 09, Art. 06. 2018.

Parker, K., Horowitz, J. Menasce and Anderson, M. “Amid Protests, Majorities Across Racial and Ethnic Groups Express Support for the Black Lives Matter Movement.” *Pew Research Center*, 12 June 2020.

Powers, Kevin. “The Moral Clarity of ‘Slaughterhouse-Five’ at 50.” *The New York Times*, 6 March 2019.

Public Law 89-665, An Act of the Senate and House of Representatives of the United States of America in Congress, 15 October 1966.

Roellinger, Mathilde. “Centenary of the French Law on Historic Monuments.” *Art Antiquity and Law*, Vol. XIX, Issue 4, December 2014.

Sacristán Murga, Luis. “Between Memory and Intervention: An Interview with Nieto Sobejano Arquitectos.” In: *Int|AR Journal of Adaptive Reuse*, Vol. 6. Basel and Boston: Birkhäuser, 2016.

Schulzinger, Robert D. *A Time for War: The United States and Vietnam, 1941–1975*. Oxford: Oxford University Press, 1997.

Silver, Roxane Cohen, Holman, E. Alison and Garfin, Dana Rose. “Coping with Cascading Collective Traumas in the United States.” *Nature Human Behavior*, Vol. 5, January 2021.

Thompson, Robert J. and Allen, Steve. “Television in the United States.” *Encyclopedia Britannica*, 1 July 2019.

US Department of Commerce. “Media Utilization – Telephone and Telegraph Systems.” In: *Statistical Abstract of the United States 1982–1983*, 103rd Edition.

https://www.auschwitz.org/en/education/

https://www.culture.gouv.fr/en/Thematiques/Monuments-Sites/Monuments-historiques-sites-patrimoniaux/Les-monuments-historiques

https://www.icomos.org/en/participer/179-articles-en-francais/ressources/charters-and-standards/157-thevenice-charter

https://libeskind.com/work/military-history-museum/

https://www.moma.org/interactives/exhibitions/2012/artistinplace/

https://museums.nuernberg.de/documentation-center/architecture

https://www.nps.gov/subjects/historicpreservation/national-historic-preservation-act.htm

https://www.unesco.org/en/brief

https://www.whitehousehistory.org/anti-war-protests-of-the-1960s-70s

Chapter: Looking Ahead

Chen, Ann and Reiss, Aaron. “The Only Living Pay Phones in New York.” *The New York Times*, 27 May 2022.

Diamant, Jeff and Mohamed, Besheer. “What the Data Says about Abortion in the U.S.” *Pew Research Center*, 24 June 2022.

Elefante, Carl. “Carbon Positive: Retrofitting Renewal and Transformation.” *Architect*, 20 June 2022.

Elefante, Carl. “The Greenest Building is One That is Already Built.” *Forum Journal*, Vol. 21, No. 4, Summer 2007.

Khanna, Parag. “Migration Will Soon Be the Biggest Climate Challenge of Our Time.” *Financial Times*, 3 October 2021.

Nguyen, Celine. “‘Never Demolish. Always Transform, with and for the Inhabitants’: Anne Lacaton Delivers Inaugural Jaqueline Tyrwhitt Urban Design Lecture.” *Harvard Graduate School of Design*, 13 April 2022.

“The Greenest Building: Quantifying the Environmental Value of Building Reuse.” The Preservation Green Lab, National Trust for Historic Preservation, 2011. https://forum.savingplaces.org/viewdocument/the-greenest-building-quantifying.

https://www.architectsjournal.co.uk/news/retrofirst

https://architecture2030.org/existing-building-actions/

https://environmentagency.blog.gov.uk/2021/03/28/construction-and-demolition-sites-do-you-know-whats-in-your-waste/

https://futuremap.io

https://www.gov.uk/vat-builders

https://lendager.com

https://madaster.com

Index

Project	Location	Year	Program	Page
Frøsilo/Gemini Residence	Copenhagen, Denmark	2005	A	*78, 87, 90, 98–99*
Garage Museum of Contemporary Art	Moscow, Russia	2015	T	*118*
Gas Station (Mies van der Rohe)	Montreal, Canada	2011	T	*108, 114, 118*
Gasholders	London, UK	2018	E	*23, 32*
Gasklockan	Stockholm, Sweden	2022–	E	*23, 32*
Gasometer Oberhausen	Oberhausen, Germany	1994	E	*22, 32*
GES-2 Art Center	Moscow, Russia	2021	E	*11, 23, 32, 34, 42–43*
Google Spruce Goose Hangar	Los Angeles, CA, USA	2018	T	*11, 109, 118*
Granville Island	Vancouver, Canada	1979	M	*59*
Gravitricity	Stařič, Czech Republic	2022	E	*32*
Green Forests Work	Virginia, USA	2022–	E	*23, 32*
Grey Nuns Reading Room	Montreal, Canada	2014	R	*149*
Guido van Helten Silo Murals	Brim, Australia	2016	A	*87*
Hedmark Museum	Hamar, Norway	1967–2005	A	*10, 87, 90, 100–101*
Hiroshima Peace Memorial	Hiroshima, Japan	1996	NH	*10, 170, 176, 179, 186, 188*
House in a Church	Rotterdam, the Netherlands	2010	R	*140, 149*
House of Air	San Francisco, CA, US	2010	T	*108, 118*
House of Vans	London, UK	2014	T	*108, 118*
Huashan 1914 Creative Park	Taipei, Taiwan	2005	M	*50, 59*
Im Viadukt Arches	Zurich, Switzerland	2010	T	*10, 111, 118, 120, 130–131*
Inujima Art Project	Inujima, Japan	2008	M	*50, 59*
Kanaal Antwerp	Antwerp, Belgium	2017	M	*51, 59*
Kanaal Wijnegem	Wijnegem, Belgium	2015	A	*51, 59, 79, 87*
Kaos Temple	Llanera Spain	2015	R	*10, 141, 149*
Karstadt Re-Parked	Berlin, Germany	2025	T	*119, 136–137, 236*
Klan KOSOVA TV Station	Pristina, Kosovo	2014	M, NH	*10, 51, 59, 171, 188*
The Kommandant's House	Westerbork, the Netherlands	2015	NH	*171, 188, 190, 196–197*
König Galerie	Berlin, Germany	2015	R	*11, 141, 149, 152, 160–161*
Kraanspoor	Amsterdam, the Netherlands	2007	T	*10, 108, 113, 118, 120, 132–133*
Kruisherenhotel	Maastricht, the Netherlands	2005	R	*140, 149*
Kunsthalle Praha	Prague, Czech Republic	2022	E	*23, 32*
Kunstsilo	Kristiansand, Norway	2022–	A	*79, 87*
La Fábrica	Sant Just Desvern, Spain	1975	M	*50, 56, 59, 62, 66–67*
Lantern Art Factory	Detroit, MI, USA	2022	M	*11, 51, 59*
Lao Ding Feng	Beijing, China	2022	M	*59*
Launchlabs	Basel, Switzerland	2014	M	*51, 59*
Le Chic Resto Pop	Montreal, Canada	2004	R	*140, 149*
Le Fresnoy Art Center	Tourcoing, France	1998	NH	*10, 174, 188, 190, 212–213*
Leipziger Baumwollspinnerei	Leipzig, Germany	2001	M	*50, 59*
Library and Lecture Hall	Madrid, Spain	2003	R	*140, 149*
Limelight David Barton Gym	New York, NY, USA	2014	R	*10, 141, 142, 149*

Project	Location	Year	Program	Page
Park Street Armory	New York, NY, USA	2007–	NH	*171, 188*
Parque Fundidora	Monterrey, Mexico	1998	M	*50, 59*
Piazza Alicia	Salemi, Italy	1997	R	*10, 140, 149, 152, 154–155*
Pixel Hotel	Linz, Austria,	2006	NH	*10, 174, 190, 214–215*
Plant Seven (Congdon Yards)	High Point, NC, USA	2018	M	*51, 59*
Pombal Castle Visitor Centre	Pombal, Portugal	2014	NH	*11, 171, 178, 188, 190, 206–207*
Porto Slaughterhouse Cultural Centre	Porto, Portugal	2022–	A	*87*
Powerhouse High School	Chicago, IL, USA	2009	E	*23, 32*
Pratt Street Power Plant	Baltimore, MD, USA	1985	E	*22, 32*
Prizrenasja Hydro Power Plant Museum	Prizren, Kosovo	1979	E	*22, 32*
Proekt Fabrika	Moscow, Russia	2005	M	*50, 59*
Professional Cooking School	Medina, Spain	2011	A	*78, 87*
Quarry Theatre at St. Lukes	Bedford, UK	2015	R	*149*
RCA Sackler Building	London, UK	2009	M	*10, 50, 59, 62, 68–69*
Rog Centre Creative Hub	Ljubljana, Slovenia	2002	M	*50, 59*
Rosa Parks House Project	Berlin, Germany/Detroit, MI, USA/Naples, Italy	2015–	NH	*11, 174, 182, 183, 188, 190, 208–209*
Royal Abbey of Fontevraud	Fontevraud, France	2014	R	*11, 141, 149*
S.21 Tuol Sleng Genocide Museum	Phnom Penh, Cambodia	2010	NH	*10, 170, 177, 188, 190, 210–211*
San Francisco Armory	San Francisco, CA, USA	2006	M	*50, 59*
San Juan de Ruesta Hermitage	Ruesta, Spain	2021	R	*140, 149, 152, 164–165*
San Telmo Museum	San Sebastián, Spain	2011	R	*10, 140, 149*
Santa María de Vilanova de la Barca	Lleida, Spain	2016	R	*141, 149*
Santralistanbul	Istanbul, Turkey	2007	E	*22, 32*
Seattle Central Waterfront	Seattle, WA, USA	2018	T	*118*
Selexyz Dominicanen Bookstore	Maastricht, the Netherlands	2007	R	*140, 145, 149, 152, 166–167*
Seoullo 7017 Skygarden	Seoul, South Korea	2017	T	*11, 109, 118*
SESC Pompéia	São Paulo, Brazil	1986	M	*10, 50, 59, 62, 70–71*
Shipyard 1862	Shanghai, China	2018	T	*109, 118*
Silo City	Buffalo, NY, USA	2023	A	*87*
Sinan Books Poetry Store	Shanghai, China	2019	R	*141, 149*
South Street Landing	Providence, RI, USA	2017	E	*23, 32*
St. Nicholas Eastern Orthodox Church	Springdale, AR, USA	2009	M	*51, 60*
Station A	San Francisco, CA, USA	2022	E	*23, 32*
Streetmekka Viborg	Viborg, Denmark	2018	M	*51, 60, 72–73*
Superkilen	Copenhagen, Denmark	2012	T	*108, 118*
Tafts Ale House	Cincinnati, OH, USA	2015	R	*141, 149*
TaoCang Art Centre	Jiaxing, China	2020	A	*11, 79, 87*
Tap Holding Headquarters	Paderborn, Germany	2020	R	*141, 149*
Tate Modern Museum	London, UK	2000	E	*10, 22, 32, 34, 46–47*

Project	Location	Year	Program	Page
Technopolis Gazi	Athens, Greece	1999	E	*22, 32*
Tempelhof Airport	Berlin, Germany	2009	T	*11, 108, 116, 118*
Temporary Contemporary	Los Angeles, CA, USA	1983	M	*50, 54, 56, 60*
Tervahovi Silos	Oulu, Finland	2017	A	*79, 87*
The Exploratorium at Pier 15	San Francisco, CA, USA	2013	T	*108, 118*
The Goods Line	Sydney, Australia	2015	T	*109, 118*
The High Line	New York, NY, USA	2009	T	*10, 111, 120, 128–129*
The Line Hotel	Washington, DC, USA	2017	R	*141, 149*
The Plant	Chicago, IL, USA	2021	M	*11, 51, 57, 58, 60*
The Rail Park	Philadelphia, PA, USA	2022–	T	*118*
The Sanctuary Museum (Museum of Divine Statues)	Lakewood, OH, USA	2011	R	*140, 149*
The Silo	Copenhagen, Denmark	2017	A	*79, 87*
The Singular	Puerto Bories, Chile	2011	A	*79, 87*
Théâtre Paradoxe	Montreal, Canada	2014	R	*141, 150*
Torre de David	Caracas, Venezuela	2007	NH	*10, 174, 188, 190, 216–217*
Transformer Fitzroy	Fitzroy, Australia	2015	M	*60*
Tripolis Park	Amsterdam, the Netherlands	2022–	NH	*185, 188, 190, 218–219*
Tsingpu Yangzhou Retreat	Yangzhou, China	2017	M	*11, 51, 60, 74–75*
TWA Hotel	Queens, NY, USA	2019	NH, T	*11, 115, 188, 190, 220–221*
University of Rome Testaccio	Rome, Italy	2013	A	*87*
Unser S(ch)austall (Pigsty Showroom)	Ramsen, Germany	2005	A	*78, 87*
USS Arizona Memorial	Honolulu, HI, USA	1962	NH	*188*
Vertige Escalade	Sherbrooke, Canada	2009	R	*140, 150*
Vienna Gasometers	Vienna, Austria	2001	E	*10, 22, 32, 34, 40–41*
Village of Ruesta	Ruesta, Spain	2022–	NH, R	*11, 188*
Waanders in de Broeren	Zwolle, the Netherlands	2013	R	*140, 150*
WaterFire Arts Center	Providence, RI, USA	2017	M	*51, 60*
Waterhouse at South Bund	Shanghai, China	2010	NH	*171, 172, 188*
West Heating Plant Condo	Washington, DC, USA	ongoing	E	*23, 32*
WUK Werkstätten- und Kulturhaus	Vienna, Austria	1980	M	*50, 60*
Yangshupu Power Plant	Shanghai, China	2022	E	*23, 29, 32*
Yellow House	Flims, Switzerland	1997	A	*10, 78, 87, 90, 102–103*
Yin Yu Tang House at the Peabody Essex Museum	Salem, MA, USA	2003	NH	*10, 175, 188, 190, 222–223*
Zeitz MOCAA Modern Museum of Contemporary Art Africa	Cape Town, South Africa	2017	A	*11, 79, 85, 87, 90, 104–105*
Zollverein Coal Mine Industrial Complex	Essen, Germany	2001	E	*10, 17, 30, 32, 186*
Zwarte Silo	Deventer, the Netherlands	2015	A	*79, 87*

Chapter: Looking Back

Graph — Adaptive Reuse over Time; courtesy of author.
IMG 1 — Jacques Peitret, L'amphithéâtre d'Arles, 1666; Gallica.
IMG 2 — Arles Arènes; Creative Commons, https://en.wikipedia.org/wiki/Arles_Amphitheatre#/media/File:FranceArlesArenes_07-2010.jpg.
IMG 3 — Ford Assembly Line 1913; Ford Company Public Domain.
IMG 4 — Ruhrmuseum; NatiSythen, CC BY-SA 3.0, https://creativecommons.org/licenses/by-sa/3.0, via Wikimedia Commons.
IMG 5 — Dr. Martin Cooper; Rico Shen, CC BY-SA 3.0, http://creativecommons.org/licenses/by-sa/3.0/, via Wikimedia Commons.

Chapter: Energy

Graph — Reuse of Structures for Energy Production + Primary Energy Consumption; data source: U.S. Energy Information Administration.
IMG 1 — Protestors at the National Capital Region Earth Day in Washington, DC; Cecil W. Stoughton, public domain, via Wikimedia Commons.
IMG 2 — Earth Day, April 22, 1970, Fifth Avenue & 51st Street, NYC; courtesy of NYC Dept. of Records & Information Services.
IMG 3 — Closed gas station during energy crisis, 1976; Seattle Municipal Archives, Flickr.
IMG 4 — Gas lines at crowded stations; Library of Congress Public Domain Archive.
IMG 5 — Zollverein Nachtaufnahme; image by Marc B. via Pixabay.

E-1–E-6 — Mini diagrams: Kayci Gallagher and Yara Hadi.
E-1 — CaixaForum Madrid; diagram: Yara Hadi; image: Alexander Lütjen, CC BY 2.0., https://creativecommons.org/licenses/by/2.0, via Wikimedia Commons.
E-2 — Coal Drops Yard; diagram: Yara Hadi; image: diamond geezer, Flickr.
E-3 — Vienna Gasometers; diagram: Kayci Gallagher; image: Martin Grill, Flickr.
E-4 — GES-2 Art Center; diagram: Kayci Gallagher; image: Evgeniy Vasilev.
E-5 — Museum of the Centrale Montemartini; diagram: Yara Hadi; image: Carole Raddato from Frankfurt, Germany, CC BY-SA 2.0, https://creativecommons.org/licenses/by-sa/2.0, via Wikimedia Commons.
E-6 — Tate Modern Museum; diagram: Yara Hadi; image: Merlijn Hoek, Flickr.

Chapter: Manufacturing

Graph — Reuse of Manufacturing Structures + Manufacturing Employment vs. Output 1939–2019; data source: Bureau of Labor Statistics/Macrotrends.
IMG 1 — Nixon at an athletic exhibition in Peking, 1972; Richard Nixon Presidential Library and Museum, public domain, via Wikimedia Commons.
IMG 2 — An Intel C4004 processor; Thomas Nguyen, CC BY-SA 4.0, https://creativecommons.org/licenses/by-sa/4.0, via Wikimedia Commons.
IMG 3 — "Cosmic Latte" by Spencer Finch at MASS MoCA; Timothy Valentine, Flickr.
IMG 4 — Temporary Contemporary; Courtesy of Ken_Ken, Flickr.
IMG 5 — Storage battery assembling department, Thomas Edison; National Park Service Digital Gallery.
IMG 6 — Gallery transformed from a textile factory; courtesy of Kaegan Walsh Architect.
IMG 7 — Entry to Tabakfabrik, Linz; courtesy of Michael Grugl.
IMG 8 — Vertical farm in The Plant; Plant Chicago, Flickr.

M-1–M-6 — Mini diagrams: Kayci Gallagher and Yara Hadi.
M-1 — Pace Gallery – 798 Art Zone; diagram: Kayci Gallagher; image: Leeluv, CC BY-SA 3.0, https://creativecommons.org/licenses/by-sa/3.0, via Wikimedia Commons.
M-2 — La Fábrica; diagram: Kayci Gallagher; image: Viennaslide/Alamy Stock Photo.
M-3 — RCA Sackler Building; diagram: Kayci Gallagher; image: courtesy of Hélène Binet/Haworth Tompkins.
M-4 — SESC Pompéia; diagram: Kayci Gallagher; image: Paulisson Miura from Cuiabá, Brasil, CC BY 2.0, https://creativecommons.org/licenses/by/2.0, via Wikimedia Commons.
M-5 — Streetmekka Viborg; diagram: Yara Hadi; image: courtesy of Rasmus Hjortshøj/EFFEKT.
M-6 — Tsingpu Yangzhou Retreat; diagram: Kayci Gallagher; image: courtesy of Neri & Wu.

Chapter: Agriculture

Graph — Reuse of Agricultural Structures + Number of People Employed in Agriculture 1947–2019; data source: WorldInData based on International Labor Organization.
IMG 1 — Brim silo mural by Guido van Helten; Brucephython, CC BY-SA 4.0, https://creativecommons.org/licenses/by-sa/4.0, via Wikimedia Commons.
IMG 2 — Pigs in a CAFO; USGS, public domain, via Wikimedia Commons.
IMG 3 — Silage bales; Sheila Russell/Silage bales.
IMG 4 — Silo No 5 Quai de la Pointe-du Moulin; Mickael Pollard, CC BY-SA 2.0, https://creativecommons.org/licenses/by-sa/2.0, via Wikimedia Commons.
IMG 5 — 1933 Slaughterhouse, Shanghai; Mad Ball, Flickr.
IMG 6 — The Silo by COBE, Nordhavn, Copenhagen; August Fischer, Flickr.
IMG 7 — Testaccio before MACRO; courtesy of author.

A-1–A-7 — Mini diagrams: Kayci Gallagher and Yara Hadi.
A-1 — Bourse de Commerce – Pinault Collection; diagram: Kayci Gallagher; image: Jean-Pierre Dalbéra, Flickr.
A-2 — Cineteca Matadero; diagram: Yara Hadi; image: Gabri Solera, Flickr.
A-3 — Egg Shed Heritage & Community Centre; diagram: Kayci Gallagher; image: Copyright Angus Bremner, courtesy of Oliver Chapman Architects.
A-4 — Frøsilo/Gemini Residence; diagram: Kayci Gallagher; image: Wirestock – Freepik.com.
A-5 — Hedmark Museum; diagram: Yara Hadi; image: Peter Guthrie, Flickr.
A-6 — Yellow House; diagram: Yara Hadi; image: Brutarchitekt, Yellow House Flims.
A-7 — Zeitz MOCAA; diagram: Yara Hadi; image: Esther Westerveld, Flickr.

Chapter: Transportation

Graph — Reuse of Structures for Transportation + Development of Operational Speed for Major Transport Modes (1750–2020); data source: Rodrigue, J.-P. (2020), *The Geography of Transport Systems*, Fifth Edition, New York: Routledge.
IMG 1 — Coulée Verte René Dumont; Guilhem Vellut from Paris, France, CC BY 2.0, https://creativecommons.org/licenses/by/2.0, via Wikimedia Commons.
IMG 2 — J. M. W. Turner, *Keelmen Heaving Coals by Moonlight*, 1835; National Gallery of Art, CC0, via Wikimedia Commons.
IMG 3 — The container ship *MSC Isabella*; Rob, PxHere.
IMG 4 — Nun's Island Gas Station by Mies van der Rohe; Niroyb, CC BY-SA 3.0, https://creativecommons.org/licenses/by-sa/3.0, via Wikimedia Commons.
IMG 5 — The Inhabited Bridge; courtesy of Sofia Paez & Shuyi Guan.
IMG 6 — Long Museum West Bund; Fayhoo, CC BY-SA 3.0, https://creativecommons.org/licenses/by-sa/3.0, via Wikimedia Commons.

T-1–T-8 — Mini diagrams: Kayci Gallagher and Yara Hadi.
T-1 — Danish Maritime Museum; diagram: Yara Hadi; image: courtesy of Stefano Corbo.
T-2 — Bicycle Parking Main Station Karlsruhe; diagram: Yara Hadi; image: courtesy of JOHNNY architecture, Nikolay Kazakov, photographer.
T-3 — FRAC Grand Large; diagram: Yara Hadi; image: courtesy of Michelle Courteau.
T-4 — The High Line; diagram: Yara Hadi; image: jerseygal2009, Flickr.
T-5 — Im Viadukt Arches; diagram: Kayci Gallagher; image: Ulrike Parnow, Flickr.
T-6 — Kraanspoor; diagram: Yara Hadi; image: futurelandscapes, Flickr.
T-7 — Musée d'Orsay; diagram: Yara Hadi; image: DAJesan, Stockphoto.
T-8 — Karstadt Re-Parked; diagram: Kayci Gallagher; image: courtesy of Lendager.

Chapter: Religion

Graph — Reuse of Religious Structures + Rise of the Religious Nones (1955–2021); data source: Gallup Poll.
IMG 1 — Club Paradiso, Amsterdam; Ville Miettinen from Helsinki, Finland, CC BY 2.0, https://creativecommons.org/licenses/by/2.0, via Wikimedia Commons.
IMG 2 — Lakewood worship; ToBeDaniel at Italian Wikipedia, CC BY 3.0, https://creativecommons.org/licenses/by/3.0, via Wikimedia Commons.
IMG 3 — MareNostrum Supercomputing Center; Martidaniel, CC BY-SA 4.0, https://creativecommons.org/licenses/by-sa/4.0, via Wikimedia Commons.
IMG 4 — Selexyz Dominicanen; giggel, CC BY 3.0, https://creativecommons.org/licenses/by/3.0, via Wikimedia Commons.
IMG 5 — Jesus, Son of Mary Mosque; courtesy of Dennis Earle, architect for the conversion.
IMG 6 — Kaos Temple; courtesy of Zoa Ma Escudero, Flickr.

R-1–R-7 — Mini diagrams: Kayci Gallagher and Yara Hadi.
R-1 — Piazza Alicia; diagram: Kayci Gallagher; image: Vladimir Korostyshevskiy, Shutterstock.

R-2 — Convento das Bernardas; diagram: Yara Hadi; image: Daniel Bettencourt, Flickr.
R-3 — Eremitani Civic Museum; diagram: Kayci Gallagher; image: courtesy of the author.
R-4 — König Galerie; diagram: Kayci Gallagher; image: Koenig Daniel Turner, Particle Processed Cafeteria, Charles Joplin, CC BY-SA 4.0, https://creativecommons.org/licenses/by-sa/4.0, via Wikimedia Commons.
R-5 — Monastery of San Juan; diagram: Yara Hadi; image: courtesy of BSA Consult, Santiago Escribano, photographer.
R-6 — San Juan de Ruesta Hermitage; diagram: Yara Hadi; image: courtesy of Sergio Sebastian.
R-7 — Selexyz Dominicanen Bookstore; diagram: Kayci Gallagher; image: Bert Kaufmann from Roermond, the Netherlands, CC BY 2.0, https://creativecommons.org/licenses/by/2.0, via Wikimedia Commons.

Chapter: New Heritage

Graph — Reuse of Structures of Negative Heritage + Death from Terrorism 1970–2019; data source: Global Terrorism Database from OurWorldinData.
IMG 1 — Mount Vernon; Michael Allen Lake, CC BY-SA 4.0, https://creativecommons.org/licenses/by-sa/4.0, via Wikimedia Commons.
IMG 2 — Waterhouse Hotel at South Bend; 準建築人手札網站 Forgemind ArchiMedia, Flickr.
IMG 3 — Kent State University shooting; National Archives Catalog from the Records of U.S. Attorneys, 1821–1994.
IMG 4 — Cast of *M*A*S*H*; Public domain via pxhere.
IMG 5 — Genbaku Dome, Hiroshima; Jakub Hałun, CC BY-SA 4.0, https://creativecommons.org/licenses/by-sa/4.0, via Wikimedia Commons.
IMG 6 — Film still from the documentary *One Day In September* (1999) about the terrorist attack at the 1972 Summer Olympic Games in Munich; PictureLux / The Hollywood Archive / Alamy Stock Photo.
IMG 7 — Demonstrators fill Boston Common in 1970 in sympathy for the victims of the Kent State Massacre on May 4th; Marmaduke St. John/Alamy Stock Photo.
IMG 8 — Dokumentationszentrum Reichsparteitagsgelände, Nürnberg; Chris Baier (chrisglub), http://www.chrisbaier.com, CC BY-SA 2.5, https://creativecommons.org/licenses/by-sa/2.5, via Wikimedia Commons.
IMG 9 — TV Department Eastlake KMart Press Photo; Phillip Pessar, Flickr.
IMG 10 — 9/11 Memorial; Billie Grace Ward from New York, USA, CC BY 2.0, https://creativecommons.org/licenses/by/2.0, via Wikimedia Commons.
IMG 11 — Shirley Chisholm poster; SecretName101, CC BY-SA 4.0, https://creativecommons.org/licenses/by-sa/4.0, via Wikimedia Commons.
IMG 12 — Audubon ballroom where Malcolm X was shot, from collection of LOC, from *NY World-Telegram & Sun*; Library of Congress Archives; Stanley Wolfson, photographer.
IMG 13 — Map of World Heritage sites color coded by UNESCO inclusion criteria, displayed using the Wikidata Query Service; NavinoEvans, CC BY-SA 4.0, https://creativecommons.org/licenses/by-sa/4.0, via Wikimedia Commons.

NH-1–NH-16 — Mini diagrams: Kayci Gallagher and Yara Hadi.
NH-1 — Bunker 599; diagram: Kayci Gallagher; image: Lluunnoo, CC BY-SA 4.0, https://creativecommons.org/licenses/by-sa/4.0, via Wikimedia Commons.
NH-2 — Castelvecchio; diagram: Kayci Gallagher; image: Jonathan Lin, Flickr.
NH-3 — The Kommandant's House; diagram: Yara Hadi; image: FaceMePLS from The Hague, the Netherlands, CC BY 2.0, https://creativecommons.org/licenses/by/2.0, via Wikimedia Commons.
NH-4 — Memorial for the Abolition of Slavery; diagram: Kayci Gallagher; image: Lionel Derimais/Alamy Stock Photo.
NH-5 — Moritzburg Museum; diagram: Yara Hadi; image: © Laurian Ghinitoiu, CC BY-SA 4.0, https://creativecommons.org/licenses/by-sa/4.0, via Wikimedia Commons.
NH-6 — Neues Museum; diagram: Kayci Gallagher; image: courtesy of author.
NH-7 — Nyamata Genocide Memorial; diagram: Kayci Gallagher; image: Adam Jones, Flickr.
NH-8 — Pombal Castle Visitor Centre; diagram: Kayci Gallagher; image: FG+SG Fotografía de Arquitectura, courtesy of COMOCO Arquitectos.
NH-9 — Rosa Parks House Project; diagram: Kayci Gallagher; image: courtesy of Fabia Mendoza.
NH-10 — S.21 Tuol Sleng Genocide Museum; diagram:Yara Hadi; image: Wagner T. Cassimiro "Aranha," Flickr.
NH-11 — Le Fresnoy Art Center; diagram: Yara Hadi; image: courtesy of Michelle Courteau.
NH-12 — Pixel Hotel; diagram: Yara Hadi; image: courtesy of Michael Grugl.
NH-13 — Torre de David; diagram: Kayci Gallagher; image: Wilfredor, CC0, via Wikimedia Commons.
NH-14 — Tripolis Park; diagram: Kayci Gallagher; image: courtesy of MVRDV.
NH-15 — TWA Hotel; diagram: Yara Hadi; image: Anthony Quintano, Flickr.
NH-16 — Yin Yu Tang House at the Peabody Essex Museum; diagram: Kayci Gallagher; image: Richard Cummins / Alamy Stock Photo.

Chapter: Looking Ahead

Graph 1 — Global Crude Oil Prices + Definition of Adaptive Reuse; data source: PB Statistical Review of World Energy from OurWorldinData.
IMG 1 — Phone Booth, NYC; Chris Ford, Flickr.
IMG 2 — Transformation of 530 Dwellings; victorsu, Flickr.
IMG 3 — Library Yoga Class; NJLA New Jersey Library Association, Flickr.
IMG 4 — New Roads Community; courtesy of the author.
IMG 5 — Co-locating energy and agriculture; National Renewable Energy Lab, DOE-InSPIRE, Flickr.
IMG 6 — Deconstruction; CC BY 2.5, https://en.wikipedia.org/w/index.php?curid=7477401.
Graph 2 — The 1970s + Warming Stripes Graphic Comparing Different Datasets of Global Mean Surface Temperature; data source of base diagram: RCraig09, CC BY-SA 4.0, https://creativecommons.org/licenses/by-sa/4.0, via Wikimedia Commons.
IMG 7 & 8 — Upcycle Studios and Resource Rows; image by Rasmus Hjortshøj, courtesy of Lendager.

Liliane Wong received her BA in Mathematics from Vassar College and her MArch from the Harvard University Graduate School of Design. She is Professor in the Department of Interior Architecture at the Rhode Island School of Design, where she was Department Chair for thirteen years. Her research focus on architectural interventions to existing structures and her teaching on this subject led her to co-found *Int|AR, the Journal of Design Interventions & Adaptive Reuse*, which promotes creative and academic explorations of sustainable environments through exemplary works of reuse. She is the author of *Adaptive Reuse: Extending the Lives of Buildings*, co-author of *Libraries — A Design Manual* and co-editor of *Interventions and Adaptive Reuse: A Decade of Responsible Practice*. She was recognized by *Design Intelligence* in 2018–2019 and 2019–2020 as one of the 25 most admired design educators in the United States. A long-time volunteer at soup kitchens, her teaching emphasizes the importance of public engagement through architecture and design. Her other teaching and research interests include design as social activism, preservation and sea level rise, the mathematics of curved space, affordable modular housing, and technical textiles.

Wong is a registered architect in Massachusetts and has practiced through her own firm, Mahon Wong Associates, as well as with the Boston firms of Perry Dean Rogers and FHCM.

Imprint

Graphic Design, Layout and Cover:
Sebastian A. Schmitt (Bureau Est, Leipzig)

Production:
Heike Strempel and Anja Haering, Berlin

Printing:
Grafisches Centrum Cuno GmbH & Co. KG
Paper:
Magno Natural 120 g/m²

Editor for the Publisher:
Michael Wachholz, Berlin

Library of Congress Control Number:
2023934135

Bibliographic information published by the German National Library

The German National Library lists this publication in the Deutsche Nationalbibliografie; detailed bibliographic data are available on the Internet at http://dnb.dnb.de.

This publication is also available as an e-book (ISBN PDF 978-3-0356-2564-6).

P.O. Box 44, 4009 Basel, Switzerland
Part of Walter de Gruyter GmbH, Berlin/Boston

Printed on acid-free paper produced from chlorine-free pulp. TCF ∞

Printed in Germany

ISBN 978-3-0356-2563-9

9 8 7 6 5 4 3 2 1

www.birkhauser.com